WORLD ®
AIR POWER

J O U R N A L

Aerospace Publishing Ltd

Published quarterly by
Aerospace Publishing Ltd
179 Dalling Road
London W6 0ES
UK

ISSN 0959-7050

Published under licence in USA and
Canada by Airtime Publishing Inc.,
10 Bay Street, Westport,
CT 06880, USA

Editorial Offices:
WORLD AIR POWER JOURNAL
Aerospace Publishing Ltd
179 Dalling Road
London W6 0ES
UK

Publisher: Stan Morse
Editors: David Donald
        Jon Lake
Production Editors:
  Trisha Palmer
  Karen Leverington
Design: Barry Savage
        Robert Hewson
Typesetting: SX Composing Ltd
Origination and printing by
  Imago Publishing Ltd
Printed in Italy

Europe Correspondent:
  Paul Jackson
Washington Correspondent:
  Robert F. Dorr
USA West Coast Correspondent:
  René J. Francillon
Asia Correspondent:
  Pushpindar Singh
Australia Correspondent:
  Greg Meggs
Switzerland Correspondent:
  Peter Gunti

The editors of WORLD AIR
POWER JOURNAL welcome
photographs for possible
publication, but cannot accept any
responsibility for loss or damage to
unsolicited material.

**World Air Power Journal
is published quarterly
and is available by
subscription**

**SUBSCRIPTION AND BACK
NUMBERS:**

**UK and World (except USA an
Canada) write to:
Aerospace Publishing Ltd
FREEPOST
MARLBOROUGH
Wilts SN8 2BR
UK**

**(No stamp required if posted
within the UK)**

**USA and Canada, write to:
Airtime Publishing Inc.
Subscription Dept
10 Bay Street
Westport, CT 06880
USA**

**Prevailing subscription rates ar
available on request.
For single and back issues of th
soft-cover edition (subject to
availability):
$17.95 each for delivery within
mainland USA, Alaska and
Hawaii. $21 (Can) each for
delivery to Canada. $21 (US)
each for delivery overseas.
Please enclose payment with
your order. Visa and MasterCar
accepted. Include your card
number, expiration date and
signature.**

Publisher, North America:
  Melvyn Williams
Subscription Director:
  Linda DeAngelis
Charter Member Services Manager
  Jill Brooks
  Janie Klanit

The publishers gratefully
acknowledge the assistance given b
M. Jacques Marmain, co-author of
MiG OKB with the current Bureau
Designer General, Rostislav
Belyakov. This authoritative work
published in French by Editions
Larivière, and provides much new
information and detail on the
MiG-23 family.

WORLD AIR POWER®

AIR POWER

J O U R N A L

CONTENTS

Military Aviation Review

International

NH-90 programme formally launched

Italy's signature on 25 June completed a four-nation memorandum of understanding officially authorising the design and development phase of the NH-90 helicopter project. Representing the interests of the customer nations is the NATO Helicopter Management Agency, which will handle all dealings with the prime contractor. The latter is NH Industries SARL, formed by the four manufacturers (whose financial shares are shown in parentheses): Aérospatiale of France (42.4 per cent), Agusta of Italy (26.9 per cent), MBB of Germany (24.0 per cent) and Fokker of the Netherlands (6.7 per cent). As with NAMMA and Panavia, the equivalents for the Tornado project, the single customer office and industry representative will be co-located, in this instance at Aix-en-Provence, France.

Financial accounting in the venture is in European Currency Units, the cost of the development phase being estimated as ECU 1,376 million. Both Tactical Transport Helicopter and NATO Frigate Helicopter sub-variants are required: 150 TTH and 60 NFHs for France; 120 German army and 114 air force TTHs, plus 38 NFHs; 150 TTHs and 64 NFHs for Italy; and 24 Netherlands NFHs. Unusually for an international project of this nature, the financial shares in the industrial programme are not proportional to the numbers of aircraft bought by each country.

A major alarm was raised late in August when semi-official reports claimed that France had indefinitely postponed its participation in NH-90 for financial reasons. The claim was swiftly denied by Prime Minister Edith Cresson, who maintained that funding was still assigned to the programme.

This West German Canberra B.Mk 2 (one of two used for survey and mapping duties) was a surprise visitor to Britain's International Air Tattoo.

Above: Under new management, the Hungarian air force has adopted the new chevron insignia seen here.

Western Europe

GERMANY:

More moves announced

Re-alignment of defences within unified Germany – principally to counter the vacuum in the east, where most Soviet-designed equipment has been retired – is expected to lead to a revised chain of command as well as moves of base for Luftwaffe wings. At present, western Germany is covered by four divisions – two air defence and two tactical fighter – whilst the east has one multi-role division (5th). Despite a separate Air Transport Command in the west, transport units in the east are directly attached to 5 LwDiv. It is proposed to copy the system in the west from 1993 onwards, reducing Luftwaffe divisions from five to three and eliminating the transport arm as an independent force.

According to data published in July, disbandment of the navy's MFG 1 strike/attack wing at Schleswig/Jagel will merely involve the arrival of Aufklärungsgeschwader 51 to take over most of its Tornados – at least some of which will be configured for reconnaissance. MFG 2 at Eggebeck will retain its reconnaissance commitment and absorb a dozen or so of MFG 1's Tornados to increase its strength to 65 – enough to mount 80 attack and 24 recce sorties per day under wartime conditions.

AKG 51 and its sister wing AKG 52 currently fly RF-4E Phantoms, these aircraft being due for disposal (and their bases at Bremgarten and Leck closed) when the Tornado ECR is fully operational. Fighter defence for the east is to be boosted with the transfer of two F-4E Phantom wings: Jagdgeschwader 72 from Hopsten to Laage and JG 73 from Pferdsfeld to Holzdorf, although the August decision to retain MiG-29s may result in only one of these wings being moved. Laage – rather than the originally announced Pferdsfeld – will also be the base of the Egrett D500 high-altitude reconnaissance aircraft from 1994. Still under development, the D500 is to be operated by a squadron known as Aufklärungsstaffel S, presently under formation at Norvenich.

Two new transport wings are also being established in eastern areas. The Transall C.160Ds of Lufttransportgeschwader 62 are scheduled to leave Wunsdorf for Neubrandenburg in 1996, whilst LTG 65 is to form at Neuhardenburg (formerly known as Marxwalde) with former LSK/LV aircraft. Gathered within the latter will be most of the communications fleet in that part of Germany, comprising three Ilyushin Il-62s, four Tupolev Tu-134s, tw Tupolev Tu-154s and Mil Mi-8s from T 44, already based at Neuhardenburg; Antonov An-26s from TS 24 at Dresde Let L410UVPs of VS 14 at Strausberg; a more Mi-8s of THG 34 at Brandenbur Briest. In all, THG 34 and LTG-65 sha some 41 Mi-8s and 25 Mi-2s. Several ba teries of air force Hawk and Patriot SAM will also move eastwards.

Announced base closures planned in t west are Bremgarten, Hopsten, Neub berg, Oldenburg and Pferdsfeld, whi flying activities will also be ended at Al horn, Diepholz, Fassberg, Fürstenfel bruck, Husum, Kaufbeuren, Leck, L pheim, Manching/Ingoldstadt a Wunsdorf. The experimental aircraft wi WTD 61 at Ingoldstadt may be transferr to the former Soviet base at Templin.

Airbuses join Luftwaffe

Three Airbus A310 transport aircr formerly operated by the East German ai line, Interflug, were receiving attentic from Lufthansa's engineering base Hamburg in August prior to entering mi tary service on 10 September. Two will used in the VIP transport role, whilst t third will be converted to a passenge freighter at a future date. Until milita crews can be trained, personnel from t defunct Interflug will operate the A310s f a year. Each wears a military serial numb and the Greek Cross, but no Luftwa livery. The Airbuses will take over sor operations from the fleet of four Boei 707s which are expected to be converted tankers and re-positioned at Brandenbur Briest. The latter will be developed into major military transport base servi Berlin.

Army aviation changes

Incorporation of eastern equipment in army aviation has involved creation Heeresfliegerstaffel (Army Aviati Squadron) 70 at Cottbus with 13 Mi-8T one Mi-8S and four Mi-9 versions of 'Hi plus HFS-80 at Basepohl with ni Mi-8TBs and four Mi-9s. Unknown un recently, Mi-9 is the Soviet designation f the tactical communications and EC helicopter known to NATO as 'Hip-G'. squadron of the Marineflieger continues operate Mil Mi-14 'Haze' helicopters fro Parow on Baltic SAR duties.

Below left: Dutch demonstration F-16s get more and more colourful every year.

Right: Gulf war veteran 'Diplomatic Service' returned to the area as part of the RAF's contribution to Operation Warden, the reinforcement of Turkey.

'Fulcrums' to stay

The Luftwaffe's announcement in July, confirming that the 24 MiG-29s inherited from the former East Germany would be retained in service, means that they will now fly until about 2002, when their 2,500-hour airframe lives will have been exhausted. Four MiG-29UB two-seat trainers are included in the batch serving with Jagdgeschwader 9, but the unit will probably be relocated from its base at Preschen, close to the Polish border. Holzdorf and the current Soviet MiG-29 base of Altenberg have been suggested. A flood of invitations to participate in dissimilar air combat is expected from other European air forces, although the German authorities have taken steps to prevent JG 9 from appearing to be merely a curiosity unit, and have banned MiG-29 appearances at air shows abroad.

Technical and operational assessments which led to the decision to retain the 'Fulcrums' note that the type has excellent combat manoeuvrability and a good pulse-Doppler radar (0I-93 Zhuk), which can track up to 10 targets and detect aircraft up to 100 km (62 miles) distant. Although 0I-93 was at first claimed to be a direct copy of the US AN/APG-65, more detailed analysis has revealed a high degree of Soviet originality. Less desirable attributes found in the MiG-29 are a limited radius of action, poor low-level performance and an engine overhaul interval of only 350 hours. Germany currently has only enough spares to keep the MiG-29s flying until 1992, and has yet to arrange a source of supply from the USSR.

Top: No. 100 Squadron has now started to re-equip with the BAe Hawk. Above: The squadron badge.

ITALY:
First Harriers

The Aviazione per la Marina Militare became a Harrier operator on 23 August when the two TAV-8B trainers ordered in 1990 for pilot continuation training were handed over at Norfolk, Virginia, and taken aboard their future seaborne base, the carrier *Giuseppe Garibaldi*. There will be some delay in receiving the balance of 16 AV-8Bs, as Italy has elected to wait until the Harrier II-Plus is available. Whilst Hughes AN/APG-65 radar will be an obvious addition to the 'Plus', this aircraft also features larger LERX, better take-off performance and a 1814-kg (4,000-lb) increase in weapon load to 5987 kg (13,200 lb). In July, a formal order for the first three Italian AV-8B+ aircraft, together with two spare Pegasus 11-61 turbofans, was approved by the US government. The 11-61 (F402-RR-408), which earlier in 1991 suffered fan clearance problems in the newest USMC Night Attack AV-8Bs in which it has been installed, is rated at 107.87 kN (23,800 lb) st – 8.9 kN (2,000 lb) st more than the output of the RAF's current Pegasus Mk 105.

Naval aviation is training 40 pilots to fly the Harrier – its first fixed-wing aircraft in four decades. Personnel are attending US Navy schools.

More paramilitary helicopters

Italy's Servizio Nazionale Protezione Civile (SNPC – National Civil Protection Agency) ordered additional helicopters from Agusta during July in the form of six Boeing CH-47C Chinooks and six Bell 412s. Both will be used for fire-fighting and associated relief: the Chinooks with either an internal 5000-litre (1,100-Imp gal) retardant tank or prefabricated field hospital and operating theatre; Bell 412s with 1000-litre (220-Imp gal) tanks or seats for 12 firefighters or medical personnel. As with other SNPC helicopters, operation will be in military markings by the army. Three Alenia G222PROCIV transports assigned to the SNPC were due to be transferred in September from the air force's 46° Brigada at Pisa to the civil operator, Tecno Avio Interventi at Ancona. Two more will be delivered shortly.

NETHERLANDS:
Helicopter plans change again

Ramifications of the latest defence White Paper were made clearer in July when it was revealed that escort and scout capabilities would also be demanded of the next-generation attack helicopters to be obtained for the KLu in army support roles. This stems from the Dutch plans to participate in NATO's forthcoming Rapid Reaction Corps, for which it will form the 11th Airmobile Brigade in 1994. The brigade will also need between 25 and 40 transport helicopters (to be based at Eindhoven), making selection from such types as the Aérospatiale AS 532 Cougar, Boeing CH–47D Chinook and Sikorsky UH-60

Black Hawk a matter of urgency. Acquisition of combat helicopters will be a two-stage process, beginning with the leasing of 20 state-of-the-art aircraft in the McDonnell Douglas AH-64A Apache and MBB PAH-1 category. These will tide over the KLu until 40 next-generation helicopters can be bought in the late 1990s. Types under consideration include AH-64C Longbow Apache, Boeing/Sikorsky RAH-66 Comanche and Eurocopter Tiger, all of which combine anti-tank capability with escort and scout potential.

NORWAY:
Defence cuts imposed

One effect of a round of defence cuts recently announced will be a still further life extension for the score of veteran Cessna O-1 Bird Dogs of the Luftvernartilleriet (Artillery Air Observation). Instead of being retired in 1993, these lightplanes will now have to wait until 1996 before seven or eight helicopters, of an as-yet undecided type, arrive as replacements. Also to be cut back is pilot training, all of which is undertaken by the USAF, and flying time. Instead of 20 students, only 16 were sent to the US in 1991, whilst 14 will go in 1992. F-16 pilots will in future be restricted to 180 hours per year, compared with up to 240 currently flown. Financial constraints appear to have ruled out any additional fighter purchases, making replacement of the KNL's remaining Northrop F-5A/B squadron less likely.

SPAIN:
Second Seahawk batch ordered

The US Congress was asked to approve in July a second batch of six Sikorsky SH-60B Seahawk ASW helicopters which is to be sold to the Spanish navy. These represent the balance of four from the original requirement, plus an extra two added early in 1990, and increase the total to 12. First-batch deliveries were made late in 1988 to Escuadrilla 010 for basing aboard FFG-7 'Perry'-class destroyers. The latest Seahawks are needed for more vessels under construction.

EdA changes organisation

A new, regionally-based organisation for the Ejercito del Aire was introduced on 1 July, having been authorised by the government on 21 March. Interceptor, tactical attack and transport aircraft were assigned to single-function commands until the disbandment on 30 June of Mando Aéreo de Combate, Mando Aéreo de Tactico and Mando Aéreo de Transporte. Their assets are now distributed among three new commands: Mando Aéreo del Centro at Madrid, for the central region; Mando Aéreo del Estrecho at Seville covering southern areas; and Mando Aéreo de Levante at Zaragoza for the north-east. Mando Aéreo de Canarias on the Canary Islands has always been a multi-function command and thus remains unchanged.

SWEDEN:
J 35J programme completed

During August (or nearly two years later than planned) the Flygvapen received the last of 66 SAAB Drakens converted from J 35F to J 35J standard. Acceptance of the first J in March 1987 launched a programme to modify the aircraft of No. 10 Wing at Angelholm as a means of maintaining credible air defences until the JAS 39 Gripen is available. Changes comprise two more weapon pylons and revised avionics, including upgrading of the infra-red seeker, radar and IFF.

TURKEY:
Fighting Falcon plans

Turkish plans for a second batch of F-16 Fighting Falcons to be built under licence by the TUSAS factory at Mürted became clearer in July when the US government revealed that 80 aircraft were involved, together with 92 General Electric F110 engines from the TUSAS factory at Eskisehir. TUSAS is in the process of building 152 Block 30/40 standard F-16C/Ds for the THK, a further eight having come complete from GD. Firm commitments are thus increased to 278, including the 46 Block 50 F-16s recently ordered from Turkish production by Egypt. The THK will buy a further 80 aircraft when they can be afforded, increasing its total to 320 and making it the second-largest F-16 operator after the USAF.

Extra defence for Kurds

Following the departure of coalition forces from the security zone in northern Iraq on 15 July, air elements were increased to meet any military action by Iraq against its Kurdish citizens. In mid-August, France sent eight Dassault Mirage F1CR reconnaissance/fighter-bombers and a C-135F(R) tanker to the Turkish base at Incirlik. On 30 August, the RAF announced that Operation Warden would involve eight SEPECAT Jaguar GR.Mk 1As flying out to Incirlik early in September. Germany's helicopter contribution to food and other aid distribution had increased to 24 Bell UH-1D and 24 Sikorsky CH-53G Stallion helicopters by early August. The US provided A-10s and F-16s, operating from Incirlik and Batman, to join the air element assigned to support the 2,500-3,000 troops of eight nations who are based just across the border from the Kurdish safety zone. RAF Chinooks assigned to Operation Warden from Silopi and Diyarbakir reached a peak of 12, including several diverted from a planned homeward journey from the Gulf War. The last of these was withdrawn on 15 July.

Despite being host to forces protecting the Kurds, Turkey has taken air action against guerrillas of the Kurdish Workers' Party who attacked a Turkish military base on 4 August. On the following day, THK McDonnell Douglas F-4E Phantoms and Lockheed F-104G Starfighters bombed guerrilla bases in northern Iraq, at the start of a week-long ground operation by 20,000 troops and light armoured vehicles.

UNITED KINGDOM:

Harriers grounded

A less-than-happy summer for the Harrier culminated in the imposition of a flying ban by the RAF on 29 July following a series of inflight fires in which one aircraft was lost. On 29 May, a Harrier GR.Mk 7 (ZG473) of No. 3 Squadron was abandoned by its pilot four miles from Gütersloh after a total electrical failure, whilst another aircraft managed an emergency landing at the same base on 16 July and a GR.Mk 5 was able to reach Wittering despite an inflight electrical failure on 29 July. The RAF has also refused to accept further Harrier deliveries, outstanding aircraft at the time of the ban being 15 Mk 7s and all 14 T.Mk 10s on order, plus 58 Mk 5s due to be upgraded to the night-attack Mk 7 standard. Harrier GR.Mk 3s, Sea Harriers and US-built AV-8Bs have different electrical systems and were unaffected by the restrictions. Suspicion has fallen on the transformer-rectifier located in the rear fuselage avionics bay and corrective modifications made to prevent chafing of electric wiring nearby.

Also at the time that Harrier flying was halted, six Mk 5s were receiving titanium patches on their rear fuselages, to the rear of the back engine nozzles, to counteract fatigue cracking between frames 31 and 32. Caused by acoustic vibration induced at certain combinations of flap and nozzle angles, the problem affects only Mk 5s and USMC AV-8Bs built before 1990.

Missile deadline

Interested manufacturers had until 6 August to register their proposals for supplying the RAF with a successor to its AIM-9 Sidewinder AAMs in satisfaction of SR(A)1234. This amounted to a reopening of the competition to all comers, following the abandonment of an agreement with the US under which Hughes developed the medium-range AIM-120 AMRAAM for NATO countries whilst a European consortium was responsible for the medium-range AIM-132 ASRAAM. Leading contenders appear to be BAe/Hughes with the missile originally designed for AIM-132 before the USAF lost interest, and GEC-Marconi/MATRA offering the MICASRAAM. Loral and Raytheon from the US, plus Germany's BGT, are offering three other proposals, at least two of which are based on upgrades of Sidewinder. Some specialists consider that the latter missile has reached the end of its 40-year development lifetime and can not be made to meet the ASRAAM specification.

RAF closures

Base closures announced on 2 July include RAF Hullavington, to be run down by the autumn of 1992, apart from an enclave for the Parachute Servicing Flight and Balloon Operations Squadron. No. 2 Squadron of the RAF Regiment will move to Catterick in the ground-defence role, replacing No. 58, which disbands there on 30 March 1992. The maintenance base at Abingdon will transfer its remaining work to St Athan and close by May 1993. No. 7 FTS will begin dispersing its fleet of Tucanos (to No. 1 FTS at Linton-on-Ouse and No. 3 at Cranwell) in April 1992, prior to closure of its base at Church Fenton. The airfield will become a reserve landing ground, but the remainder of the site will be sold. West Raynham is also to close at an undetermined date.

Eastern Europe

YUGOSLAVIA:

Air actions in civil war

Hungary issued a formal protest to the federal government in Belgrade after JRV aircraft entered its airspace whilst manoeuvring to attack Croat militia positions and civilian targets in the town of Osijek on 23 August. Thereafter, Hungarian border guards were instructed to fire upon any military aircraft straying out of Yugoslav airspace. Aircraft bombed the Croatian villages of Nova Grabiska, south of Zagreb, on 18 August and Sarvas on 21 August.

Croat forces claimed destruction by ground fire of two SOKO G2-A Galeb armed trainers on 26 and 28 August, although the federal government reported that one had been able to return to base despite being damaged. The aircraft were bombing the Croatian town of Vukovar, in support of a joint ground operation by Serb guerrillas and the federal army.

EC attempts to end the fighting have been largely unsuccessful. A Netherlands air force Aérospatiale Alouette III carrying a monitoring party was hit by six rounds of small-arms fire which forced it to make a precautionary landing near Novska, south-east of Zagreb, on 16 August.

Mystery arms consignment

An unresolved side-issue to the civil war was the shipment of 35,000 tonnes of arms which was unloaded and then confiscated at Bar, in the province of Montenegro, during July, having reportedly arrived from Lebanon. Included in this massive consignment were eight or more helicopters (of which four were Aérospatiale Gazelles) which were said by some sources to have been supplied to Lebanon by Iraq. Availability of such a stock of equipment could also have been the result of the recent disbandment of private armies in Lebanon. In late August, two Americans were charged in Miami with attempting to sell General Dynamics FIM-43A Redeye and FIM-92A Stinger shoulder-launched SAMs to the Croat militia.

SOVIET UNION:

Post-coup military

Few of the world's armed forces will b unaffected by the momentous event which unfolded in the Soviet Unio during the closing days of August. A lef wingers' coup of 19 August initiall threatened a return to the Cold War an caused considerable alarm in the easter European nations from which Sovic forces had just withdrawn, or were in th process of leaving. Just three days late however, the army's refusal to crack dow on popular opposition to the coup resulte in the collapse of the coup, the liberatio from house arrest of President Gorbache and his return to Moscow to reassume h position. In this, he was not complete successful, because of the enhanced statur of Boris Yeltsin, who had courageously re sisted the plotters and made use of th vacuum following their downfall to tak considerable, formerly national, powers t himself as leader of the Russian Federatio – the largest of the 15 republics constitutin the USSR. Other republics (Byelorussi Georgia, Moldavia and the Ukraine) fo lowed in proclaiming their independenc effectively shattering the central contro which had kept the USSR together (reluc antly in most cases) since the 1920s. Th was expected to lead to a looser federatio of self-governing states, the prospect of further backlash to reform being greatl weakened by decrees outlawing the Com munist Party.

The still-confused military situation the end of August was that several repub lics were claiming jurisdiction over arme forces on their territory (and had appointe Defence Ministers for that purpose), bu would be likely to allow Moscow to cor tinue to have national control – althoug with a measure of republican veto – ove external defence policy and strateg nuclear forces. Western leaders appeare satisfied with that possibility, yet ther were still fears that tactical nucle: weapons might get into the 'wrong' hanc if the ongoing ethnic disputes among autc nomous republics developed into civ war. Approximately 35 per cent of nucle: forces, including 20 per cent of the ICBM are stationed outside the Russian Republic

If the threat of massive destabilisation averted, a further round of cuts of Wester armed forces may become possible. Cu rent reductions are based on the USSR inability to launch a sudden surface thru: through eastern Germany and the othe Eastern European nations from which it withdrawing. Disbandment of the Con munist Party and depoliticisation of th army – including replacing 80 per cent c the higher echelons with 3,000 younge more liberal officers – means that th USSR is no longer committed to using i military forces as a 'legitimate' means c spreading socialism throughout the fre world. This further reduces the need fc Western deterrence.

Left: A Federal Yugoslav Jastreb runs in for a strafing pass at Osijek airport. A militiaman dives for cover.

Below left: The Soviet air forces in former East Germany made history by holding a small open day at Eberswalde Finow during August 1991.

Left: This Soviet army Mil Mi-24 was another Finow visitor.

Middle East

EGYPT:
First order for Aero L-59

Launching production of a 'Westernised' Albatros, the L-59, Egypt placed an order in August for 48 of these advanced jet trainers, of which delivery will take place in 1992-93. The L-59 differs in several respects from the standard Warsaw Pact L-39 Albatros which Egypt received only in March 1990 when Libya presented 10 to the EAF. With additional thrust and operating economy derived from replacing the 16.86-kN (3,792-lb) st Ivchenko AI-25W by a 21.57-kN (4,850-lb) st Lotarev/ZVL DV-2 turbofan, the L-59 is fitted with US avionics, making it more acceptable to export customers. A similar version, with DV-2 power and unchanged avionics, is being delivered to the Soviet air force under the designation L-39MSU. Requirements are for 110 to be supplied between 1991 and 1995. In July, Garrett, the US engine manufacturer, signed an agreement with Aero Vodochody concerning trial installation of a TFE731-4 turbofan in an L-39 Albatros, due to fly before the end of 1991.

IRAN:
Soviet combat aircraft sought

A visit to Moscow in July by an Iranian military delegation was reported to be for the purpose of negotiating a second batch of MiG-29 'Fulcrums' and attempting to order Sukhoi Su-24 'Fencer' interdictors. Iran received 14 MiG-29s in 1990, whilst four more, plus 24 'Fencers', sought sanctuary from coalition attacks on Iraq earlier this year. Iran has shown little inclination to return the aircraft and may be contemplating upgrading its air force through their incorporation. The only impounded Iraqi aircraft which Iran proposes to release are one Airbus A300C-620 and five A310-200s seized from Kuwait Airways during the August 1990 invasion.

Above and below: This rarely seen Boeing 747 is operated by the Islamic Republic of Iran air force.

JORDAN:
Mirage 2000s cancelled

In a statement of the already apparent, Jordan cancelled its order for 12 Dassault Mirage 2000s on 28 August. The aircraft – 10 2000EJs and two 2000DJs – were ordered in April 1988 and due for delivery from early 1991 onwards. They were to have been financed by Saudi Arabia, which has withheld all aid to Jordan since it supported the Iraqis in the Gulf War. Also likely to have been affected is an upgrading of the RJAF's 15 Mirage F1CJ interceptors to multi-role F1EJ standard.

KUWAIT:
Air bases to be rebuilt

An interim operational capability is to be achieved at Kuwait's two military air bases through a contract placed with the US government and involving essential reconstruction by the Army Corps of Engineers. Both Ali al Salem and Ahmed al Jaber were severely damaged by coalition bombing and Iraqi vandalism, and will require extensive additional work which will be undertaken later through civilian contracts. Kuwait's first McDonnell Douglas F/A-18 Hornet left the production line at St Louis in July and is due for delivery in January 1992. The US has offered temporary basing facilities until the aircraft can be operated from Kuwaiti airfields.

The UK and the US have declined a request made in August by Kuwait to keep residual forces in Kuwait as a deterrent, although naval vessels will continue to operate in the Arabian Gulf and reinforcement can be made rapidly by air. Arab sensitivity to a permanent Western presence resulted in initial plans for Egyptian and Syrian troops to be stationed in Kuwait, but unsatisfactory conditions imposed by these two countries resulted in the troops' withdrawal and the most recent Kuwaiti request.

SAUDI ARABIA:
F-15 Eagle force increased

Two McDonnell Douglas F-15 Eagles handed over to Saudi Arabia on 13 August were the first of nine F-15Cs and three tandem-seat F-15Ds ordered as attrition replacements three years before the Gulf war. Delivery of the remaining aircraft is taking place at two per month. Three squadrons (Nos 5, 6 and 13) were equipped with Eagles from original deliveries of 47 Cs and 15 Ds, whilst a further 24 (including two Ds) were supplied from USAF units in Europe as emergency aid in August 1990, forming No. 42 Squadron. Production in the US of the pure interceptor Eagle ends in 1992 after five F-15Ds for Israel, leaving the multi-role F-15E on the St Louis assembly line. However, Saudi Arabia hopes to gain US government authorisation to buy 24 of the projected single-seat F-15F, which lacks the E's full range of air-to-ground weapon delivery options.

Southern Asia

AFGHANISTAN:
Guerrilla action continues

Anti-government guerrillas, though no longer supported by the US, have continued sporadic attacks against the armed forces. On 26 July, a Mil Mi-8 'Hip' transport helicopter of the AAF was shot down by ground fire, killing 30 personnel, including 20 women of a forces' entertainment dance troupe.

INDIA:
LCA programme slippage

Having been intended to fly in 1990 and enter service in 1997, India's LCA (Light Combat Aircraft) is now understood to be as far away as ever. In a statement to parliament in July, Defence Minister Sharad Pawar revealed that the two aircraft which will fly in 1995-96 are regarded as merely demonstrators and that it is upon their performance that a decision will be made on the number of LCA prototypes to be built. On this reckoning, Mr Pawar's estimate of production deliveries to the IAF before the end of 2005 would appear optimistic. India is planning to manufacture 250 LCAs powered by the indigenous GTRE GTX-35VS Kaveri afterburning turbojet, which is also in the development stage. The Defence Minister said in August that the Kaveri will be ready for testing in December 1993 and enter production five years later. General Electric F404 turbofans were bought as long ago as 1986 as interim power for the five prototype LCAs, which were to have begun flight-trials last year.

MYANMAR:
'Fishbed' deliveries

Working-up was proceeding in mid-year of a squadron of 11 Chinese-built Chengdu F-7M Airguard versions of the MiG-21 'Fishbed' which had been handed-over to Myanmar (Burma) on 3 May. In conjunction with the six SOKO G-4 Super Galeb armed jet trainers received from Yugoslavia only a few months previously, the F-7s represent a massive upgrading of the MAF, whose jet combat equipment formerly consisted of six aged Lockheed AT-33As. According to unofficial reports, two squadrons of Shenyang F-6s (MiG-19 'Farmers') have also been ordered.

Far East

CHINA:
'Flankers' delivered

As expected, news was received during August confirming receipt by China of Sukhoi Su-27 'Flanker' air superiority fighters which were apparently ordered following demonstration flights at Nanyan in March by this type as well as MiG-29 'Fulcrums' and Su-25 'Frogfoots'. Eight 'Flankers' were in the initial batch, whilst a further 14 will be supplied in January/ February 1992 to complete the order. Interestingly, the aircraft will be based on the island of Hainan, the most southerly part of China, off the coast of Vietnam.

This Il-18 'Coot' (above) and Il-76 'Candid' (below) serve with the North Korean air force. Both were seen visiting Berlin's Schonefeld airport, perhaps picking up MiG spares or overhauled engines.

JAPAN:
E-3 Sentry doubts

Having procrastinated over its planned purchase of Boeing E-3 Sentry AWACS until the type was out of production – following completion of the last RAF E-3D airframe in May – Japan is now complaining to Boeing at the high cost being quoted for re-opening the line. Publication in August of 1992 defence spending plans indicated that Japan has spent the funds originally set aside for its first E-3 on a battery of Raytheon MIM-104 Patriot SAMs. The four large AWACS needed by the ASDF to complement its 13 Grumman E-2C Hawkeyes may now be obtained by converting civilian Boeing 707s or switching to the new EC-130V Hercules.

Second customer for Beechjet

Following its selection for the USAF's tanker/transport lead-in trainer requirement, designated T-1A Jayhawk, the Beechjet 400T executive turbofan-twin gained a second military customer when the JASDF named it as the winner of the similar TC-X competition. Nine of the type will be bought by 1995, of which the first three are to be included in the 1992 defence budget. The selection also represents a homecoming for the Beechjet, the design of which was acquired by Beech from Mitsubishi, by which it was previously known as the Diamond II.

BAe wins HS-X – again

What it is hoped will be final confirmation of its success in the HS-X jet-powered SAR aircraft competition was received by British Aerospace in August. The decision, announced by the Japan Defence Agency, had first been made a year previously, then suspended in deference to US objections. Japan plans to buy an eventual 27 BAe 125-800s for SAR, fitted with 360° radar, FLIR, flares and droppable rescue equipment. Following earlier purchase of three of the same variant for navigation aids checking as U-125As, the rescue version is designated U-125A. Three are included in the 1992 defence budget, the eventual deployment being pairs of U-125As at 12 bases – the first operational in 1995 and the last in 2003. Delivery of aircraft to Japan will be in 'green' condition for equipment installation by a local contractor.

TAIWAN:
Ching-Kuo setback

Implications for the ambitious Indigenous Defence Fighter programme were under assessment following the crash into the Strait of Taichung on 12 July of second prototype AIDC Ching-Kuo (serial number 10002). The accident, which killed project test pilot Colonel Wu Ke-Chen, was understood to be the result of acute transsonic buffeting causing damage to the stabilators and consequent loss of control at about 16,500 ft. Following preliminary investigation, the programme director

announced that production of the Ching-Kuo would not be delayed. RoCAF requirements are for some 250 Ching-Kuos to replace F-104G Starfighters and F-5E Tiger IIs.

Kfir purchase possible

Undeterred by the prospect of Chinese ire, Israel has been attempting to sell to the RoCAF up to 95 of its mothballed IAI Kfirs. Agreement is believed to have been reached recently for transfer of 34 Kfir C-7s and six TC-7 two-seat trainers.

THAILAND:
Corsair request

In a request to the US for weapons, published in July, Thailand asked for 30 LTV Corsairs, which it plans to base at Satahip/U-Tapao as the basis of its first maritime attack and Marine Corps close air support wing. Having recently retired large numbers of Corsairs, the US Navy would have no difficulty in supplying the 24 A-7Es and six TA-7C conversion trainers needed. Delivery could begin in 1993.

Above: A South African Air Force Gemsbok (a Puma locally upgraded to virtual Super Puma standards).

Right: Seen at Patrick AFB, Florida, this P-3C is soon to be exported to Pakistan, whose markings it already wears.

Australasia

AUSTRALIA:
Training changes begin

Some 50 NZAI CT-4A Airtrainers of the RAAF's No. 1 Flying Training School were earmarked for civilian sale in July as the RAAF began a 12-month run-down of its base at Point Cook. The sale is part of an economy programme in which some services will be contracted out, and it is expected that private flying schools will be assigned the role of screening pilot applicants in future. Students will then gain their wings on RAAF turboprop-powered Pilatus PC-9As, with prospective fast-jet pilots then flying the Aermacchi M.B.326 – first with No. 25 Squadron at Pearce for conversion, then No. 76 Squadron at Williamtown for lead-in fighter training.

NEW ZEALAND:
Training moves

Plans to close Wigram aerodrome resulted in an announcement during July that the resident Flying Training Wing would be transferred to an alternative base on North Island. The unit operates 15 NZAI CT-4B Airtrainers and similar AESL T6/24 Airtourers, plus four Bell 47Gs. The decision was made in advance of a report, due in September, examining joint RAAF-RNZAF aircrew training. This could result in basic training on Pilatus PC-9s in Australia, followed by advanced training

on Aermacchi M.B.339Cs in New Zealand. Joint training of Hercules and Orion crews in Australia is also under consideration. In the longer term – perhaps over a 20-year period – the RAAF and RNZAF might be forced by financial constraints to amalgamate completely as a single air arm.

Three M.B.339s were delivered in March and three more were due in September from a total of 18 on order. Fresh urgency was added to deliveries when fatigue cracks were discovered in the wings of seven of the RNZAF's 15 BAe Strikemasters during July. Two were determined to be beyond economical repair and a third has been cleared for restricted manoeuvring. The remaining aircraft had returned to flying by September.

PHILIPPINES:
BAe Hawk interest

An enthusiastic appraisal of the BAe Hawk advanced trainer and light fighter/attack aircraft by the PhilAF's commander has greatly increased the prospects of an order for 12. Although no formal agreement has been reached, it is expected that the order will go ahead on the basis of 100-per cent trade offsets. Speaking in August, C-in-C Brigadier General Rogelio Estacio said the Hawk was better and cheaper than its US and Soviet counterparts and would most likely be bought by other ASEAN countries, following sales already made to Indonesia and Malaysia.

The AM-39 Exocet-armed Agusta Sikorsky ASH-61 (left) and rocket-armed Ecureuil (below) were displayed at São Pedro to celebrate Brazilian Naval Aviation's 75th anniversary on 31 August 1991.

Left: The prototype EMB-312H Tucano is stretched, up-engined and has a modern cockpit.

Africa

BOPHUTHATSWANA:

New transport aircraft

Having recently been upgraded from an Air Wing of the Defence Force to a fully-fledged Air Force – Tshireletso ya Bophuthatswana – this unit was anticipating receipt of its 12th aircraft in mid-year. The latest addition, an Airtech CN.235, joined two CASA C.212s, three PC-7 Turbo Trainers, one PC-6 Turbo Porter, two BK-117s, two Alouette IIIs and an AS 365 Dauphin.

MOROCCO:

US offers Fighting Falcons

Sales proposals revealed in the US during July name Morocco as only the second nation on the African continent (after Egypt) authorised to receive General Dynamics F-16 Fighting Falcons.

SOUTH AFRICA:

Rooivalk renaissance

Originally thought to have been relegated to a research programme after the SAAF requirement evaporated with withdrawal of forces from Angola and Namibia, the Atlas CSH-2 Rooivalk attack helicopter returned to the headlines in July when plans were revealed to construct a second prototype and launch production. Because the Rooivalk remains a private venture, the exercise would appear to be prohibitively

costly for Atlas, as the initial, but undisclosed, foreign customer requires only about five helicopters. By mid-1991, the XH-2 first prototype had flown over 100 hours since 11 February 1990, the only obvious change resulting from these trials being a minor modification to the vertical fin. The second Rooivalk is expected to be fitted with the full attack avionics, including target acquisition systems reportedly developed in conjunction with Israel.

Oryx and Gemsbok revealed

Having gained wide experience of supporting a fleet of 70 Aérospatiale SA 330 Pumas, South Africa wisely used the dynamic systems of this helicopter as the basis for the Rooivalk, thereby considerably reducing development costs. Surprise was nevertheless generated by reports that one or two upgraded versions of Puma had entered SAAF service recently, known as the Oryx and Gemsbok. The former, apparently delivered from late 1990 onwards, is a Puma re-engined with the Super Puma's Makila turboshaft engines – a conversion already undertaken with Portuguese helicopters – and additionally modified with a ventral fin, new horizontal stabiliser and nose radar. The Gemsbok helicopter also reported to be in SAAF service may be basically the same helicopter adapted for gunship roles. Operational trials by three Oryx were under way by mid-1991.

Right: The first Brazilian two-seat AMX takes off on its first flight. Brazil is already working on a radar for the AMX, which is flying in a BAe 125 test aircraft.

South America

BRAZIL:

First two-seat AMX

A successful 65-minute maiden flight of the first two-seat AMX built by EMBRAER in Brazil was accomplished by test pilot Gilberto Pedrosa Guimaraes at São José dos Campos on 14 August. Wearing the designation A-1 (as the single-seat variant, instead of the anticipated TA-1, the aircraft carried its serial number in the USAF style: FAB5650. Two AMX-Ts have already flown in Italy during 1990, and A-1 5650 would also have been airborne before the end of that year had it not been for a slow-down in deliveries caused by the government not making its payments to EMBRAER on time. By August, nine AMXs had been delivered to the FAB – mainly for 1°/16° GAvCa at Santa Cruz – and two more were undergoing flight-testing. Brazil plans to obtain 79 AMXs and 15 AMX-Ts, of which 30 and four, respectively, are on firm contract in the first two production batches. Plans to fit the AMX with nose radar were advanced when a BAe 125 began flight trials at São José dos

Campos with a Tecnasa Elettronca-SMA SCP-01 multi-mode radar.

Hopes for new Tucano

EMBRAER is hoping that its flagging financial fortunes can be revived by the latest EMB.312H version of Tucano turboprop trainer, a prototype of which was under construction in July. The Tucano H will be fitted with a five-bladed propeller and an 820-kW (1,100-shp) Pratt & Whitney PT6A-67 powerplant offering a considerable boost in performance over the -25C (559 kW/750 shp) of the previous Brazilian-built model. Offering jet-like speeds already attained by the uprated Shorts Tucano in the United Kingdom, the EMB.312H is capable of light attack and target-towing, in addition to basic pilot instruction. The prototype is due to begin a sales tour late in 1991 and will be easily identifiable by reason of two fuselage plugs increasing its length by 1.56 m (5 ft 1½ in). Production of the Tucano in Brazil is presently suspended pending further orders.

North America

CANADA:

EH.101 powerplant selected

Following the lead set by Italy in September 1990, Canada announced selection of 2,000-shp (1491-kW) General Electric CT7-61A turboshaft engines to power its EHI EH.101 helicopters, thus rejecting the Rolls-Royce/Turboméca RTM322 to be installed in UK naval variants. CT7s, which are civil versions of the widely-used military T700, have also been fitted in all nine prototype EH.101s. Standard Aero of Winnipeg will be responsible for assembly of the engines installed – three each – in Canadian Forces' EH.101s. Unless requirements are reduced by defence cuts, the CF requires 35 of the type for anti-submarine duties ashore and afloat, plus 15 configured for SAR.

Jet Squalus production plan

Despite rejection by the Canadian govern-

ment of requests for a subsidy, it appeared in August that the path had been cleared for Promavia to establish a Jet Squalus production plant in Saskatchewan when Arab financing was obtained. Plans of the Belgian company are to offer the Jet Squalus for the USAF's JPATS jet trainer requirement and to the Canadian Forces as a Canadair Tutor replacement. A civil flying school in Canada is also envisaged. In 1989, Promavia agreed plans with OGMA in Portugal for production of up to 100 aircraft, including 30-35 for the local air force as Lockheed T-33 replacements. The current status of this arrangement is unknown.

UNITED STATES:

Independence *to relieve* Midway *in Japan*

USS *Independence* (CVA-62) was scheduled to arrive in Yokosuka, Japan, on 11 September 1991 to relieve USS *Midway* (CV-41). *Midway* has been home-ported at Yokosuka since 1973, when the United States sought to pre-position two aircraft-

carriers, including crews' families, abroad, but was unsuccessful in obtaining a second home-port berth in Greece. *Midway* was scheduled to depart Yokosuka on 10 August 1991 to return to the US to prepare for decommissioning, the actual 'turnover' of operations between the two carriers to be conducted at Pearl Harbor, Hawaii.

Bede wants military customers for supersonic, kit-built BD-10J

Bede Jet Corporation in St Louis, Missouri, hopes for foreign military sales of its BD-10J, which has the distinction of being the world's first supersonic, home-built jet aircraft. Powered by a General Electric CJ610 engine, the BD-10J, according to designer Jim Bede, is capable of Mach 1.4 at altitudes up to 13932 m (45,000 ft). The 'amateur-built' aircraft makes use of conventional aluminium alloys, has a gross take-off weight of 1877 kg (4,140 lb), and will have non-boosted controls and a pressurised cockpit.

First flight is still some months away. The company claimed to have 52 orders

from non-military clients when a partially-completed BD-10J was demonstrated at the Experimental Aircraft Association's 39th annual convention in Oshkosh, Wisconsin, in July 1991. One purchaser is the Holiday Inn aerobatic team.

Designer Jim Bede told *World Air Power Journal* that the BD-10J was created with a specific civilian market in mind but that his firm recognises the potential military application as an *ab initio* trainer. "We also see a possible RPV [remotely piloted vehicle] use." Bede feels the aircraft has strong potential, as well as a simplicity certain to appeal to Third World purchasers. "It has no hydraulics, no cables. The flight surfaces are operated by push-pull rods, rod ends and ball-bearings. It has manual controls. This may seem unusual in today's world, but remember that Learjets use them and the X-1 [the first supersonic aircraft] was all manual-controlled." Though it can "go supersonic quite nicely," a drawback, acknowledges Bede, is that the craft "doesn't have the maximum manoeuvrability you'd get with a boost system."

The BD-10J is unique in having two control sticks: a side stick and centre stick, mechanically connected, both of which move at the same time. "The centre stick is comfortable at high speed. The side stick [of the kind employed by the F-16 Fighting Falcon] is better for the novice at low speeds."

S-76 helicopter being offered in SAR role

Sikorsky is vigorously promoting its S-76 SAR (search and rescue) helicopter to foreign military purchasers, following entry of three S-76A(Plus) SAR aircraft into service with the Royal Hong Kong Auxiliary Air Force (RHKAAF).

The manufacturer is also looking for customers for its S-76C version, powered by twin Turboméca Arriel 1S1 engines, which received Federal Aviation Administration Category A certification in 1991.

Spain has ordered eight S-76C helicopters for use by the Spanish air force for flight instrument training, search and rescue, and utility missions. Bond Helicopters of Aberdeen, Scotland, has contracted for seven S-76C helicopters for offshore oil service.

The S-76 can also be equipped for SAR missions with Omega navigation system, Honeywell Primus 700 weather avoidance radar, GEC forward-looking infra-red, Racal RNAV II navigation management system, and high-density Spectrolab Nite-sun illuminator.

With deliveries to Hong Kong completed, the RHKAAF now has three S-76A(Plus) airframes assigned to general-purpose duties, three S-76A(Plus) assigned to SAR, and three S-76C helicopters assigned to general-purpose duties.

FB-111A fleet is retired

The last flight by a Strategic Air Command FB-111A was made on 10 July 1991, when Colonel J. Paul Malandrino, Jr, commander of the 380th Air Refueling Wing at Plattsburgh AFB, NY, flew the final aeroplane (68-0249, nicknamed '*Little Joe*') to the AMARC storage facility at Davis-Monthan AFB, Arizona.

The last four FB-111As to fly departed Plattsburgh on that date, the other three going to Barksdale AFB, Louisiana, Offutt AFB, Nebraska, and K. I. Sawyer AFB, Michigan, to be placed on static display. Other bases which have already received static-display FB-111As are Castle AFB, California; Kelly AFB, Texas; Ellsworth AFB, South Dakota; and March AFB, California. One aircraft (68-0286) is being retained for outdoor exhibit at Plattsburgh.

The USAF had 59 FB-111As, of which 29 were turned over to the Tactical Command, redesignated F-111G, and assigned to the 27th Tactical Fighter Wing at Cannon AFB, New Mexico. Sixteen more FB-111As will be stored at AMARC. The remainder not placed on display will be used for ground crew training.

The 380th Bombardment Wing at Plattsburgh was one of two SAC FB-111A wings for many years, before converting to the KC-135A Stratotanker and acquiring its present name on 1 July 1991. On that date, the wing's 528th Bombardment Squadron and 530th Combat Crew Training Squadron were deactivated, while the 529th Bombardment Squadron was placed in 'caretaker' status. The wing now operates the 310th and 380th Air Refueling Squadrons. In fiscal year 1994, Plattsburgh is slated to convert to the KC-135R model of the Stratotanker.

VMFA-321 says 'so long' to F-4 Phantom

US Marine Reserve Squadron VMFA-321, 'Hells Angels', commanded by Lieutenant Colonel Alan Davis, held ceremonies at Andrews AFB, Maryland, on 13 July 1991 to mark the departure of the squadron's last F-4S Phantom.

To mark the occasion, an F-4S Phantom, BuNo 153904, was painted in special markings reminiscent of those employed by the squadron in the early 1970s. For the ceremonies, VMFA-321 also borrowed '*Sageburner*' an early F4H-1F (F-4A), BuNo 145307, which was the 11th Phantom built and which set a world air speed record of 902.769 mph on 28 August 1961. The historic '*Sageburner*' belongs to the National Air and Space Museum and is usually out of public view, in storage at Silver Hill, Maryland.

VMFA-321 will be without aircraft until January 1992, when the unit is scheduled to begin receiving F/A-18A Hornets. With the departure of this squadron's last Phantom, VMFA-112 'Wolf Pack' at NAS Dallas, Texas, becomes the last formation in US Navy/Marine aviation to operate the McDonnell fighter. The Dallas-based unit has not announced a date for conversion to the F/A-18.

US Army seeks Huey replacement in training role

The US Army is lobbying hard to maintain 1992 funding for an NTH (New Training Helicopter) for IERW (Initial Entry Rotary Wing) training at Fort Rucker, Alabama, where the UH-1 Huey now handles primary flight training.

The Army has defined a requirement for 150 to 200 new helicopters to provide initial primary and instrument training for its aviators prior to their transition to the type they will fly in service. Since the retirement of the Hughes TH-55 in 1988, the Army has been employing the expensive, not fully satisfactory – and ageing – UH-1 Huey in this role, for which the Huey was not designed. The NTH programme is aimed at sharply reducing helicopter operating costs and, hence, training costs. Any aircraft chosen would also be a prime candidate to replace 100 TH-57C helicopters employed for rotary-wing training (but only after fixed-wing training in the T-34C) by the US Navy.

The Army was scheduled to release a Draft Request for Proposals (DRFP) for the new helicopter in July 1991, an event subsequently postponed until September.

Differences in how to handle the NTH programme are serious and, coupled with a general reduction in US defence funding, could threaten the programme. The US Army strongly wants to lease the new training helicopter, together with a 'turn key' maintenance package. In consecutive fiscal years (1991-92), Congress has included authority for the lease but has strongly urged the Army to purchase the aircraft.

Almost any small helicopter with side-by-side seating which meets simple requirements – it must be turbine-powered, FAA-certified for both VFR and IFR oper-

Above: The Missouri ANG's 131st TFW at St Louis has re-equipped with the F-15.

Above: Unusually, this Alabama ANG RF-4C carries AIM-9L Sidewinders

Above: The MAC C-141B colour scheme, to be applied to C-5s and C-130s

ation, and seat three – is a possible candidate for the NTH. But three aircraft types appear to be ahead in the running.

The Schweizer 330, powered by a derated 200-shp Allison 250-C20W turbine engine, with 185-km/h (115-mph) cruising speed, seats three in the training role. The helicopter "is unique in many ways [sic]," says Schweizer's Barbara Tweedt. "Its three-seat configuration and three sets of controls make it the ideal training helicopter. The wide body allows plenty of room for three pilots." Based on the maker's 300C aircraft, the 330, says Tweedt, "is designed for reliable, maintenance-free operation." A drawback is that FAA certification is pending.

The Aérospatiale AS 350B Astar, powered by a 641-shp Turboméca Arriel turbine engine (possibly to be replaced by 616-shp Lycoming LTS101-600A.2 in a production version), with maximum speed of 274 km/h (170 mph), cruising speed of 225 km/h (140 mph), also seats three as a trainer. The aircraft, which would be assembled in Grand Prairie, Texas, is based on the highly successful AS 350 Ecureuil (Squirrel), some 500 of which have been delivered as a six-seat, general-purpose civil helicopter. The AS 350B is fully FAA-certificated.

The Enstrom TH-28/480, powered by a fully rated 420-shp Allison 250-C20W turbine engine, also cruises at 225 km/h (140 mph) and seats three as a trainer. En-

strom's Robert M. Tuttle says the build has paid special attention to the Army need for crashworthiness: "lightweigh crashworthy crew seats [built by Simul Inc.] will be tested beginning in the sum mer of 1991. The leading French manufa turer of crashworthy fuel cells, Aerazu was selected to develop the crashworth fuel system." As of August 1991, t TH-28/480 had entered the flight stra survey portion of FAA certification flig testing.

A 'dark horse' in the NTH competitic is the LTV Panther 800, a version of the S 365M Dauphin to be powered by t 1,200-shp LHTec T800 turboprop engi also destined for the Army's RAH-6 Comanche light helicopter. The Arm likes the idea of engine commonality (ar continues to fund testing of a T80 powered HH-65A Dauphin even thoug the Coast Guard, which owns the test ai craft, has lost interest). However, t Panther 800 has most of the disadvantag of the present Huey for the NHT role size, cost, complexity.

The push for a new trainer comes at time when all of the US armed forces ha a surplus of pilots in the junior ranks. T US Army is currently reducing its streng by more than 25 per cent, from 18 comb divisions to 12 and from 740,000 personr to 490,000. Any NTH aircraft will have compete for funding with the RAH-66 ar other programmes.

Above: A Spangdahlem-based McDonnell Douglas F-4G.

Right: A Thunderbirds F-16 during the team's recent European tour.

Left: A 149th TFS (VA ANG) F-16C.

F-15 STOL/MTD aircraft makes final flight

The US Air Force's STOL/MTD F-15B Eagle (71-0290) made its 138th and final flight on the night of 12 August 1991. Swan song for the short-field demonstrator Eagle was a short landing beneath a simulated 62-m (200-ft) ceiling in total darkness using only the aeroplane's ALG (Autonomous Landing Guidance) system. Lieutenant Colonel Felix Sanchez later said that the difficult landing could have been accomplished "even if we'd had a 30-kt crosswind and a wet runway." Although primary pilot for the F-15S/MTD programme has been McDonnell's Larry Walker, USAF Major Michael J. Costigan and the manufacturer's Steven M. Herlt made the 12 August flight, using a Hughes AN/APG-70 radar to locate the runway and designate a desired landing spot.

The landing completes a three-year flight test programme which was tailored to demonstrate technologies for an autonomously guided landing in a 464.4 by 15.48-m (1,500 by 50-ft) runway area at night in weather – meaning wet and icy conditions, with up to 30-kt crosswinds, a half-mile of visibility and a 62-m (200-ft) ceiling – with no external landing aids. The programme also sought to demonstrate 'up and away' performance equal to or better than the basic F-15. Both purposes were closely linked to the US Air Force's air base operability programme, aimed at developing various means (rapid reconstruction teams, decoy aircraft to deceive strafers, and short-field warplanes) to allow airfields to continue to generate combat sorties while under the kind of attack envisaged in a European scenario during the Cold War era. In the 1990s, air base operability funding has been slashed dramatically. Further, the F-15S/MTD's vectored-thrust nozzles have reached the end of their useful lives and have been returned to Pratt & Whitney.

During its flying life, the F-15S/MTD made numerous vectored take-offs, with rotation demonstrated at speeds as low as 68 km/h (42 mph) for a 38-per cent reduction in runway take-off roll. The shortest landing made by the F-15S/MTD, in June 1991, used 422 m (1,366 ft). A basic F-15 routinely needs 2322 m (7,500 ft) of runway to land.

The US Air Force plans to spend $4 million to install the F-15S/MTD's ALG system in its F-15E fleet in 1993.

MH-60K special operations helicopter delivered

The first Sikorsky MH-60K special operations helicopter (89-26194), which has been flying at the manufacturer's Stratford, Connecticut, facility for some time, was formally delivered to the US Army on 20 August 1991.

The MH-60K, based on the US Army's UH-60A/L utility helicopter, is equipped with terrain-avoidance radar and FLIR (forward-looking infra-red) systems for low-level missions at night and in adverse weather. The airframe has structural reinforcement and some improved internal systems, when compared with the UH-60A/L. The aircraft is equipped to carry two 230-US gal external fuel tanks and also carries additional fuel inside the cabin. It is also equipped with an air-refuelling probe.

Sikorsky has a US Army contract valued at $315 million to deliver 11 MH-60Ks, with an option for 11 more. US Army documents submitted to Congress state a need for 38 aircraft, with the first full production machine to be delivered in the summer of 1992.

Hornet scores aerial 'kill' of E-2C Hawkeye

An E-2C Hawkeye belonging to Squadron VAW-122 had to be shot down over the Mediterranean on 8 July 1991 after its crew bailed out to escape an uncontrollable engine fire.

The engine of the Hawkeye (BuNo 161343, coded AE-601) caught fire during a mission from USS Forrestal (CV-59) off the coast of Cyprus during Operation Provide Comfort – the effort to assist Kurdish refugees in Iraq. After the five crew members parachuted from the E-2C, the aircraft continued flying. An F/A-18A Hornet from VFA-132, also aboard Forrestal, was ordered to shoot down the E-2C to prevent it from endangering civilians or property. The Hornet pilot achieved the 'kill' with 20-mm cannon fire.

The E-2C crew members were rescued by helicopters from Forrestal and the guided-missile cruiser USS Yorktown (CG-48).

AFTI F-16 resumes flying; F-16 production threatened

The US Air Force resumed flight testing of the AFTI (Advanced Fighter Technology) F-16 Fighting Falcon close air support (CAS) aircraft (75-0750) on 10 July 1991. Though the future of F-16 production is now uncertain, the service continues to want an F/A-16 version in the CAS role. Under a $44-million contract, the test programme at Edwards AFB, California, will evaluate single and dual line-of-sight, head-steerable FLIR systems and an integrated night-vision helmet-mounted display system.

The flight test programme is a joint US Air Force/NASA effort. The first phase will concentrate on problems of first-pass target acquisition, including target cueing and data-link operations with air- and ground-based forward air controllers. A projected second phase of flight tests will examine two-aircraft attack operations in the close air support role with a second, standard F-16 participating.

The fate of the fiscal year 1992 funding for F-16 production was uncertain after the US Senate approved an Armed Services Committee recommendation to 'zero' funding for what was billed as the USAF's final purchase of 72 F-16C block 50 fighters. Instead, the Senate added $1 billion to 1992 appropriations for purchase of 24 F-117 'Stealth Fighters', which the USAF has not requested and does not want. While the F-117 purchase was unlikely to materialise, it was also uncertain that F-16 funding could be restored by the time a defence bill became law in October 1991.

The USAF has been planning to retire F-16A block 10 aircraft (now serving in Air National Guard units) and to invest heavily in resolving the problem of wing stress cracks in the remainder of its F-16 fleet.

The USAF and General Dynamics, during routine inspections, discovered minute wing cracks in 14 F-16s – a discovery that prompted the service to initiate a $280-million field upgrade programme. Far from being "plagued with cracks," as one journal reported, the F-16 fleet simply requires structural improvements to some 667 F-16C block 25 and block 30 models. Hairline cracks are expected to surface in the future in F-16A block 10 and block 15 models, and the USAF has long wanted to dispose of the former, anyway, since converting F-16A block 10s to the 'big tails'

used by all other airplanes in the series would be prohibitive in cost. USAF officials blame the problem of cracks – which they say has been exaggerated in the press – on increased weight and greater than anticipated flying hours. Added avionics and radars have raised the average mission weight of an F-16 from 10206 kg (22,500 lb) to 12201 kg (26,900 lb).

USAF Major General Joseph Ralston has acknowledged that wing cracks surfacing later in the 1990s could shorten the F-16's expected life from 8,000 hours to around 6,000. A typical F-16 is flown just 250 hours per year.

Some $1.2 billion in already-programmed F-16 funding is available from which to cover crack-repair costs. This may be accomplished by 'stretching' a planned F100-220E engine upgrade or F/A-16 close air support modifications, or by delaying plans to install the probe-and-drogue refuelling system.

A separate F-16 problem is a fan blade fault discovered on those few F-16Cs currently powered by the Pratt & Whitney F100-P-229 IPE (Improved Performance Engine). One of these made a belly landing at Edwards AFB, California, in June. Subsequently, engineers discovered that the IPE's fourth blade is out of specification by millimetres, a situation which could, in the extreme, produce a blade crack. The USAF temporarily refitted this handful of F-16Cs with older-model F100s until a correction, thought to be possible by October 1991, could be achieved. This is expected to produce a minor delay in developmental work on the F-16C block 50 programme.

The USAF wants – and expected to begin funding in 1992 – 72 F-16C block 50 aircraft which would have LANTIRN navigation/targetting systems and would be 'wired' for AGM-88A HARM (high-speed anti-radiation missile) and TSSAM (tri-service stand-off attack missile). Despite its current force reduction from 36 to 26 wings, the USAF wants to keep the F-16 in production into the late 1990s in order to obtain its much-wanted A-16 CAS aeroplanes from existing inventory and to field block 50 Fighting Falcons in front-line units. In Operation Desert Storm, the F-16 Fighting Falcon flew more sorties – 13,500 – than any other fixed-wing aircraft type.

100th AH-1W Supercobra delivered

The 100th production AH-1W Supercobra, or 'Whiskey' Cobra, was delivered to the US Marine Corps on 8 August 1991 at Bell's Fort Worth, Texas, facility.

The occasion brought comments from Marine officers about the AH-1W's performance in Operation Desert Storm. Forty-nine AH-1Ws participated in the war against Iraq, 28 operating from land bases and 21 aboard ships. The AH-1W was flown for 8,500 hours with no shortened blade lives experienced and no engine changes required. Also during the war, some AH-1Ws surged to as many as 16 flight-hours per day.

The Marine Corps has no plans for a new helicopter type comparable with the Army's RAH-66 Comanche, and expects to continue acquiring AH-1Ws well into the 1990s at a rate of about two per month.

Above: Future USN NFOs will be trained in the T-39N Sabreliner.

Right: A VF-213 Tomcat flies patrol over Kuwait's still-raging fires, August 1991.

Boeing abandons plans to resume 707 production

Faced with an "absence of sufficient new orders," Boeing announced on 30 August 1991 that it has abandoned efforts to restart production of military versions of the Boeing 707 aircraft. The military production line re-opened in 1977 shortly before the last commercial model 707 was delivered in 1978, and subsequent production has focussed on E-3 AWACS and E-6 Hermes submarine communications aircraft. The builder's last order for a military 707 was received in early 1987 and "the gap in orders has now widened to more than four years, making re-establishment of a production programme costly and difficult."

The decision appears to end Japan's quest for a version of the E-3 AWACS. Japanese plans called for an order of only two AWACS initially, to be followed a year later by two more. Boeing felt it needed orders for a minimum of 14 aircraft to enable a re-start of the 707 production line.

Boeing is close to completing the last of 16 E-6A Hermes for the US Navy, seven E-3D Sentry AEW.Mk 1s for Britain, and four E-3F Sentries for France. Other countries had shown interest in new AWACS aircraft including Austria, Italy, South Korea and Spain, but firm orders eluded the manufacturer. When production ends in 1993, 68 AWACS will have been produced for the US, NATO, Saudi Arabia, Britain and France.

US Navy seeks to re-start P-3 Orion production

The US Navy announced in August 1991 that it will seek funding for new-production P-3C Orion maritime patrol aircraft in fiscal year 1993 to fill a 'gap' left by the July 1990 cancellation of the P-7A aircraft, which was to have been a P-3C replacement. The Navy wants a version of the P-3C Update III to be known as the P-3C (Plus).

An obstacle to re-opening a P-3 production line had been the Navy's unwillingness to shoulder the cost alone. But an order for eight P-3s by South Korea in December 1990 (a figure which may increase to 12) has made it possible for Lockheed to open new production at Marietta, Georgia, even as the last of previously-ordered Orions is being completed at Palmdale, where the manufacturing facility will shut down. One source indicates that the Korean aeroplanes will be designated P-3D, even though the D suffix has long been used for NOAA (National Oceanographic and Atmospheric Administration) WP-3D and for VXN-8 (below) RP-3D aeroplanes.

At the end of August, the Navy had reduced its 24 active and 13 reserve P-3 squadrons to 20 and 13 respectively. By the end of fiscal year 1993, those figures will drop to 18 active and nine reserve squadrons.

The US Navy maritime patrol community is still feeling the impact of a 21 March 1991 loss of two P-3s which collided 96 km (60 miles) off the Californian coast, killing 27 crew members. The P-3C Update III retrofit aeroplanes, which were working with the USS *Abraham Lincoln* (CVN-72) battle group, were BuNos 159325 (coded SG-1) and 158930 (SG-8) belonging to VP-50 'Blue Dragons'.

The US Navy also announced in August that it is delaying work on its hoped-for ATS (Advanced Tactical System), a single aircraft type which would replace the E-2C Hawkeye early warning aircraft, EA-6B Prowler jammer, and S-3 Viking anti-submarine platform. The Navy now says that ATS is "perhaps 15 years away" and is working on service-life extensions of the types it would replace.

In other P-3 developments, Squadron VP-44, 'Golden Pelicans', which flew the P-3C Update II, was disestablished on 31 May 1991 at NAS Brunswick Maine; VP-19, 'Big Red', which had operated the P-3C Update I, was disestablished on 31 August 1991 at NAS Moffett Field, California; VP-48, 'Boomers', operating the P-3C Update III, was disestablished at Moffett Field on 31 August 1991; VP-56, 'Dragons', flying the P-3C Update III, was disestablished on 28 June 1991 at NAS Jacksonville, Florida; VP-MAU (VP Master Augmentation Unit), which had trained reserve crews in P-3A, UP-3A and P-3C Update II aircraft, was disestablished on 30 June 1991 at Brunswick.

VXN-8, or Oceanographic Development Squadron Eight, located at NAS Patuxent River, Maryland, held a retirement ceremony on 11 July 1991 for RP-3A Orion BuNo 150500, nicknamed '*Arctic Fox*' and employed for 18 years in Operation Birdseye ice-reconnaissance missions in northern climes. With 20,200 flight hours, the '*Arctic Fox*' will have all survey mission equipment removed and may eventually acquire a civilian owner. The well-known Orion will be replaced by a P-3B, BuNo 154587, which is now being converted to RP-3D standard. VXN-8 will then have five RP-3Ds on strength, including Birdseye aeroplanes nicknamed '*Roadrunner*' and '*El Coyote*'.

CILOP (conversion in lieu of procurement) of the EP-3E Aries II electronic reconnaissance versions of the Orion was assumed by the Naval Aviation Depot at NAS Alameda, California, on 31 July 1991. The depot will convert the last 7 of 12 P-3Cs selected to become EP-3Es for squadrons VQ-1 and VQ-2, the first five conversions to Aries II standard having already been accomplished by Lockheed AeroMod Center.

B-1B readying for SRAM II, conventional bomb tests

The US Air Force's B-1B Lancer bomber, hampered by recent groundings for engine problems and structural cracks, has begun tests with the AGM-131A SRAM II (Short-Range Attack Missile) designed to augment, and eventually replace, the AGM-69A SRAM-A now in service. In a separate development, even though the USAF's Air Staff has long denied any interest in a conventional bombing role for the B-1B, one example of the bomber (85-0068) is being modified at Rockwell's Palmdale, California, plant to support possible conventional weapons testing.

The B-1B has been awash in criticism and plagued by groundings since it became operational in September 1986. The bomber's Eaton AIL AN/ALQ-161 defensive electronics system – actually a suite of systems, comprising over 100 elements – has been called ineffective, and evaluations have been under way by the B-1B CTF (Combined Test Force) at Edwards AFB, California, with a downsized version of the system. In August 1991, the USAF acknowledged that 14 B-1B aircraft had cracks in the 25° longeron, requiring a 'fix' in the form of a boron epoxy plate attached to the affected area at a cost of $50,000 per aeroplane. Worse, an August 1991 study by the Institute for Defense Analyses (IDA) – mandated two years earlier by Congress – determined that costly plans to retrofit the scaled-down version of the AN/ALQ-161 would not enable the B-1B to defeat Soviet defences.

In early 1991, the B-1B assigned to the CTF carried out stores separation tests with the SRAM II at speeds up to Mach 0.85 and altitudes as low as 93 m (300 ft). Actual 'live' launches of the SRAM II from the B-1B are scheduled for early 1992 at White Sands Missile Range, New Mexico. Twenty-five SRAM II launches are scheduled over a 30-month period. The missile will have improved range and accuracy as compared with the SRAM-A and is viewed by Air Force officers as a new weapon rather than as an update to the SRAM-A. If the system survives budget challenges and technical hurdles to become operational, the B-1B will carry eight SRAM IIs on each of three rotary launchers.

The tactical version of the new missile, the AGM-131B SRAM-T, will apparently be tested by the Edwards-based CTF in 1995, although the SRAM-T is intended for use with the F-15E Strike Eagle.

The B-1B now being modified for conventional weapons testing is the same ship (one of two on charge with Air Force Systems Command, not SAC) previously employed for tests involving the AGM-129A ACM (advanced cruise missile). Ironically, the USAF has no known plans to employ the ACM aboard the B-1B and has publicly stated that it has no plans to employ the B-1B in a conventional bombing role. The B-1B will, however, be highly effective as a platform from which to evaluate various kinds of ordnance.

Third B-2 flying, future uncertain

On 18 June 1991 and 3 July 1991, landing gear problems caused the US Air Force to curtail two separate B-2 bomber flights. In both cases, as a routine safety precaution, the bombers were diverted to landings on Rogers Dry Lake at Edwards AFB, California. The B-2s landed without mishap. The two incidents, according to USAF spokesmen, were unrelated.

The third B-2, known as AV-3 (Air Vehicle 3), resumed flying in August 1991 after a six-week lay-up for maintenance. The third ship is reportedly to be first in the series to be equipped with a Northrop defensive countermeasures system, identified as the ZSR-2, intended to enable the bomber to penetrate or evade air defence radar systems. The USAF and Northrop

VMFA-321 painted up this F-4 in old style high-vis colours for their disbandment.

have kept close wraps on the bomber' defensive system, refusing even to confirm its designation, but sources indicate tha the system is much more than a jamme and includes an intelligence-gathering capability directed towards such difficul targets as mobile ICBM launchers. Whil officials have maintained for years that th B-2 does not need to emit energy (an hence, render itself vulnerable to detection in order to carry out its mission, source now say that the ZSR-2 emits 'miniscul amounts' when employed to deceive defensive radar system.

Sources indicate that a stand-off weapon for the B-2, not yet identified by name, i being developed in a 'black' programm which the USAF refuses to acknowledge This weapon is said to be a different system from the AGM-129A ACM (advance cruise missile) or AGM-131A SRAM I (short-range attack missile).

In July 1991, the Senate Armed Service Committee gave a tentative go-ahead t the administration's request for additiona production funding for the B-2 (for fou aeroplanes, ships Nos 16-19, in fiscal yea 1992), but failed to support a sub-committee recommendation for an accelerate buy-out of all 75 planned B-2s by fisca year 1996.

Fifteen B-2 bombers had been paid fo and seemed 'safe' at the end of fiscal yea

Left: This P-3C Update II.5 belongs to VP-16 'Eagles'.

Above: Yellow stripes enliven a Jacksonville-based SH-3. Jacksonville's Sea King units are transitioning to the SH-60F.

Above: Also present at the ceremony was the record-breaking 'Sageburner', the 11th Phantom built.

1991 from any budget-cutting measures. Despite resistance in the House of Representatives, it appeared likely that the Bush administration would win approval of its bid for four B-2s, to be built in fiscal year 1992 (beginning 1 October 1991). The future of the B-2 bomber after that would remain uncertain, with the flying-wing aircraft a target for almost every special-interest group in domestic US politics.

Having already reduced its planned purchase of the B-2 from 132 aircraft to 75 (as a result of Defense Secretary Dick Cheney's Major Aircraft Review of spring 1990), the US Air Force is now under strong pressure to agree to a fleet of 50 B-2s. Dialogue on the issue is confused – critics of the bomber insisting that they can kill future acquisition entirely, supporters arguing that a 50-plane fleet would be too small to maintain SIOP (Single Integrated Operations Plan) nuclear alert status – and would allow the USAF to field fewer than two wings.

Subject to Congressional funding and the outcome of domestic debate, the USAF/Bush administration's schedule for purchase of a fleet of 75 B-2s (two wings of 30 each plus 15 for other purposes) is as follows: 15 aircraft in pipeline (including three now flying); four in FY (fiscal year) 1992; seven in FY 1993; seven in FY 1994; 11 in FY 1995; 11 in FY 1996; 11 in FY 1997; nine in FY 1998 (for a total of 75).

Douglas C-17 airlifter makes first flight

The Douglas C-17 made its first flight on 15 September 1991, flying from the manufacturer's Long Beach, California, facility to Edwards Air Force Base where developmental testing was to begin. Crew of the first C-17, known as T-1, was pilot William Casey, co-pilot Lieutenant Colonel George London, flight test engineer Vanm De Graaf, and loadmaster Ted Venturini.

The C-17 flight-test programme, now underway with Edwards' 6510th Test Wing, will eventually use five aircraft, of which four will later become operational with MAC (Military Airlift Command). Ten C-17s are now in assembly, including two non-flying ground-test airframes, the prototype, and the first seven production aeroplanes. The USAF's planned purchase of C-17s was reduced from 210 aircraft to 120 as a result of Defense Secretary Dick Cheney's MAR (Major Aircraft Review) in March 1990.

The three-man C-17, which will eventually replace some C-141B StarLifters, is the first four-engined airlifter to have a two-member cockpit crew, a single loadmaster, and all-digital FBW (fly-by-wire) flight controls. Its short-field landing capability is based on powered lift using an externally-blown flap principle, directed-flow thrust-reversers, and avionics for the air crew, including the first HUD (head-up display) in a transport.

The C-17 is powered by four 18915-kg (41,700-lb) thrust Pratt & Whitney F117-PW-100 (PW2040) engines. Maximum gross weight is 263083 kg (580,000 lb). Maximum payload is 781081 kg (172,200 lb).

The first C-17 is scheduled to be delivered to MAC in late 1992, with IOC (initial operating capability) by the 17th Airlift Squadron, 437th Airlift Wing, Charleston AFB, SC, in 1994.

Last fleet Corsair squadrons disestablished

The final two Fleet A-7 Corsair II squadrons were disestablished during a ceremony at NAS Cecil Field, Florida, on 30 May with their official demise following at the end of June. The last two squadrons were VA-46 and VA-72, which served with CVW-3 aboard CV-67/USS *John F. Kennedy* and whose last cruise was during Desert Shield and Desert Storm between 15 August 1990 and 28 March 1991. The squadrons have been replaced within CVW-3 by VFA-37 and VFA-105.

Surprisingly, front-line Fleet A-7 squadrons outlived the Corsair in Naval Reserve service, as the type was retired by VA-204 at NAS New Orleans, Louisiana, on 13 April. The squadron was redesignated VFA-204 on 1 May in preparation for the delivery of the first F/A-18A. NAS New Orleans received the latest Naval Reserve transport unit when VR-54 was established on 1 June to operate six examples of the C-130T.

USS Lexington ceases training duties

After 29 years in the training role, the carrier AVT-16/USS *Lexington* ceased operations on 8 March, several months earlier than planned, as the ship was originally due to have remained in service until being decommissioned on 26 November. However, due to the high cost of operating the elderly vessel it was decided the ship would not put to sea again and would be temporarily replaced in the training role by other Atlantic Fleet carriers until 1992, when CV-59/USS *Forrestal* will be permanently assigned. A C-2A Greyhound from VRC-40 had the distinction of performing the 493,760th, and last, arrested landing aboard the *Lexington*.

Navy squadron news

VAQ-35 was established at NAS Whidbey Island, Washington, on 1 June, joining sister units VAQ-33 and -34 performing electronic warfare 'aggressor' training as part of the Fleet Electronic Warfare Support Group (FEWSG). The squadron has four EA-6Bs assigned, which were formerly flown by VAQ-142, until the latter was disestablished at NAS Whidbey Island on 31 March.

After having retired most of its A-7 Corsair aircraft several months earlier, VA-122 was disestablished at NAS Lemoore, California, on 31 May. The squadron has been responsible for training Pacific Fleet A-7 pilots for more than two decades. VAQ-34, which moved from NAS Point Mugu, California, to NAS Lemoore in May, is the only Navy squadron operating the A-7, with this unit taking over the responsibility for training the few Corsair pilots still required.

With E-6A Hermes deliveries to VQ-3 well advanced, VQ-4 at NAS Patuxent River, Maryland, has begun receiving its initial complement. The first aircraft arrived on 25 January and, after a work-up period, operational missions began in June. VQ-5 formed at NAS Agana, Guam, on 15 April in anticipation of receiving the first operational ES-3A Elint Viking for the Pacific Fleet, while VQ-6 was formed at NAS Cecil Field, Florida, in August for Atlantic Fleet ES-3A operations.

HS-3 at NAS Jacksonville, Florida, commenced transition from the SH-3H to the SH-60F in April, to become the Atlantic Fleet's first unit to convert to the latter type, with completion due in October.

The majority of squadrons which together composed CVW-13 have transferred elsewhere or disestablished in recent months. The Carrier Air Wing was itself disestablished on 1 January 1991, even though the last cruise aboard CV-43/USS *Coral Sea* ended in late September 1989. At the completion of this cruise, Marine Corps F/A-18A Squadron VMFA-451 returned to shore-based duty at MCAS Beaufort, South Carolina, while VFA-132 and VFA-137 were both transferred to CVW-6 during 1990. Of the two A-6E squadrons, VA-65 moved to CVW-8 immediately after the 1989 cruise, while VA-55 officially disestablished on 1 January 1991. As stated earlier, VAQ-142 disestablished on 31 March 1991, with HS-17 standing down at NAS Jacksonville on 2 July 1991. This accounts for all of CVW-13's squadrons except for VAW-127, whose present status is unknown.

In preparation for the transfer of CV-62/USS *Independence* to be home-ported at Yokosuka, Japan, to replace CV-41/USS *Midway*, several changes of complement have taken place to CVW-5. F/A-18A squadron VFA-151 moved to NAS Lemoore from NAF Atsugi on 30 September 1991, while the S-3Bs of VS-21 will arrive at Atsugi from NAS North Island around the same time as the USS *Independence*. The remainder of the Carrier Air Wing complement will continue as before.

Military Aviation Review

New 'Air Force One' visits London

President of the United States George Bush arrived in London on 14 July aboard new 'Air Force One' VC-25A 86-28000 of the 89th MAW, to attend the G7 economic meeting. The VC-25 landed at Heathrow Airport shortly after 7.00 p.m. on its first visit to the UK, and was followed next day by second example 86-29000 with Secretary of State James Baker aboard. The two aircraft remained at Heathrow until 18 July, when the President left the United Kingdom. Three HMX-1 VH-3Ds, consisting of 159351, 159353 and 159254, were on hand to provide the President with helicopter transport within the capital, arriving at Heathrow from RAF Mildenhall on the afternoon of 14 July. The trio of VIP Sea Kings was airlifted in a C-5 Galaxy on 10 July from Andrews AFB, Maryland, to Mildenhall, where they were test-flown prior to their relocation to London.

The VH-3s were joined at Mildenhall by UH-60As 81-23580, 81-23616, 86-24555, 87-24634 and 88-26056 of the 6th Battalion, 158th Aviation Regiment from Wiesbaden, and CH-47D 87-0077 from 7th Battalion, 158th Aviation Regiment at Mainz-Finthen, which ferried Army special forces from Germany. UH-60A 24555 and the Chinook remained at Mildenhall while the other four Black Hawks, containing the special forces personnel, provided escort to the three VH-3s. Upon arrival at Heathrow, President Bush travelled to central London by road although his helicopter escort was airborne for the duration of the journey.

C-20C 86-0403 of 89th MAW spent the period of the G7 meeting on standby at RAF Northolt. The wing is reported to have changed designation from Military Airlift Wing to Military Special Missions Wing earlier this year, and adopted a second retitling on 12 July when it became the 89th Airlift Wing (officially abbreviated simply to 89th ALW). The most recent change is in line with the decision by the Commander in Chief of Military Airlift Command General H. T. Johnson to drop the words 'Military' and 'Tactical' from MAC unit titles in order to eliminate the segregation between intercontinental and theatre airlift prior to the delivery of the C-17, which is intended to perform both roles.

Former 'Air Force One' C-137C 62-6000 returned to Andrews AFB on 20 June to rejoin the 89th MAW fleet as a normal VIP transport after having spent nine months at Greenville, Texas, where E-Systems Inc. reconfigured the interior and removed the Presidential special communications equipment.

Chrysler C-27A programme on schedule

Chrysler Technologies (CTAS) is completing modification of the first of 10 C-27A intra-theatre airlifters for the US Air Force and claims to be on schedule. The C-27A is a conversion of the Alenia G.222 twin-turboprop transport, the first of which arrived at Chrysler's Waco, Texas, plant for modification on 19 April 1991. This initial aircraft was scheduled for

delivery in August to the USAF, which will operate it for US Southern Command (Southcom) headquartered at Howard AFB, Panama.

In August 1990, CTAS was awarded an $80.2-million contract to produce five C-27As. In February 1991, the USAF exercised an option valued at $72.6 million for five additional aircraft.

The C-27A is expected to facilitate US military operations in Latin America, where few established air bases are in use, transport missions cover a broad area, and operating conditions are austere. The C-27A is expected to be capable of carrying up to 6739 kg (14,859 lb) of cargo, 24 paratroopers or 34 combat-equipped troops, 24 litters with four medical attendants, or a variety of wheeled vehicles. The C-27A is capable of making parachute drops.

In addition to modifying the aircraft, CTAS will provide training for USAF crews with initial maintenance and aircrew training taking place at the Alenia facility in Naples, Italy. In due course, transition training will be located at the Waco facility.

The requirement for the C-27A arose in 1987, at a time when US Southern Command, which is responsible for American military operations in Central and South America, faced conflicts in Nicaragua and El Salvador, plus anti-drug operations in Colombia and Peru.

Strategic reconnaissance unit news

Strategic Air Command reconnaissance units have been the subject of changes in recent months. At RAF Alconbury the 17th Reconnaissance Wing was inactivated on 28 June as the controlling element of the TR-1As serving in Europe, with the 95th RS being directly assigned to the 9th SRW at Beale AFB, California. However, much of the unit's day-to-day tasking will be co-ordinated through the 7th Air Division (SAC) at Ramstein. The squadron was to have had a complement of 16 TR-1As, although it is doubtful if it ever operated this number. The elimination of the threat from the Warsaw Pact has considerably reduced the operational requirement of the TR-1A in Europe, with the result that the 95th RS will be assigned just four aircraft in due course. At present the unit has only five pilots assigned, plus the squadron commander and his deputy, despite having more than seven TR-1s based. The 9th SRW has several U-2Rs and TR-1As stationed at Taif, Saudi Arabia, providing an ongoing commitment to monitor activities inside Iraq, with aircraft rotated between Beale, Alconbury and the Middle East on a regular basis.

The 9th SRW has activated the 5th SRS and 6th SRS at RAF Akrotiri, Cyprus, and Osan AB, South Korea, replacing Detachments 3 and 2 respectively. The upgrading of the units to squadron status will permit an increased number of aircraft to be operated when necessary. Four additional detachments have deactivated in recent years, three associated with the SR-71A, while the fourth operated the TR-1A/U-2R. Detachment 5 at Patrick AFB, Florida, which operated one TR-1A/U-2R, flew its last mission in October 1990 and was inactivated in February 1991.

Above: A VIP VH-3D of HMX-1 deployed to Britain to carry George Bush to the G7 summit.

Left: The Marines have their own fixed-wing VIP aircraft, including this Sabreliner.

Below: The US Army's Berlin-based Pilatus Turbo Porters have been re-assigned for new duties Stateside.

Detachment 1 at Kadena AB, Okinawa, and Detachment 4 at RAF Mildenhall both flew the SR-71A until January 1990, when the aircraft returned home, permitting the dets to inactivate. Detachment 6 at Norton AFB, California, was associated with the SR-71 programme, although it did not operate any aircraft directly. Instead, the det was responsible for logistics support, providing the link between Lockheed, the parent wing at Beale and the overseas detachments. This has inactivated.

The 9th SRW also operates the majority of KC-135Q tankers, which until early 1990 were dedicated to providing air refuelling to the SR-71s, until the latter's premature retirement. Subsequently the KC-135Qs have been reassigned to support the F-117A 'Stealth Fighter'. 9th SRW KC-135Qs were active during Desert Shield and Desert Storm, ferrying personnel and equipment between the USA and Khamis Mushait, Saudi Arabia, before basing a sizeable complement of tankers at Riyadh Military City Airport to conduct refuelling sorties for the F-117A. The 9th SRW at present operates 40 Q models, and will possess a disproportionate number even with the planned inactivation of the 349th ARS and the transfer of nine aircraft elsewhere. The large number of KC-135Qs remaining with the 350th ARS indicates the unit's continued support of the F-117A programme, although the move by the 37th TFW from Tonopah Test Range, Nevada, to Holloman AFB, New Mexico, will be less than convenient. The distance from Beale AFB to Tonopah is approximately 400 miles, whereas Holloman AFB is more than 600 miles further away. One solution could be to detach a number of tankers to Holloman, and it may be that the 'Stealth Fighter'/KC-135Q combination could be another candidate to become a composite wing.

Marine Corps overseas deployments

Marine Corps Reserve Squadron VMAQ at NAS Whidbey Island, Washington, was mobilised on 11 March prior to commencing a six-month deployment to MCA Iwakuni, Japan, as part of the USMC Unit Deployment Program (UDP). VMAQ began operating the EA-6B on 2 April having earlier transferred its EA-6As to VAQ-33. With transition to the Prowler complete the squadron flew to Japan in June to relieve VMAQ-2 Det X, whose six-month deployment began in June 19 and was extended by a further seven months due to Operation Desert Storm. A number of other Marine Reserve units were mobilised to fulfill UDP commitments in the Far East, including HML-7 and HML-776 operating the UH-1N

Above: The Enstrom TH-28/400 is a contender for the US Army new training helicopter requirement.

Below: Marsh Aviation have now flown a prototype ASW-configured Turbo Tracker.

Left: The KC-130T-30H, the newest C-130 variant, takes shape. This will be a stretched tanker.

1,000th Hornet delivered

The Marine Corps became the recipient of the 1,000th Hornet when VMFA (AW)-242 at MCAS El Toro received F/A-18D 164237 on 22 April.

USAFE unit change details – update

Additional details have been made available concerning the withdrawal of certain units and the relocation of others from within the United States Air Forces in Europe (USAFE). The 10th TFW at RAF Alconbury is preparing the withdrawal of its two squadrons of A-10As, which will start in the autumn of 1991 and should be completed by the spring of 1992. The 509th TFS will be the first to withdraw, followed by the 511th TFS, although many of the wing's aircraft have been operating without fin-tip colours since July, indicating they may be operating on a 'pool' basis. During early 1992 the 39th SOW will begin moving to Alconbury with the MH-53Js 'Pave Low III' of the 21st SOS and HC-130N/P Combat Rescue Hercules of the 67th SOS, both relocating from Woodbridge, and the MC-130E 'Combat Talon I' version of the Hercules of the 7th SOS relocating together with the parent wing from Rhein Main AB, Germany. Completion of the move will mark the first occasion when Europe-based USAF special operations have been grouped to-

NAS South Weymouth, Massachusetts, and NAS Glenview, Illinois, respectively, and HMH-772 with the CH-53A based at NAS Dallas, Texas. Front-line Marine Corps F/A-18 Hornet squadrons currently located in the Far East are VMFA-531 from MCAS El Toro (which deployed in February 1991 to replace VMFA-323, which had also exceeded its six-month Iwakuni detachment by four months due to Desert Shield/Desert Storm), and VMFA-122 (which left MCAS Beaufort, South Carolina, for Iwakuni in April 1991 to relieve MVFA-312, which had been delayed in Japan a further three months for the same reason). AV-8B Squadron VMA-513 from MCAS Yuma, Arizona, flew to Iwakuni during December 1990, while VMA(AW)-332 from MCAS Cherry Point, North Carolina, completed the UDP commitment commencing January 1991.

gether at one facility, although the nature of their mission will ensure they are operated from a variety of locations in Europe. At present the majority of 39th SOW assets are supporting the ongoing Provide Comfort operation in eastern Turkey, which may delay the plans for the move and preparations to upgrade to the MC-130H 'Combat Talon II'.

Once RAF Alconbury has completed the return of its A-10s to the USA, it will be the turn of the 81st TFW at RAF Bentwaters and RAF Woodbridge, who will commence in April 1992 and continue for the next 12 months. The 81st TFW has 80 A-10As divided equally between the two bases, with Woodbridge initiating the retirement process when the 78th TFS begins going home over a three-month period commencing in April. The 91st TFS will follow in July before the 510th TFS at Bentwaters returns its aircraft to the USA between October and December, although the latter squadron is to transfer the best of its aircraft to the 92nd TFS. This will ensure the 92nd TFS is composed of A-10s with the lowest airframe hours and the best maintenance records, prior to the squadron relocating to Spangdahlem to join the 52nd TFW between January and March 1993. Six of the Thunderbolts will be to OA-10A configuration. Once transition is complete the 52nd TFW will be the first composite wing in USAFE. The 81st TFW ceased forward operating location (FOL) duties to Sembach mid-May, with detachments to continue to Leipheim and Norvenich until the end of 1991. The 10th TFW had ceased deploying to its FOL at Ahlhorn by the autumn of 1991.

At RAF Lakenheath the 48th TFW has begun the first stages in preparation for the arrival of the F-15E and the transfer of the F-111Fs to the 27th TFW at Cannon AFB, New Mexico. The 495th TFS, which has a training role in addition to its operational commitment, is to deactivate before the end of 1991, followed by a second squadron during 1992. The identity of this other squadron has yet to be confirmed, although it will either be the 493rd or 494th TFS as the 492nd TFS will be the first to convert to the F-15E. The wing is to be assigned two squadrons, each equipped with 24 aircraft.

The 10th ACCS at RAF Mildenhall has been retiring its EC-135H post-attack airborne command posts (PAACP) since the end of May, with the remaining two and its WC-135B trainer due to return to the USA by the end of 1991. The 'Silk Purse' command centre ceased operations at the end of August, enabling the Control Group and the 10th ACCS to be inactivated at the end of the year. Overseas-based airborne command posts are being retired or reassigned to the 55th SRW at Offutt AFB, Nebraska, including those from the 9th ACCS at Hickam AFB, Hawaii, and the Mildenhall squadron. In addition the SAC EC-135A/G/L variants based at Ellsworth AFB, South Dakota, with the 28th BW and the 305th ARW at Grissom AFB, Indiana, are included in this consolidation of PAACP assets along with the EC-135Ps of the 6th ACCS at Langley AFB, Virginia. However, there will be a limited ongoing requirement for airborne command post duties overseas, with 55th SRW aircraft detached to Mildenhall and Hickam as required.

In Germany several bases have ceased flying duties within the last few months. Zweibrücken AB transferred a dozen of its RF-4Cs to the 67th TRW at Bergstrom AFB, Texas, during March and April, while the remaining eight were retired for storage or ground training duties before the 26th TRW deactivated and the base closed. Several of the airframes employed in the battle damage repair role at Zweibrücken were transported by road to museums in Germany and France. The 43rd ECS at Sembach AB inactivated on 6 May, with its last three EC-130H 'Compass Call' versions of the Hercules relocating to the 41st ECS at Davis Monthan AFB, Arizona. The 66th ECW inactivated shortly afterwards, prior to the base reverting to German control on 1 August. The wing was the controlling authority for the EF-111As of the 42nd ECS at Upper Heyford which have been transferred to the 20th TFW for the remainder of their stay in Europe. Sembach still houses Headquarters 17th Air Force, which is responsible for USAF activities in Germany but has no aircraft assigned.

The 52nd TFW at Spangdahlem initiated a reorganisation earlier this year in readiness for equipment changes. For many years the wing was assigned three squadrons flying a mixture of F-4G 'Wild Weasel' versions of the Phantom, together with the F-16C Fighting Falcon in an anti-SAM hunter/killer team. However, the 81st TFS transferred its F-16Cs to the 480th TFS in exchange for that squadron's F-4Gs, resulting in the two units operating just the one type. The 23rd TFS is the only squadron operating both types and will continue in this mode until the end of 1991, when the F-4G will be replaced by additional F-16Cs, including some obtained from the 401st TFW at Torrejon. The F-4Gs of the 81st TFS will remain operational until 1992 when it is to return to the USA for service with the Air National Guard, permitting the squadron to deactivate before the 92nd TFS arrives from Bentwaters.

The 36th TFW at Bitburg has been approximately 12 aircraft under strength since September 1990, when a batch of two dozen USAFE F-15Cs was transferred to the Royal Saudi Air Force as part of the Desert Shield build-up of forces. The other 12 aircraft were drawn from the 32nd TFG at Soesterberg AB, Netherlands, that squadron likewise being operated on a reduced capability basis. However, the 525th TFS is to inactivate by early 1992, permitting the two squadrons remaining at Bitburg to be fully equipped while the residue of F-15s will transfer to the 32nd TFG.

As stated in an earlier edition of *World Air Power Journal*, the 401st TFW at Torrejon AB, Spain, deactivated the 613th TFS in June and has since disbanded the 612th TFS in September. The 614th TFS will follow in December, although the wing is understood to be relocating to Aviano AB, Italy, without personnel or equipment pending a decision on the future of Crotone AB, Italy. One report suggests the wing will remain active for the time being and will be assigned three 'other USAFE squadrons, which will remain at their home bases except in time of crisis. If this report is true, the 52nd TFW at Spangdahlem and the 86th FW at Ramstein would be likely candidates.

BRIEFING

Right: The Staff Flight of MFG 1 uses this unusual flying suit patch. Axel Ostermann is the deputy commander of this unit. Main picture: The AIM-9 is already curving away towards its hapless target as the launch aircraft manoeuvres to engage another target.

Panavia Tornado

Live missile launch

Staffelkapitan Axel Ostermann, whose 'From the Cockpit' photo feature appeared in the last volume of *World Air Power Journal*, has since sent us this breathtaking photo of a Marineflieger Tornado loosing off an AIM-9 Sidewinder. Marineflieger Tornados use the AIM-9 for self defence, and also use the HARM anti-radiation missile and the Kormoran anti-ship missile in their anti-shipping role.

Left: This is one of the ageing Lim-6bis aircraft used by 45 LPSz-B (Lotniczy Pulk Szkolno-Bowojy) at Babimost. The prominent brake chute fairing and inboard underwing pylons (here with an indigenous Mars-2 rocket pod attached) are clearly visible. Poland's last Lim-6s were used to give tactical training to newly qualified fast-jet pilots, who would then go on to Su-20s or MiG-21s.

Below: The simple (almost Korean War-vintage) cockpit of the Lim-6bis was dominated by a broad vertical white line painted down the centre of the panel. In the event of entering a spin, the pilot merely has to centralise the stick by lining it up with the painted line.

Mikoyan-Gurevich MiG-17/PZL Lim-6

Old soldiers fading away

Today, the MiG-17 is widely regarded as being obsolete and an anachronism, fit only to serve with Third World air arms, and then in secondary roles. In fact, many MiG-17s remained in front-line Warsaw Pact ser-

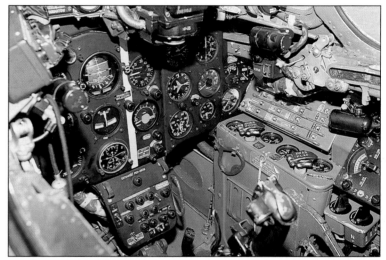

Left: The cannon pack can quickly be winched down to be reloaded, as in the contemporary British Hawker Hunter. Pre-loaded cannon packs cannot be exchanged for an exhausted pack, however. The three-digit tactical code comprises the last three digits of the constructor's number.

Below: Engine running – a tethered Lim-6bis with its Klimov VK-1F turbojet in full afterburner. Underwing fuel tanks are an almost permanent fixture on these elderly fighter-bombers. The entire rear fuselage could be removed for access to the powerplant.

MiG-17/PZL Lim-6 fading away

Above: The pilot of this taxiing Lim-6bis wears an old-fashioned cloth flying helmet, there being no room for a modern 'bone-dome'.

Top right: This battered-looking Lim-6bis shows its age, with huge areas of silver paint showing through the peeling camouflage.

vice into the 1980s, finally being replaced by MiG-23BNs in the early 1980s. Even after their withdrawal from the front line, small numbers of MiG-17s remained in use for other duties in a number of European countries.

The Polish MiG-17 connection began in the mid-1950s, when the type was adopted as a successor to the MiG-15. Licensed production began in 1956. The first Polish MiG-17 variant was based on the MiG-17F 'Fresco-C' and designated Lim-5. A total of 477 was delivered (with c/n's between 1C 00-01 and 1C 19-14) between 28 November 1956 and 30 June 1960. The MiG-17PF 'Fresco-D' all-weather fighter was delivered between 18 January 1959 and 29 Decem-

Below: The ventral recce pack of this Lim-6bisR contains an AFA-39 camera.

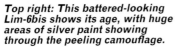

ber 1960 as the Lim-5P. A total of 129 was built, ending with c/n 1D 06-41. A handful of Lim-5Rs was also delivered, and these were basically MiG-17Fs equipped with an under-fuselage camera pack.

In an attempt to produce a dedicated ground-attack fighter, the Poles produced 60 Lim-5Ms, which had thickened wing roots housing extra fuel, twin-wheel main undercarriage units, and provision for RATO gear. The first made its maiden flight on 2 July 1959 and the last was delivered on 10 May 1961. They never reached service status.

Next was the similar 'thick-winged' Lim-6, which had modified flaps and a drag chute in a conical fairing at the base of the rudder. Forty were completed (c/n's 1J 04-01 to 1J 04-40) but proved no more successful than the Lim-5M.

Most of the Lim-5Ms and Lim-6s were modified back to a more standard configuration as the Lim-6bis from 23 May 1963, with conventional undercarriage and inner wings, and without the new flaps but with new inboard underwing pylons. The Lim-5Ms also received the Lim-6-style brake parachute. A handful of Lim-5Ps was upgraded to Lim-6bis standard (retaining their radar nose contours) as Lim-6Ms.

Above: This pristine-looking 'Fresco' is seen outside its camouflaged hardened aircraft shelter at Babimost.

With the conversion programme complete, 70 new aircraft were built to Lim-6bis standard, the last, c/n 1J 06-40, being delivered on 25 February 1964. The conversions and new-build Lim-6bis aircraft included a number of Lim-6bisRs, with a ventral camera pack.

Left: For conversion and continuation training 45 LPSz-B uses a handful of licence-built MiG-15UTI 'Midgets', some of them converted from single-seat MiG-15s. They are actually designated SBLim-2M in Polish service, the M suffix indicating a variety of improvements, including increased area airbrakes. Some were previously SBLim-2A reconnaissance aircraft, with a ventral camera pack and a periscope in the front cockpit.

Below: The front cockpit of an SBLim-2M. The instrument panel layout is virtually identical to that of the MiG-17, making the older aircraft an excellent conversion trainer.

Left: Instructor and pupil pose beside one of the unit's SBLim-2Ms. They both wear standard Polish air force flying kit, including the antique-looking cloth flying helmets necessitated by the lack of headroom in the MiG-15UTI.

One Polish air force unit was still using the Lim into the 1990s. 45 PLM (fighter squadron) received the Lim-5 in 1961, and was later redesignated 45 PLM-Sz (fighter attack squadron) and then in 1982 45 PLM-B (fighter bomber squadron). Finally, in 1986, the unit became a fighter-bomber training squadron as 45 LPSz-B.

Below: Seen from above, the different wing planform of the MiG-15/SBLim-2 by comparison with the Lim-5/Lim-6bis can clearly be seen, along with its smaller, unstiffened airbrakes and different wing fence arrangement.

BRIEFING

Take Charge And Move Out II

For many years, the vital role of maintaining communications links with the US Navy's nuclear missile-launching submarines was undertaken by the Lockheed Hercules in its EC-130G and EC-130Q variants. Although it performed well in the role, the Hercules suffered from a lack of patrol endurance, and the airframes were old. The US Navy embarked on a programme to replace the aircraft known as TACAMO (Take Charge And Move Out) II.

On 29 April 1983 Boeing was given the contract to develop TACAMO II, and naturally chose the military 707 airframe as a basis. In all, 16 aircraft were required for the mission, these accounting (along with some E-3s for France and the United Kingdom) for the last airframes from the 1,000-plus Boeing 707 production line.

In essence the new TACAMO II (designated E-6A and later named Hermes) is based on the later production E-3 aircraft, and indeed shares great commonality with the Sentry. However, it is fitted with the CFM International F108-CF-100 turbofan,

Previous TACAMO equipment was the Lockheed EC-130Q Hercules, this example being from VQ-4. Having been upgraded throughout its career, much of the communications equipment, including the AVLF, was taken out and installed directly into the replacement E-6As.

rated at 106.76 kN (24,000 lb) thrust, higher even than the similar engines of the later E-3s. These engines feature very low fuel burn, allowing the E-6 to perform an unrefuelled patrol of 10 hours 30 minutes 1850 km (1,150 miles) from base, or nearly 29 hours with one refuelling. With multiple refuellings the E-6 is designed to perform a 72-hour mission.

Internally the E-6 has three areas. Forward is the crew area, comprising a four-man flight deck and a rest area. The latter has standard amenities such as toilet and galley, and eight bunks for the carriage of spare crew members during long patrols or deployments. In the overwing area is the main mission compartment, with five communications stations, one of which is for the Airborne Communications Officer, who oversees the relay and transmission of messages. In the rear of the cabin is the equipment area, with access for inflight maintenance.

As one would expect, the E-6 is packed with communications equipment. No less than three VHF/UHF and five HF radios are carried, with secure voice capability, a feature also shared by the crew intercom system. UHF satellite communications aerials are housed in distinctive wingtip pods, underneath which are probes for the HF system. Also in the wingtip pods are receivers for the ALR-66(V)4 electronic support measures system, providing the E-6 with a passive warning system should it come under attack and a means of providing information about hostile surface ships that may be operating in its area. The central communications area is

equipped with a vast array of recorders, teletypes and cryptographic systems, and a downlink receiver for the ERCS (Emergency Rocket Communications System). The comm gear is hardened against the effects of nuclear blast and radiation.

In its TACAMO role, the E-6 would be airborne in time of tension using the large array of systems at its command to be in contact with the Air Force's airborne command posts, the Presidential Boeing E-4 National Emergency Airborne Command Post, the ERCS and ground stations. From a variety of sources it could receive messages for the SSBN (ballistic missile submarine) fleet. These are

BuNo 162782 was the first E-6A completed for the US Navy. Its first flight took place on 19 February 1987, and was a short hop from the Renton manufacturing facility to Boeing Field, Seattle.

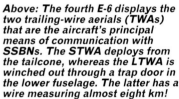

Above: The fourth E-6 displays the two trailing-wire aerials (TWAs) that are the aircraft's principal means of communication with SSBNs. The STWA deploys from the tailcone, whereas the LTWA is winched out through a trap door in the lower fuselage. The latter has a wire measuring almost eight km!

Above: Now that the nuclear threat has receded considerably, the E-6's mission is not so vital, allowing the eventual basing of the fleet at Tinker, sharing central servicing with the USAF's E-3 fleet. The Soviets have an E-6 equivalent in the shape of the Tu-142 'Bear-J', similarly equipped with TWAs.

Below: A close-up of the wingtip shows the pods that house Satcom UHF downlink receivers and ESM equipment. Standard HF probes are carried underneath.

downlinked to the submarines using the AVLF (Airborne Very Low Frequency) suite, which consists of two trailing wire aerials. An STWA (Short Trailing Wire Aerial) acts as a dipole, and deploys from the tailcone. This wire is 1220 m (4,000 ft) long. The main aerial is the LTWA (Long TWA) which is a massive 7925 m (26,000 ft) long and deploys from the lower rear fuselage.

When wishing to communicate with SSBNs, the E-6 reels out the TWAs and enters a tight orbit. The LTWA has a 41-kg (90-lb) drogue attached which pulls the aerial down, and the tight turn of the aircraft causes the wire to stall and hang vertically. Over 70 per cent of the wire must be vertical for communications to be undertaken. The entire LTWA weighs some 495 kg (1,090 lb), a figure which nearly doubles in drag effect when fully deployed. Messages are passed using 200 kW of power, and are received by SSBNs towing antenna arrays.

As noted, a total of 16 E-6s has been funded, comprising BuNos 162782/4 in Fiscal Year 1986, BuNos 163918/20 in FY 87, 164386/8 in FY 88 and 164404/10 in FY 89. The first of these took to the air from Boeing's Renton, Washington, plant on 19 February 1987, and full systems trials began on 1 June. During the course of aerodynamic trials the aircraft lost part of its fin during a dive.

2 August 1989 was the date of the first delivery, a pair of E-6s going to NAS Barber's Point, Hawaii, for use by VQ-3. Five were in place by October, although all were being used for crew training. Flight crew training is also undertaken by McDonnell Douglas at Waco, Texas, using a pair of civil Boeing 707s with E-6 cockpit systems and dummy refuelling receptacles. It was not until November 1990 that VQ-3 (named the 'Tacamopac') was up to its full strength of eight aircraft for support of the Pacific Fleet. Early 1991 saw the delivery of E-6s to the East Coast squadron, VQ-4 'Shadows' at NAS Patuxent River, Maryland, allowing the replacement of the EC-130Qs.

Changes envisaged for the E-6 fleet include the move by VQ-4 to Tinker AFB, Oklahoma, in June 1992 so that the aircraft can enjoy the benefits (and the Navy the cost-saving) of basing the machines alongside the USAF's E-3 Sentry fleet. VQ-3 may also move to Tinker at a later date, but the distances involved in travelling to the Pacific operational areas may prevent this. In any case, the E-6 with its ultra-long range and full remote deployment capability can easily operate autonomously from any runway large enough to take it.

Slovenian Air War

For many years the Yugoslavian confederation of separate republics was held together with tenuous chains by the federal government in Belgrade. In late June 1991 Slovenia became the first republic to break away, resulting in fierce fighting between Slovenian and federal forces.

On 26 June 1991 the Slovenian nation was celebrating outside the parliament buildings in Ljubljana. The previous day Slovenia had formally declared its independence from the rapidly disintegrating federation of Yugoslavia. However, the state government in Belgrade was far from happy at the turn of events in the north, and tanks were sent from their barracks to attempt to rein in the breakaway republic, and to consolidate the central grip on the borders. Opposing the Yugoslav army were the well-motivated but ill-equipped Slovenian territorial defence forces. For the state forces, the aircraft of the Jugoslovensko Ratno Vazduhoplovstvo (JRV) were ready to mount attacks against key targets.

Belgrade's initial orders were to secure the northern borders with Italy, Austria and Hungary, and to seize control of Ljubljana-Brnik, the main airport in Slovenia. Early in the morning of 27 June, tanks rolled out of their barracks and headed towards their targets, but Slovenes had been hard at work putting up barricades, using buses and trucks to halt their progress. The armoured columns suffered many technical problems, and even after using their guns to clear barricades could not make fast enough progress to avoid running into freshly-built barriers. The 30-32 tanks sent to take Brnik never achieved their goal.

Brnik airport is the main base for Adria Airways, and was a natural choice for early attack so that the Slovenes could not receive foreign arms directly into the republic. On this first day of war, the JRV planned an attack on the runway using J22B Oraos armed with MATRA Durandal cratering munitions, but this was called off due to very bad weather. However, JRV helicopters were used throughout the day, causing one Mil Mi-8 to be damaged near the Jezersko border pass. Due to an unfortunate underestimation of Slovenian defences, the helicopter had been ordered to fly at only 305 m (1,000 ft), as the groundfire threat was thought to be minimal.

This tactical mistake was graphically illustrated later in the day when a pair of Mi-8s was re-routed around bad weather, their new track taking them close to Ljubljana, where territorial defence forces shot one down with a shoulder-launched SA-7 'Grail' missile, with the loss of all on board. Then, a single Gazelle which had been making low passes across the centre of Ljubljana was hit by another SA-7 launched from the top of the Slovenian parliament building itself. The first day of the war ended with more successes for the republic: a helicopter assault in the town of Trzin resulted in a Slovenian police unit taking the first prisoners of war, while a Gazelle landed on a hill near Celje to change sides.

After an evening of violent storms throughout Slovenia, the weather cleared to allow the JRV to strike back the next day. At 10:15 a.m. local time, a pair of SOKO G-4 Super Galebs hit Ljubljana airport in the most publicised attack of the 10-day war. Armed with underwing rocket pods and an underbelly 23-mm cannon, the G-4s carried out

two low-level attacks against Adria's buildings at Brnik. The damage was extensive, hitting buildings and hangars.

Caught outside Adria's hangar were de Havilland Canada Dash Seven YU-AIE and McDonnell Douglas DC-9-33 YU-AHW, both of which sustained some damage, while inside the hangar Dash Seven YU-AIF and Airbus A320 YU-AOE were both peppered with shrapnel, causing extensive damage. The aircraft are now back with their manufacturers being repaired but, in the case of the two aircraft in the hangar, it will be many months before they are back in service. The only direct hit from the G-4s punctured the A320's fin.

Adria's buildings suffered considerable damage in the attack, as did the employees' parking lot, with many cars burned. None of the air-

The devastation in the Adria Airways' car park followed the Super Galeb rocket attack on Ljubljana Airport. In the background are a Republic F-84 and North American F-86 of the airport's small museum collection. No-one was hurt in this area, but out on the airfield two Austrian journalists lost their lives.

line staff were killed, but a car out on the airfield containing two Austrian journalists received a direct hit, with fatal results. The attack on Brnik caused much damage but, given the size and vulnerability of the main target (Adria's hangar), and the virtual lack of any defences, it can be considered as surprisingly ineffective. Although the airline feared further attacks, the JRV did not return in anger to Ljubljana airport after the 28 June strike until much later.

That evening, Slovenian territorial defence

Above: Particularly active during the short fighting in Slovenia was the JRV's Gazelle force. These were used mainly for spotting and liaison, at least one being shot down in the course of such operations.

Left: Although Oraos have been used in Yugoslavia for some attacks with cluster bombs and precision missiles, the majority of air strikes have consisted of unguided rocket and strafing attacks. The elderly MiG-21 has been used on many occasions.

war started). Other attacks that day were made against the Slovenian communications network, striking five or six TV/radio transmitters at Krvavec, Boc, Kum, Nanos and Domaale. These attacks were undertaken by G-4 Super Galebs, Oraos and MiG-21s, most using unguided rockets as the principal weapon. Considerable damage was caused, but with no loss of life.

Border attacks

On 29 July the JRV began a series of attacks against Slovenian territorial defence force positions, which lasted until the end of the war. The first of these attacks was made against the border pass at Sentilj, where more than 20 tanks were caught, and several civilians killed. Super Galebs and Oraos were involved in the strike, and following the weapons run made a turn which took them into Austrian airspace. Austrian Saab Draken interceptors were scrambled and were only a few seconds late to intercept the intruders. During a later JRV mission, at least one jet strayed into Italian airspace.

The next morning saw JRV jets streaking across Ljubljana as a show of force following Slo-

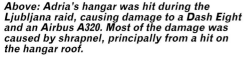

Above: Adria's hangar was hit during the Ljubljana raid, causing damage to a Dash Eight and an Airbus A320. Most of the damage was caused by shrapnel, principally from a hit on the hangar roof.

Right: Mil Mi-8 'Hips' disgorge parties of troops during the fight against Slovenian militia. The Mi-8 allowed the federal forces a great degree of mobility in mounting quick strikes against the Slovenes.

forces struck at the only JRV air base in the republic at Cerklje, firing mortars at the base but damaging no aircraft. Fearing more attacks, the JRV withdrew its aircraft to other bases; the exodus comprised 15 J22B Oraos, a few J-1 Jastrebs, 20 Mil Mi-8s, six Gazelle-maljukta attack helicopters and a Dassault Falcon 50, the latter carrying the newly-installed JRV commander General Jurjevic Zvonko (not surprisingly, the former JRV commander, General Marjan Tus – a Slovene – had been replaced a few days before the venian refusal to end opposition to federal troops by a 9:00 a.m. deadline. Fierce fighting occurred on the Slovenia-Croatia border, particularly along the main Zagreb-Ljubljana road. Here armoured trucks were trapped and attacked by JRV aircraft, Oraos employing the BL755 cluster-bomb against the vehicles. Super Galebs, MiG-21s and elderly J-1 Jastrebs joined in the attacks, which were largely centred around the towns of Medvedjek and Krakovski Gozd. In the course of this campaign the Slovenes lost many men, and several foreign truck drivers were killed.

Elsewhere, the JRV mounted strikes to relieve the Yugoslav barracks at Dravograd, which was surrounded by Slovenian territorial defence forces. Two MiG-21s attempted a rocket attack, but the town lies in the bottom of a deep valley and the MiGs could not fire their weapons effectively, the rockets falling harmlessly into a river. A Mil Mi-8 was forced to land near Maribor, and was captured by the Slovenes. It was later returned to the JRV after the end of hostilities.

Throughout the short conflict, the air base at Cerklje had not been used for mounting strikes, mainly due to militiamen blockading it. All strikes were flown by aircraft from bases outside Slovenia, namely Zadar, Pula, Bihac and Zagreb. Oraos were the most potent aircraft available, but they were dogged by unserviceability, and the defection to the breakaway republic by about 40 pilots from northern bases, many of whom flew the Orao. As the JRV turned its attention to Croatia later in the year, jet fuel shortages became a problem. G-4 Super Galebs and MiG-21s were used on rocket attacks, and even Jastrebs were involved.

Helicopter assets such as Gazelles and Mi-8s were used on armed reconnaissance and assault transport missions, respectively. Antonov An-26 transports also undertook war-related missions. The JRV's most potent weapon, the MiG-29, put in only brief appearances in Slovenian skies, on medium-level patrols intended primarily as shows-of-force. During one of these missions a 'Fulcrum' (local designation L.18) was forced to land at the beleaguered Cerklje airfield with a fuel shortage. It managed to return to the JRV base at Bihac unscathed.

Missile defence

Opposing the JRV, the Slovenian territorial defence forces could muster only small-calibre anti-aircraft weapons, which posed little threat to the Yugoslav warplanes, and a few of the SA-7 missiles. Some time before the war, the Slovenian national guard had received some elderly SOKO Kraguj piston-engined light attack aircraft, but these had been taken back by the JRV prior to the outbreak of hostilities to prevent their use in the Slovenian cause. Airpower of an unlikely sort was used by the Slovenes in the form of microlights, which were used for spotting federal positions.

By 2 July, observers were conceding that the Yugoslav army had largely been defeated by the Slovenian militia, and by the end of 3 July an uneasy cease-fire was taking hold. The following day federal Prime Minister Markovic admitted that the Yugoslav army had acted on its own when it moved into Slovenia, and the atmosphere began to defuse considerably. On 8 July delegates from Belgrade and Ljubljana met with

Above: A MiG-21 taxis for take-off, complete with underwing rocket pods. This type accounts for six regiments of the JRV's fighter force, but the main thrust of the air attacks against Slovenia and Croatia has been undertaken by G-4 Super Galebs and J-1 Jastrebs.

Right: On the ground, the Slovenes halted the federal forces by erecting roadblocks using trucks, buses and farm vehicles. This proved remarkably effective, and required tank fire and air strikes to clear them. While the federal forces were clearing one block, the Slovenes were erecting another down the road.

Left: It is believed that Yugoslavia has two regiments of Mil Mi-8 'Hips', these providing the assault helicopter force. Attempts to land troops in Slovenian territory resulted in' at least one 'Hip' being downed.

Right: G-4 Super Galebs are assigned to the JRV's Academy for advanced training, but has been widely used on rocket attacks. This aircraft is seen in the Krakovski Gozd region attacking Slovenian trucks.

Below: In addition to regular scout Gazelles, the JRV operates a sizeable number of Gazelle-maljukta helicopters, armed for anti-armour missions with four AT-3 'Sagger' missiles. These can also carry two SA-7 'Grail' AAMs.

European Community delegates on the island of Brioni, and worked out the details of Slovenia's immediate future. The republic would delay its secession for 90 days to allow negotiations, while the Yugoslav army would withdraw from Slovenian bases, a process eventually initiated in the latter half of July. Slovenia continued to move towards full independence, controlling its own borders and severing ties with Belgrade. However, it still remained within the confederation and some control, notably over airspace, remained in federal hands.

Federal military attention turned from Slovenia to Croatia, and the JRV has been involved in many strikes against Croatian militia. The federal units should be neutral in the battle between Serbs and Croats, but have come down heavily on the Serbian side to prevent Croatia joining Slovenia in breaking away from the confederation. In ground attack missions in Croatia, at least two Jastrebs have been shot down, and Oraos have employed Maverick precision attack missiles against a grain storage at Osijek.

On 31 August JRV MiG-21 interceptors forced down two aircraft at Zagreb airport. One was the infamous Uganda Airlines Boeing 707 which was headed for Vienna with 19 tons of South African arms for the Croatian forces, the aircraft

Left: *Mi-8s were used for heliborne assaults, but these resulted in the Slovenes taking many prisoners of war as the helicopter landed its troops.*

Above: *The JRV MiG force is large, based around the MiG-21. The single squadron of MiG-29s has been little employed in the fighting.*

and load being confiscated. The second was a Tarom Tupolev Tu-154 leased to Adria, which after inspection was allowed to continue its flight. At the same time, Ljubljana airport again came under threat as MiG-21s and Super Galebs overflew the area. The federal authorities ordered the airport to close, but in view of the previous JRV attack, Adria decided to evacuate its aircraft in short order.

In all, five airliners got out of Ljubljana, led by Adria MD-82 YU-AJY. This machine was chased by a fully-armed G-4, but as the MD-82 was empty it outran the fighter and headed into the hills and safety in the clouds. Its safe escape was no doubt enhanced by the fact that its pilot had spent his air force career flying MiG fighters! Following were two DC-9-32s of Adria, and a pair of MD-82s also owned by the airline but leased to Croatia Airlines, which had only just escaped from Zagreb airport. The airliners made

their way to Klagenfurt in Austria, just a few minutes' flight time away.

Since the Brioni Accord, an uneasy peace has been maintained in Slovenia, while fierce fighting in Croatia has continued sporadically, despite several attempts to implement a truce. At the time of writing federal forces are determined to defend Zagreb airport, which is a major JRV fighter base, against equally determined opposition from Croatian police and militia. The airport remains technically open, but under effective military control. Croatia's future is far from settled, its own attempts at independence being seriously confused by internal ethnic violence between the Croats and Serbs. However, Slovenia has shown that fierce national determination, led by the examples of the government, territorial defence forces and organisations such as Adria Airways, can triumph even against the well-equipped federal forces.

From the cockpit of Mike Lumb
War and Peace
in the Tornado

Flight Lieutenant Mike Lumb joined the RAF as a Direct Entrant in 1984. After successfully completing Initial Officer Training at the RAF College, Cranwell, he began pilot training on the Jet Provost at RAF Linton-on-Ouse, before switching to navigator training. He underwent type conversion at the Trinational Tornado Training Establishment at Cottesmore, and operational training at the Tornado Weapons Conversion Unit at Honington. His first operational tour was with No. 14 Squadron at RAF Brüggen, during which he deployed to the Gulf during Operation Granby. He is currently on a 'ground tour' as an Air Liaison Officer with No. 24 Air Mobile Brigade.

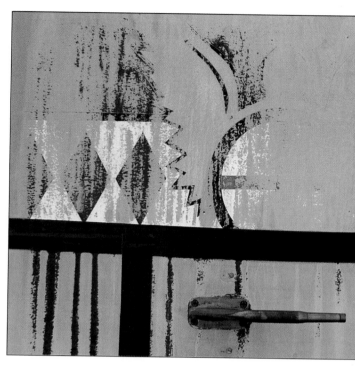

Main picture, far left: A pair of Tornado GR.Mk 1s of the Muharraq Tornado Detachment rendezvous with a tanker over the Saudi desert during Operation Granby. The Tornados flew by day and night, and attacked heavily defended targets from low and medium level, using a variety of weapons.

Above: The markings of No. 14 Squadron show through as the desert pink paint is removed from one of the unit's Tornados after the Gulf war. The difficulties experienced in stripping the paint from these aircraft (due to it being baked on by the hot sun) led to many aircraft being left in desert warpaint for many months. Mike's tour with No. 14 drew to a close soon after his return from Muharraq.

Left: The regular Red Flag exercises were always regarded as being the closest thing Tornado aircrew would get to a shooting war, but the lessons learned in the Nevada skies were soon to be put into practice over Iraq. Here a No. 14 Squadron Tornado GR.Mk 1 shares the ramp at Nellis with a quartet of USAF A-10A Thunderbolts.

Below: A self-portrait taken during the Gulf war. A pair of Tornados and a VC10 tanker can be seen reflected in Mike Lumb's visor. Despite the unfavourable conditions, the Tornado aircrew carried out their tasks with exemplary efficiency.

Left: Tornado 'Bravo X-Ray' of No. 14 Squadron at Gibraltar, dwarfed by the famous rock. Tornado crews could typically expect one or two 'Lone Rangers' per year, allowing them to practise overseas flying, and using foreign air traffic agencies. Lumb's 'Ranger' to Gibraltar went via Istres. There is no permanent RAF presence at Gibraltar, whose tricky approach makes it a challenging destination for pilots.

Below: A group from No. 14 Squadron holds up an AIM-9G during a missile practice camp at RAF Valley during 1989. The Sidewinder firing profiles gave the man in the front seat very high-value training, with a higher workload than he encountered at any other time. The elderly AIM-9G does not have all-aspect capability, and the newer, more-capable AIM-9L would be fitted in wartime.

Left: Three Tornados of No. 14 Squadron. The nearest aircraft carries a pair of practice bomb containers under the belly, with fuel tanks under the inboard underwing pylons. Unusually, the BOZ chaff/flare dispenser and Sky Shadow ECM pod are not carried. Different types of practice bombs simulate the ballistic characteristics of different full-sized weapons.

Right: Flight Lieutenants Nigel Cookson and Mike Alton pose in front of their Tornado at RAF Lossiemouth. Before participating in Red Flag exercises, or before deploying to Goose Bay, RAF Germany Tornado crews could use remote Scottish low-flying training areas to work down to flying at 100 ft. (The normal limit in most of Britain is 250 ft, and in Germany even higher.)

Right: A No. 14 Squadron Tornado GR.Mk 1 on the flight line at Goose Bay is tended by a typically North American refuelling bowser. Deployments to Goose Bay, with its vast, virtually unpopulated low-flying area, allow Tornado crews to realistically practise low-flying techniques and tactics.

Above: Inert weapons can be dropped on Goose Bay's weapons range, which even includes a dummy airfield with mock runways. Large-scale attacks can be conducted, with four-ship formations of Tornados being opposed by Canadian aggressors. Each Tornado can carry and drop eight inert 1,000-lb bombs during such attacks, making them extremely realistic training.

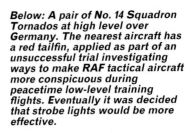

Below: A pair of No. 14 Squadron Tornados at high level over Germany. The nearest aircraft has a red tailfin, applied as part of an unsuccessful trial investigating ways to make RAF tactical aircraft more conspicuous during peacetime low-level training flights. Eventually it was decided that strobe lights would be more effective.

Right: A No. 14 Squadron Tornado taxis at Brüggen. No. 14 Squadron's crusader and winged shield emblem is carried on the nose, flanked by the blue diamonds first applied to the unit's Hawker Hunters. Blue diamonds with a white 'shadow' are repeated on the tailfin. Two-letter squadron codes commence with 'BA'.

Above: A Tornado GR.Mk 1 of No. 14 Squadron in its HAS (Hardened Aircraft Shelter) at RAF Brüggen. RAF Germany airfields were hardened against nuclear, biological or chemical attack during the 1970s and 1980s, with a major construction programme providing HASs, and hardened accommodation, operations and planning facilities.

Below: An unusual view of a taxiing No. 14 Squadron Tornado. This aircraft is fitted with the detachable bolt-on retractable inflight-refuelling probe. This is not routinely carried by RAF Germany Tornados, whose wartime role would not have necessitated inflight refuelling.

Right: A Tornado on approach, wings swept fully forward, and with leading-edge slats and trailing-edge flaps deployed. Thrust reversers will be actuated automatically, as soon as the main wheels hit the runway. The Tornado has excellent short-field performance, allowing it to take off and land on undamaged strips of runway or taxiway after an enemy airfield attack, but unlike the Jaguar which it replaced (and unlike current Soviet tactical aircraft types) cannot operate from grass, or from rough strips.

Below: No. 14 Squadron is one of the oldest and proudest RAF squadrons, with a long and distinguished history. For their 75th anniversary, the unit painted '75 Years, 1915-1990' on the tails of four of its Tornados, three of which are seen here. One of No. 14 Squadron's claims to fame is that it has not been based in the United Kingdom since 1946, and has only been based in the UK twice (once for one month in 1919, and then from October 1944 to March 1946) in an unbroken period of service since 1915.

Inset, above: The proximity of its shadow shows how low this Tornado is flying. Peacetime low-flying restrictions left RAF aircrew unprepared for the realities of war, and the first few weeks in Saudi Arabia were spent in intensive low-flying training. Above: A Tornado releases an IR countermeasures flare at low level over the desert.

Right: A gaggle of Tornado GR.Mk 1s from the Muharraq Tornado Detachment approaches the refuelling drogues trailed by a Victor tanker. The desert warpaint has already started to flake and stain.

Below: The Muharraq Tornado Wing's staff car! Armed with a (dummy) machine-gun, equipped with furry dice and camouflaged in desert pink, this vehicle certainly looked the part. Viewers of British TV's 'Only Fools and Horses' may appreciate the legend 'Trotters Independent Trading Co. New York, Paris, Peckham'.

Right: Local scenery in Bahrain. This mosque was located only a short distance from the luxury hotel used by the Muharraq Tornado aircrew as an officers' mess. The Tornados flew from Muharraq, a former RAF station and the present international airport.

War and Peace in the Tornado

Above: Flight Lieutenant Mike Lumb is pictured in front of his Tornado GR.Mk 1 at Muharraq. Transformed into a busy military airbase, Muharraq also housed RAF Jaguar fighter-bombers and Victor tankers, and a host of other aircraft, including the US Marine Corps KC-130s seen here. Despite the primitive and unpleasant conditions, RAF ground crew kept the detachment's aircraft in tip-top condition. Their morale was indicated by the abundance of nose art which was applied.

Below: Two RAF Tornados over the 'Sea of Sand', whose ripple-like dunes look almost like the sea. By moonlight, the resemblance becomes even more acute. The aircraft are each armed with four 1,000-lb bombs underfuselage, and carry the 495-Imp gal 'Hindenburgers' designed for the Tornado F.Mk 3 in place of the normal 330-Imp gal tanks. This dramatically increased the range of the Tornado GR.Mk 1, without imposing any major limitations.

Above right: 'Awesome Annie' displays her nose art and bomb log. (This was almost invariably confined to the port side of RAF Tornados.) Mike Lumb is in the back seat in this picture, being flown by Squadron Leader Jerry Rimmer. The photo was taken by Flying Officer Larry Williams.

Right: Tornados armed with JP 233, the RAF's airfield attack weapon. This was used in anger against various Iraqi airfields, and proved devastatingly effective at closing runways and taxiways, bottling up Iraqi aircraft in their shelters.

Left: An appropriate sticker applied to a JP 233 dispenser. The Tornados quickly switched from low-level anti-airfield attacks to medium-level attacks against other targets, using a variety of other weapons. Losses were surprisingly light, contrary to some scare stories which circulated in the media at the time.

Above and left: Conditions were hard for the Tornado aircrew, who lived in the same luxury hotels as Gulf Air aircrew and stewardesses and who were able to play various sports when not flying. It must have been strange to sit by the pool, enjoying the scenery in the afternoon, and then have to undergo the tension and stress of operational missions at night. Flight Lieutenants Don Evans and Douggie Potter are seen here enjoying the Jacuzzi!

Right: Inflight refuelling played a vital part in Tornado operations in the Gulf, with the tanker aircrews doing everything possible to support the Tornado bombers. Probably the most important RAF tanker asset in the Gulf was the Vickers VC10. Here a VC10 K.Mk 2 refuels Muharraq-based Tornado GR.Mk 1s. The aircraft plugged in the starboard drogue is venting fu from the fuel dump pipe at the top of its fin.

Left: A Tornado cautiously approaches the port drogue streamed by an RAF Handley Pag Victor K.Mk 2. The Gulf war almos certainly represented the swan song of the Victor, although fatigu was used up more slowly during the conflict because the punishing routine of peacetime circuit training was much reduced, and the hours flown tended to be on long missions!

Right: They sometimes say that the cockpit of a modern fighter aircraft is like a high-tech video arcade game, but this is not quite what they had in mind. A Tornado navigator holds up his 'Space Battle' game, used by him to pass the time during a boring transit, or while waiting to refuel.

Above: A Tornado GR.Mk 1 refuels from one of No. 216 Squadron's Lockheed TriStar K.Mk 1 tanker/ passenger aircraft. Two of these received a desert pink fuselage, and were dubbed 'Pinky' and 'Perky'. Although the TriStar accommodates a pair of HDUs in its fuselage, only one of these can be used at once, making the aircraft effectively a single-point tanker.

Right: Five Muharraq Tornados, four of them carrying JP 233, in formation with a Victor K.Mk 2 of No. 55 Squadron high over the Gulf. The hemp colour scheme applied to Marham's Victors was retained in the Gulf, and proved surprisingly effective as a desert colour scheme. Muharraq's Tornados were drawn from a number of units, and therefore wore no squadron insignia, although they did retain their pre-war two-letter tailcodes.

Above: Post-war, a Tornado GR.Mk 1 armed with practice bomb carriers and carrying normal GR.Mk 1 style fuel tanks cavorts for Mike Lumb's camera. The Muharraq Tornados remained in-theatre for several weeks following the cessation of hostilities, providing a symbolic presence and reminding Saddam Hussein of the likely consequences of backtracking on the terms of the ceasefire. Aircrew continued to be rotated out to staff the detachment.

Above right: The effect of modern PGMs (precision-guided munitions) on a hardened aircraft shelter. RAF Tornados used Paveway laser-guided bombs against a variety of targets, including bridges, with designation provided by Tornados carrying the new TIALD pod, or by Pave Spike-equipped Buccaneers.

Above: Everyone who visited freed Kuwait wanted some sand as a souvenir. Shame they didn't put the sign up before the war, as a warning to Saddam Hussein.

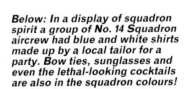

Below: One of the Tornado aircrew sips reflectively at his drink as he reads the newspaper. Within hours he was over hostile airspace, under fire, carrying out an operational bombing mission.

Below: In a display of squadron spirit a group of No. 14 Squadron aircrew had blue and white shirts made up by a local tailor for a party. Bow ties, sunglasses and even the lethal-looking cocktails are also in the squadron colours!

Below: A 'nodding donkey' oil pump livened up, perhaps to present less of an affront to the environment?

Right: RAF Tornados share the Muharraq ramp with Gulf Air TriStars. Ironically, some of the RAF's VC10 tankers (the K.Mk 2s) had previously served as Super VC10s with Gulf Air!

Below: The nearest of these two Tornados has an impressive bomb log, and a typical scantily clad woman on the nose. The significance of the penguin is unknown! Inset below: Squadron Leader Jerry Rimmer and Flight Lieutenant Gary Harrison goof about for Mike Lumb's camera. Real press photographers had probably been pestering them to give 'Top Gun'-type salutes and thumbs-ups for weeks!

MIKOYAN
MiG-23/-27

In service in huge numbers with the Soviet air forces and with virtually all its former client states, the MiG-23 is one of the most widely built jet fighters ever. The key to its enduring success lies in its basic design and configuration, which have conferred a unique blend of robustness, performance and versatility. The same basic variable-geometry wing and fuselage have been given different noses and engines to produce two entirely separate families of aircraft: fighter-interceptors, and dedicated ground attack/strike fighters. Yet in the West, these remarkable aircraft have been widely dismissed.

Had the Cold War turned hot in the mid-1980s, NATO pilots would have been most worried about the new generation of Soviet fighters that were just beginning to enter service, aircraft like the MiG-29 'Fulcrum' and the Sukhoi Su-27 'Flanker'. Although such aircraft were indisputably very capable, they were only available in very small numbers, and the backbone of Warsaw Pact air power was provided by the variants of a single family of aircraft, the MiG-23 and -27 'Floggers'. Even today, 'Floggers' outnumber 'Fulcrums' except in the most front-line military districts, and yet these obviously popular and versatile aircraft have often been dismissed as obsolete and ineffective. Many have rated them as easy prey for any halfway competent Western fighter pilot, capable of being bettered by every Western fighter from the F-4 Phantom onwards, although such an assessment is far from the truth.

At one time such a view did not seem unreasonable, since it appeared to be supported by combat experience. Syrian MiG-23s, for example, operating in an environment in which their ground control network had been entirely paralysed by Israeli action and jamming, were shot down in huge numbers (at least 36) over the Bekaa in 1982, and two Libyan MiG-23s were rapidly despatched by a pair of US Navy F-14 Tomcats in 1989. In both cases, the 'Floggers' proved unable to inflict any losses themselves. The aircraft's reputation sank to an all-time low.

In fact, the results of each of these incidents said far more about pilot quality, training and tactics than it did about the intrinsic worth of the MiG-23. It also gave a useful insight into the lack of BVR capability of the export version of the aircraft. Thus, when Syrian air force Major Abdul Bassem defected to Israel in his 'top-of-the-range' MiG-23ML 'Flogger-G', the Israeli evaluation of his aircraft was expected to be a foregone conclusion. In fact, and much to everyone's surprise, the MiG-23 emerged from the searching evaluation with a much enhanced reputation, impressing the IDF/AF evaluation pilots with its easy-to-use avionics, relatively

Main picture, right: This is one of the MiG-23MLs operated by Jagdfliegergeschwader 9, 'Heinrich Rau', of the former East German air force at Peenemünde. Several of these aircraft found their way to the USA for evaluation.

Inset, right: A MiG-27M 'Flogger-J2' of the Brand-based 116th Fighter Bomber Regiment, part of the 105th Fighter Bomber Division, headquartered at Grossenhain in what used to be East Germany. This represents the latest and most capable attack 'Flogger' variant, and is in service only with the Soviet air forces.

'FLOGGER'

Above: The Mikoyan-Gurevich Model 23-11, first variable-geometry member of the MiG-23 family, was designed when it became apparent that the lift-jet-equipped Model 23-01 would not be practical.

Above right: This early MiG-23S 'Flogger-A' is retired from service and is now displayed in a Moscow museum.

Right: Wearing the new post-WarPac Hungarian air force chevron, a MiG-23MF 'Flogger-B' of the Saman squadron, Stromfeld Regiment, blasts off from the runway at Papa. Hungary has lost four of its 16 'Floggers' in accidents. The MiG-23MF 'Flogger-B' featured a host of improvements to its avionics and systems, and gained a new powerplant, the 8300-kg Khatchatourov R-29-300. The tail surfaces were moved aft and the jet pipe was shortened, giving a very different appearance.

benign handling at high angles of attack, and phenomenal acceleration, which allowed it to better even the F-15 and F-16 in some circumstances. In particular, IDF/AF pilots found the HUD's integrated radar display easy and logical to use, and significantly more powerful than intelligence reports had indicated.

More recently, examples of ex-East German MiG-23MFs, MiG-23MLs and MiG-24BNs have been extensively tested and evaluated at the Luftwaffe test centre at Manching. Results of these tests have not yet been fully made public, although some conclusions have 'leaked out'. Again, the 'Flogger' has emerged with its reputation intact. Many Luftwaffe pilots reportedly favoured integrating the 'Flogger-Gs' to augment the F-4 force, and some openly rated the 'Floggers' more highly than their own F-4s. Some former East German 'Floggers' have also been shipped to the USA for evaluation, and perhaps to join the famous but top-secret 'Red Hats' adversary unit, which is believed to operate from Groom Lake in Nevada. This unit already operates a number of ex-Egyptian MiG-23MS 'Flogger-Es'. The much-improved 'Flogger-K', never exported and seldom seen by Western analysts, has never been evaluated in the West but, even based on the evaluation of earlier variants, this type could be very capable indeed.

The 'Flogger's' own pilots are fond of it. Even by comparison with the MiG-29, they will assert that they have a good fighter aircraft: "Not as good as the -29, maybe, but tougher, maybe a little faster and, I think, better looking," was how one Czech pilot described it. In Soviet service, the aircraft bears the popular nickname 'Chiborashka' (a Soviet cartoon hero) or 'Krokodil' (after the animal, not the satirical magazine!). Showing their disdain for the lightweight MiG-21, 'Flogger' pilots dub the earlier aircraft 'flat irons' for

their lack of power and triangular shape, or, more dismissively, 'Svistks' (whistles) because they are thought to be inconsequential, and easily lost on the wind.

Perhaps the greatest testament to the MiG-23 is provided by the sheer volume of its production run. The Soviet Union and its client states seldom use the industry's less successful products in large numbers, yet the 'Flogger' remained in production until 1984, by which time some 4, 500 had been built. Seven years later, the aircraft remains in widespread use, even with front-line elements of Soviet Frontal Aviation. In the Group of Soviet Forces in Germany, for example, one air defence regiment retains MiG-23MLD 'Flogger-Ks' and three more operate MiG-27 fighter-bombers. In many other air arms, the 'Flogger' is the most numerous front-line aircraft in service, or the most important, and it is seldom outnumbered by more modern and more glamorous aircraft like the MiG-29.

MiG-21 replacement

Design of the MiG-23 began in the early 1960s, when the Mikoyan Gurevich OKB began studies for a replacement for its MiG-21 tactical fighter. Aware of the shortcomings of the MiG-21, the Design Bureau wanted to produce a fighter with greater payload, range and firepower, with more powerful sensors to give freedom from the constraints of tight GCI control. The new aircraft was also to be faster, and faster climbing than the 'Fishbed'. All these factors made it obvious that the new fighter would have to be larger and heavier, and in the normal run of events this would have brought with it increased field lengths and relatively poor take-off and landing performance.

In Russia, as in the West, where Britain was working on the P.1127 Kestrel, France on the Dassault Balzac and Ger-

Left: Most early Soviet MiG-23MFs, especially those delivered to the IA-PVO, were initially delivered in an overall light-grey colour scheme. In Frontal Aviation service this was very soon replaced by a three-tone green and brown camouflage.

Above: The significance of the 'eye' marking on this MiG-23MF, now displayed in the Frunze museum, is unknown. Most of the aircraft in this fascinating and relatively new collection are former development airframes or prototypes.

many on a ZELL (ZEro Length Launch) system for its F-104s, STOL/rough field performance was felt to be vitally important, and the Soviet air force actually wanted an aircraft with better off-airfield take-off and landing capabilities than the MiG-21. Mikoyan engineers studied many alternative approaches to the problem of producing a STOL fighter, and two were felt to be promising enough to warrant the construction of flying prototypes or, perhaps more accurately, proof-of-concept aircraft.

The first of these, designated Model 23-01 (and later MiG-23PD) was a conventional-looking supersonic aircraft with a fixed delta wing, and conventional tailplanes, powered by a single main engine (a Tumanskii R-27-300 rated at 5200 kg thrust, or 7300 kg with afterburner) and with two 'Sustainer' engines or lift jets for take-off and landing. These lift jets (actually 2350 kg Koliesov RD-36-35s) were located in the centre fuselage, and were intended only to reduce take-off and landing speeds, and so shorten the take-off run and landing roll. They did this by reducing the need for wing-generated lift, and thus reducing the speed at which the aircraft had to fly in the circuit. They were never intended to allow vertical take-offs. When in use a hinged, shuttered trap door opened to provide airflow to the engines. Below the fuselage, the lift jets exhausted through variable rotating nozzles which allowed the pilot to vary the direction of the 'jet lift vector', like those of the P.1127 Kestrel/Harrier. On landing, these could thus be used as primitive 'thrust reversers'.

Designed by V. A. Mikoyan (nephew of 'Old Man Artem' himself), the Model 23-01 had lateral air intakes, leaving the nose free to accommodate a large pulse-Doppler radar, which was to be purpose-built for the new fighter. The wing was a scaled-up version of the basic delta shape used on the MiG-21, while the one-piece tailplane was similar to that found on previous MiGs. The aircraft used the same SPS blown flaps that had been fitted to most late MiG-21 variants, to further improve take-off performance. Only the engine air intakes broke new ground. These were of semi-circular cross-section, and were equipped with variable shock cones, similar to those fitted to the French Mirage III. Standing proud from the fuselage the intakes avoided most boundary layer ingestion problems. In fact, the Ye 23-01 was so much a scaled-up MiG-21 derivative that many Mikoyan engineers still classify it as a member of the MiG-21 family, and refer to it as such. This raises the fascinating thought that the MiG-23 itself could be seen to be a MiG-21 derivative!

The Model 23-01 was intended to provide the basis of an operational aircraft, and as such could be fitted with a twin-barrelled GSh-23 cannon below the fuselage and a pair of K-23 (AA-7 'Apex') missiles underwing. The aircraft made its maiden flight on 3 April 1967, in the hands of Piotr Ostapenko. The trials programme was supervised by V. M. Timofiev, and also involved Alexander Fedotov, the Bureau chief test pilot. After only 14 flights, Mikoyan realised that the lift-jet concept was seriously flawed, and the remainder of the aircraft's life was spent preparing for, and participating in, the Domododevo air show in July 1967. This air show was held to celebrate the 50th anniversary of the October Revolution (the change from the Julian to the Augustine calendar accounting for the apparent disparity).

The 23-01 suffered from many problems. In particular, the lift jets were felt to impose too great a weight penalty, and their installation prevented the provision of sufficient internal fuel. Flawed or not, the Model 23-01 demonstrated an astonishing take-off distance of 180 m with SPS and lift jets, and a landing distance of 250 m with SPS, lift jets and cruciform brake chute. Its appearance at Domododevo led to the assignment of the NATO ASCC (Air Standards Co-ordinating Committee) code name 'Faithless'.

At the same time that some of the OKB's engineers were working on the Model 23-01, another team, directed by A. A. Andreyev and including engineers like Rostislav Apollovich Belyakov (now the OKB's designer general), attempted to validate the alternative approach to STOL performance, that is to say, the variable-geometry wing concept. Using a wing which could be swept at different angles allowed the pilot to select a low-drag, narrow-span wing for supersonic flight, or a longer-span, high-lift wing for slow speed and for optimum take-off and landing performance. This was examined in extensive wind-tunnel testing and with a flying proof-of-concept aircraft, the Model 23-11. Recent publication of a book by Belyakov and a French author has shattered many myths about the MiG-23, including several spurious designations applied to the 23-11, such as the Ye 231, or the Ye-23I or IG. This project began during the construction of the lift-jet aircraft, when doubts began to arise concerning the viability of separate lift-enhancing engines.

This work was soon given a very high priority, and in 1965 the Minister of the Aviation Industry issued a decree stating that the Mikoyan OKB was to construct a second MiG-23 (the first being the 23-01), equipped with a variable-geometry wing. Responsibility for pivot design was assigned to the Rodina (Motherland) OKB led by Selivanov.

Variable geometry

Serious variable-geometry research originally began in Germany during World War II. The Messerschmit P.1101 was never flown, but featured a ground-adjustable, three-position, variable-sweep wing, and formed the basis of the Bell X-5. Flight trials of the latter aircraft showed that the variable-geometry (VG) wing suffered from several problems. The most important of these was the fact that the aerodynamic centre of pressure actually moved aft as the wings were swept back, turning a stable, controllable configuration into an unstable one, with unacceptable levels of instability and drag. The solution to this problem, which should properly be credited to Barnes Wallis of Vickers (inventor of the bouncing bomb and designer of the Wellington), was to move the wing pivots outboard, giving a large stub of fixed wing and a relatively small moving outer wing, which kept centre of pressure shifts within tolerable limits.

The Mikoyan Design Bureau did not have to solve the problems of variable-geometry configuration alone. As well as drawing on the experiences of the West, they were also able to draw on the resources of TsAGI, the central aerodynamics research establishment. The latter organisation drew up a basic VG configuration which was used by Sukhoi for its Su-7IG (later Su-17), by Tupolev for its Tu-22M (later Tu-26), and by Mikoyan for the Model 23-11.

Even with a basic TsAGI-approved VG configuration, Mikoyan still had to solve many problems to tailor the basic shape to its aircraft. Wing sweep angles were determined by the requirements of slow-speed landing performance, transonic handling requirements and Mach 2 capability. The location at which the wing should actually pivot in order to give the optimum degree of static stability in pitch throughout the sweep range was probably the most critical decision, although controllability problems were also addressed by tailoring vortex flow over the wings and tail surfaces. Final-

Above: Romanian 'Flogger-Bs' wear a wide variety of colour schemes. This aircraft has an unusual 'Tiger Stripe' disruptive camouflage. All Romanian air force aircraft now wear the old national roundel in place of the Communist star.

Left: The MiG-23MF was the first 'Flogger' variant to feature a wing with extended leading edges and 'dogteeth'. Originally introduced without slats as the No. 2 wing, it was developed into the slatted No. 3 wing on later MiG-23MFs.

ly, Mikoyan had to design a flight control system which would be able to change wing sweep, and to operate the differential tailplanes and the control surfaces on the variable-sweep wing.

The variable wing of the MiG-23 was never as simple as some Western analysts have assumed. From the beginning, the wing was designed to incorporate an extensive array of high-lift devices on the leading and trailing edges, and wing-sweep angles were fully and continuously variable from 16° to 72°, although three most-used values (16°, 45° and 72°) were chosen to act as easily selectable 'stops'. The high-lift devices consisted of virtually full-span trailing-edge flaps in four sections, leading-edge slats and two-section spoilers. These function as ailerons, except at 72° sweep, when roll control is provided by differential movement of the tailerons.

Although the 23-11 was specified as a VG version of the original 23-01, the two aircraft shared only the same nose and empennage design, and the same powerplant. Tumanskii's R-27F-300 was actually designed for the MiG-23 before the choice between VG and lift-jet configurations had been made. The engine was quite deliberately a turbojet, and not a turbofan, to gain the best possible take-off performance, acceleration and climb figures. Mindful of development problems with hotter-running Western turbofans, reliability was also a vital consideration for the engine designers. Range and fuel

litre and 710-litre capacity) and in three integral tanks in each wing (of 62.5-litre, 137.5-litre and 200-litre capacity). Production aircraft also had provision for external fuel to be carried, initially on the centreline, and later underwing as well.

The 23-11 forward fuselage was of a vertical oval cross section, which faired back to a rectangular cross section at frame 18 rearwards. Between frames 18 and 20 are the wing pivots, inlet ducts and the No. 2 internal fuel tank. At frame 28 the rear fuselage can be detached for access to the engine, and at frame 31 are the airbrake and stabilator attachment points. The same basic structure has been retained by all subsequent MiG-23 variants.

Thanks to the high priority accorded it, the 23-11 made its maiden flight on 10 April 1967, only one week after that of the 23-01. The pilot was Alexander Fedotov, who initially flew the aircraft with the wings fixed fully forward, at 16°. On the next flight, on 12 April, he swept the wings throughout their range, and on his third flight flew the aircraft to beyond Mach 1.3. Within weeks he was displaying the new aircraft to the public at Domododevo, where NATO assigned it the reporting name 'Flogger', although they were then still unaware about which OKB had designed it!

Like the 23-01, the VG aircraft was intended to serve as the prototype for a production combat aircraft, and as such it was armed. It carried four K-23 (AA-7 'Apex') missiles under the wing gloves and fuselage. Sometimes K-13 (AA-2 'Atolls') were substituted for live firing trials, since the prototype did not, in fact, have any radar. Between 8 April and 24 April 1968 the aircraft, flown by Ostapenko and Komarov, fired 16 missiles at altitudes from 5000 to 17000 m and over a wide speed range. No engine surges were encountered during these trials.

Flight trials

The basic OKB flight trials ended in July 1968, after 98 flights (and two of the early short-lived trials engines!). The aircraft was then handed over to the air force, along with two further 23-11 prototypes, and has now been retired to the museum at Monino, near Moscow.

The early flight trials soon showed that the new type had great potential, and the aircraft demonstrated a minimum take-off run of 320 m, and a minimum landing roll of 440 m. These figures were substantially greater than the distances achieved by the 23-01, but were nonetheless impressive enough to comfortably meet the STOL requirement, while the aircraft's combat radius (2045 km) and maximum speed

economy, which would have been better with a turbofan, were held to be less important.

Derived from the R-11F2S-300 (used by MiG-21 and Yak-28 versions), the excellent R-27 laid firm foundations for the success of the aircraft. The engine, rated at 5200 kg, or 7800 kg with afterburner, gave the 23-11 a fuel consumption 25 per cent lower than that of an R-11F2-300-engined MiG-21, with much greater thrust. By comparison with the same-weight US J79, the engine developed some 25 per cent more thrust from four fewer stages (11 instead of 15). The greater pressure rise generated at each stage was achieved by advanced aerodynamics and metallurgy. The new engine was not all good news, however, at least in the early stages of development. Its 25-hour life ended after the 45th flight, grounding the 23-11 until January 1968, when a second engine (and a three-axis autopilot) had been installed. Frequent speculation that the 23-01 and 23-11 were powered by the Lyul'ka AL-7 is incorrect.

Whereas the 23-01 featured lateral semi-circular inlets, with Mirage-style variable shock cones, the 23-11 and production MiG-23s feature rectangular section intakes with perforated variable intake ramps similar in some respects to those fitted to the F-4 Phantom. These tiny holes helped remove sluggish boundary layer air, while the whole ramps move to control shock wave formation, optimising airflow into the engine.

Fuel was carried in three fuselage tanks (of 1920-litre, 820-

(1178 km/h at 13000 m) were significantly better than the figures for the lift-jet-equipped aircraft.

On the strength of the flight trials with the three 23-11 prototypes, the aircraft was ordered into production as the MiG-23S. (MiG-23 is the air force designation for the Mikoyan Model 23-11.) The production aircraft was intended to feature both the production Sapphire radar (hence the S suffix) and a more powerful engine. However, development did not progress entirely without problems, and while the more powerful engine in the shape of the 6900 kg (10000 kg with afterburning) R-27F2M-300 was ready in time, the radar was not. Accordingly, the RP-22 (NATO 'Jay Bird') radar fitted to the MiG-21S (erroneously known as the MiG-21PFMA) ('Fishbed-J') was adopted for the first, interim variant of the new fighter, which therefore had a shorter radome. The visual difference was unimportant, but the difference in capability was profound. At a stroke, the new fighter was incapable of carrying the SARH AA-7 'Apex' missile, and thus totally lacked any Beyond Visual Range capability. The radar did, however, have an illuminator, allowing the carriage of the semi-active, radar-homing version of the AA-2 'Atoll', as well as the IR-homing version. The former missile, designated AA-2C by NATO, and sometimes referred to as the 'Advanced Atoll', was broadly equivalent to the US AIM-9C, the semi-active, radar-homing version of the Sidewinder.

Armament of the MiG-23S was restricted to four AA-2 'Atolls', and a twin-barrelled 23-mm cannon. The 'Atoll' is an inferior IR- and radar-homing, short-range missile similar to the very earliest members of the AIM-9 Sidewinder family. The MiG-23S was also fitted with an ARK-10 radio

compass, an ASP-PF sight and ranging system, and a TP-23 infra-red search and track system. The first production MiG-23S made its first flight on 28 May 1969, in the capable hands of the OKB chief test pilot, Fedotov. It had no operational equipment at all. The interim radar first flew in the fifth aircraft, and surprisingly few problems emerged. A batch of 50 MiG-23S aircraft was built between mid-1969 and the end of 1970, when production switched to the MiG-23M, which first flew in June 1972. This sequence has been confirmed by the Mikoyan OKB, but is contrary to the views of many Western experts, who have stated that the MiG-23S was followed by the refined MiG-23SM, or even by the export MiG-23MS.

The MiG-23M (the M suffix stood merely for Modified) was the first definitive version of the MiG-23 family, since it featured the intended S-23D-ch Sapphire (NATO 'High Lark') radar. This was a pulse-Doppler radar operating in the J-band and was reportedly based on, or at least incorporated, technology from salvaged F-4J Phantom (AN/AWG-10) radars recovered from aircraft shot down in Vietnam. Transistorised circuitry (the AN/AWG-10 being the first Western radar to incorporate such technology) was not used, however, the Soviets preferring to stick to bulkier, heavier valves, which had the advantage of allowing greater power output. Like the AWG-10, the 'High Lark' had look-down, but not shoot-down, capability.

With the introduction of 'High Lark', the MiG-23 was freed from dependance on the ageing and ineffective AA-2 'Atoll', and was able to carry the AA-7 'Apex'. Some analysts have suggested that this missile was broadly equivalent to the AIM-7E version of the Sparrow. Two were usually

carried (one IR-homing, one semi-active radar homing) and these would normally have been ripple-fired to increase the likelihood of a hit. Shorter-ranged than Western missiles of equivalent size and weight, the 'Apex' had a huge warhead and multiple fusing systems for maximum kill probability. IR-homing AA-2s were usually carried as a short-range back-up to the 'Apex'.

Improving the 'Flogger'

As a result of experience with the MiG-23S, a host of other improvements was also made, significantly changing the appearance of the aircraft. NATO allocated the new variant a new reporting name, 'Flogger-B', retrospectively assigning 'Flogger-A' to the -23S and -23-11 prototypes. The MiG-23M featured, for example, a new autopilot with artificial feel (known to the Soviets simply as a 'Control Column Force Regulator System'), as well as a new sight and ranging system (ASP-23D). More obvious externally was the provision of ribbed airbrakes and the adoption of a new engine, the 8300-kg (12500-kg with afterburning) Khatchatourov (as the Tumanskii OKB was properly known) R-29-300. The latter dramatically improved performance, and made the MiG-23 an extremely 'hot' fighter by the standards of the day, whereas the original MiG-23S had been judged slightly disappointing and 'sluggish'. Moreover, the new engine had variable throttled reheat.

A new wing (known officially as the No. 2 wing, and less formally as the 'wing with teeth') was also introduced on the MiG-23M. This featured a new extended leading edge, which gave a dramatic leading-edge 'dogtooth' or 'claw'. The aim of this modification was to increase wing area by increasing chord along the whole span. It also increased leading-edge sweep by 2°40' (thus changing the normal sweep settings to 18°40', 47°40' and 74°40', although cockpit indicators and flight manuals were never amended). Leading-edge slats were deleted from the No. 2 wing, and then re-introduced on the otherwise identical No. 3 wing, which was phased in during 1973.

At the same time that the No. 2 wing was introduced, the MiG-23's horizontal tail surfaces were moved aft, leaving a

larger gap between wing trailing edge and tailplane leading edge. This increased control authority and reduced stability, making the new aircraft slightly more agile in pitch. It also made the rear fuselage look totally different, since at the same time the jet pipe was made shorter.

Following a structural failure and a fortunately non-fatal crash on 14 March 1972, it was found that the wing pivots and the No. 2 fuel tank (which formed the basic structure of the centre fuselage) tended to crack, and had failed at only seven *g*, when the nominal service limit was eight *g*. To solve this problem new metallurgical processes were introduced (the failure had been caused by bubbles of hydrogen in the metal), along with better quality control measures, and local strengthening plates were added to existing aircraft. It is probable that most of the MiG-23Ss were not modified, and were merely given a lower *g* limit and shorter fatigue life. Most were probably retired as the MiG-23M began to enter service in large numbers. This cured the problem, but heavy attrition continued, often due to wing-sweep mechanism failures. At one stage, the accident rate was so high that the aircraft was picking up a reputation similar to that gained by NATO F-104 Starfighters.

Above: A Soviet air force MiG-23UB 'Flogger-C' at Wittstock, home of the MiG-29 'Fulcrum'-equipped 36th Fighter Regiment. This aircraft was reportedly the personal mount of Colonel Komisarov, the regiment commander.

Above left: A Luftwaffe pilot compares notes with the ground crew after a training sortie in a MiG-23UB, as the instructor climbs down from the rear cockpit. The 'Q' symbol on the nose is an award given in recognition of the excellent technical state of the aircraft.

Above: The ill-fated '04', an Hungarian MiG-23MF 'Flogger-B', whose dramatic demise is shown below.

Introduction of the MiG-23M, with its BVR missiles and radar, and its powerful engine, allowed the development of new tactics and procedures. The initial MiG-23S had been unsuitable for much more than pilot conversion training, lacking any greater capability than the MiG-21s it had been designed to replace. The MiG-23M itself changed slightly during its production life. The canopy gained a frame along the centreline, trim tabs were added to the tailerons, and the rudder gained a second hinge. Firepower was improved by

the adoption of the AA-8 'Aphid' short-range IR-homing missile in place of the AA-2 'Atoll', and these were often carried on twin launch rails. Production built up steadily, from two, to four, to eight aircraft a week by 1976.

Most MiG-23Ms went to Frontal Aviation for battlefield air superiority. They were the first Soviet fighters with a genuine (though limited) look-down/shoot-down capability, and usually operated in fours, flying under strict ground control to make slash attacks on enemy fighters and

low-level bombers. They also had an important, though secondary, ground-attack role, using unguided bombs and rockets. Substantial numbers of MiG-23Ms were also delivered to the IA-PVO, where they supplemented MiG-21s and Sukhoi Su-15/21 'Flagons' in the air-defence role. When a Sukhoi Su-21 destroyed the Korean Airlines Boeing 747 over Sakhalin on 1 September 1983, two MiG-23s were airborne at the same time, supporting the 'Flagon'.

Sanitised for export

The success of the MiG-23M, especially in VVS service, led to a demand for an export version of the aircraft; in fact, two down-graded export derivatives of the MiG-23M were manufactured. The first of these was the MiG-23MS, which bore the NATO reporting name 'Flogger-E'. By comparison with the MiG-23M, it differed by returning to the RP-22 radar and AA-2 'Atoll' armament, and thus lacked any AA-7 'Apex' capability. In most respects it was no better than a late-mark MiG-21 variant, and the prestige value of operating swing-wing 'Floggers' probably accounted for the type's popularity with Third World air forces, as did the type's improved reliability and maintainability.

As an interesting aside, there is no evidence to suggest that the Libyan air force ever received any fighter MiG-23s apart from the export MiG-23MS. Since these aircraft have no BVR capability, it is thus clear that the two destroyed by US Tomcats on 4 January 1989 cannot have presented a threat at the range at which they were engaged, and cannot have been carrying BVR missiles, as was claimed by the US Navy at the time. A handful of MiG-23MSs was taken on charge by Frontal Aviation, probably during a period of shortages of MiG-23Ms; photographs of these aircraft led some analysts to believe that 'Flogger-E' actually predated 'Flogger-B'.

The other export version of the aircraft was the MiG-23MF, which retained the 'Flogger-B' reporting name, and which was supplied in large numbers to various Warsaw Pact and other important export customers. Retaining 'High Lark' radar, the MiG-23MF differed from the MiG-23M in detail only, and was first delivered to Bulgaria in 1978, followed by East Germany, Czechoslovakia, Poland, Romania, Hungary, Syria, Angola, Iraq and India.

It was decided from an early stage that there would need to be a two-seat version of the MiG-23. Development of such an aircraft was authorised in May 1968, six months after authorisation for the combat version. Some confusion exists over the exact configuration of the prototype two-seater. Some sources suggest that the first aircraft was basically a two-seat version of the MiG-23S, with the R-27F2M-300 engine and associated lengthened rear fuselage, while others maintain that the aircraft (Bureau designation 23-51) was a two-seat version of the MiG-23M. A published photo of what may be the prototype, in Mikoyan colours and coded 251, seems to show an aircraft powered by the R-29-300, or at least with the empennage shifted to the rear, and with ribbed airbrakes. The original wing, however, without claws, seems to have been fitted to the two UB prototypes. This may indicate that the MiG-23UB prototype marked an interim step between the MiG-23S and the MiG-23M, with the latter aircraft being based on the airframe and engine improvements of the two-seater, coupled with the full-up weapons system and radar. Such a conclusion might be supported by the fact that Komarov made the two-seater's maiden flight in May 1969, three years before the first MiG-23M.

Designated by the air force as MiG-23UB (Uchebno Bitva, or combat trainer), the two-seater was designed from

On 16 September 1990 assistant squadron commander 39-year-old Major Karoly Soproni of the Hungarian air force was due to perform a flying display in MiG-23MF '04' as the last item on the programme of the (first ever) open day at Papa. He was selected to perform the display because he was reckoned to be the squadron's best pilot. After taking off in company with a MiG-21bis he positioned his aircraft to make an opposition pass down the runway. In this turn he had the wings swept back instead of fully forward, and his afterburner was not properly ignited. Consequently he lost height and speed. He tried to ease the aircraft back into the air, while simultaneously turning away from the crowd, but his jetpipe hit the ground. This slammed the nose down on to the airfield surface with a force estimated at some 60 g, killing the pilot instantaneously. The main fuel tank was ruptured in the impact. Although the pilot was killed, the engine kept running and the aircraft reared up into the air, spewing out burning fuel as it flew. The intense fire in the rear fuselage quickly melted through the control runs, and the aircraft veered out of control, crashing on the airfield in a ball of flame. The ejection seat fired on impact.

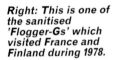

Above: The first sight of the MiG-23ML 'Flogger-G' came in 1978, when six of these aircraft visited Finland and France. They were sanitised and lacked even the undernose IRST sensor.

Right: This is one of the sanitised 'Flogger-Gs' which visited France and Finland during 1978.

the start for both pilot training and for weapons training and operational use. Since the two-seater had no Sapphire radar, a separate guidance and illuminator pod had to be provided to allow the aircraft to fire AA-7 'Apex' missiles, and this was fitted below the starboard wing root, on the leading edge.

Other changes to the two-seater included the reduction of internal fuel capacity and the replacement of single-slotted, trailing-edge flaps with twin-slotted flaps. Production two-seaters all had the No. 3 wing, allowing the aircraft to carry three external fuel tanks. The smaller-winged prototypes could carry only one, under the centreline. All two-seaters had either an AoA limiter or an AoA warning system, and have a much better avionics fit, with improved navaids and sophisticated threat and emergency simulation devices in the front cockpit. The rear cockpit was fitted with a retractable periscope to give the instructor a better view over the nose, and the head of his pupil, on take-off and landing.

Production of the UB continued until 1978, and today the aircraft remains in widespread use, having become a popular hack. Even MiG-29 and Su-27 units often have a handful of MiG-23UBs on charge, for instrument training and other duties. Conversion to the MiG-23 is, in fact, very simple, since the cockpit layout is very similar to that of late-mark MiG-21s, and handling techniques are similar.

The MiG-23 family has always been subject to constant change and improvement, and by 1976 a new fighter variant was ready for production and service. Designated 23-12 by the OKB and MiG-23ML (L for Logiky, or lightened) by the air force, the new aircraft was derived from the 'Flogger-B'

but featured improved aerodynamics, avionics and other systems in the interests of enhancing capability and perform-ance. The MiG-23ML was basically the first production variant to take advantage of a host of improvements designed by Mikoyan to provide better handling qualities (especially at high angles of attack), to improve manoeuvrability, to in-crease *g* limits, and to improve combat capability.

The airframe of the MiG-23ML was lightened by removal of the fourth fuselage fuel tank (added in the MiG-23M). This improved directional stability and allowed the removal of the dorsal fin fillet and a reduction in size of the folding ventral fin, saving further weight. By comparison with the original MiG-23M, the ML was some 1250 kg lighter. As well as lightening the airframe, the opportunity was taken to provide yet more thrust, by installing the Khatchatourov R-35-300 turbojet (rated at 8550 kg, or 13000 kg with after-burner).

Lightweight fighter

The aircraft's autopilot was redesigned, along with the navigation system. The Sapphire radar was significantly im-proved, gaining a new dogfight mode, an improved display and easier switchology, and the ageing IRST was dramat-ically improved, becoming the TP-23M. This necessitated enlarging the IR fairing below the nose. On the new variant, the SRO-2M 'Odd Rods' IFF antennas were moved aft, and the AoA vanes and some air-data probes were relocated. Two new RWR fairings were added to the rear fuselage, ahead of the airbrakes. Despite the many improvements, tac-tics remained largely unchanged, although the VVS began to place greater emphasis on autonomous action in the close-in engagements that occurred if or when targets survived the initial BVR engagement.

Other improvements included the replacement of the original four-section slats with lighter, stronger three-seg-ment units and by the provision of two extra underfuselage hardpoints, to replace the seldom-used hardpoints mounted on the bottom of the intake ducts. The nosewheel oleo assembly was considerably strengthened, giving better rough-field capability.

No exact first-flight date for the MiG-23ML is known, nor

Above: An interesting view of three Soviet air force MiG-23MLs, only one of which (the far aircraft) has an IRST. The latter aircraft also wears the modern darker camouflage scheme, while the nearer aircraft both wear a paler camouflage more often associated with export aircraft.

Far left: Full standard MiG-23MLs normally have an IRST sensor under the nose, as seen on these German examples. All MiG-23MLs have one less fuselage fuel tank, which allowed a reduction in keel area, which was achieved by removing the dorsal fin fillet and reducing the size of the folding ventral fin.

Below: This sanitised MiG-23ML seen visiting Finland carries a long-range fuel tank under the belly. No other pylons are carried, nor is the usual gun pod.

is it known who flew the first aircraft on that maiden flight. It was almost certainly during 1976, the year that the aircraft entered its five-year production career. The new variant made its public debut in 1978, when a six-aircraft detachment from Kubinka, near Moscow, led by Lieutenant Colonel Belenkov, visited Finland as part of a long-standing squadron exchange programme. These aircraft were stripped of external pylons and did not carry the sensitive undernose IR sensor, leading some observers to mistakenly conclude that they represented a new down-graded export version of the MiG-23. Assigned the reporting name 'Flogger-G', the new variant made a second appearance when the same unit sent six aircraft to Rheims for a squadron exchange with the 'Normandie-Niémen' fighter squadron.

Exports of the 'Flogger-G' were made to North Korea in late 1984, and then to Czechoslovakia and East Germany, where the new variant partly replaced and partly augmented existing 'Flogger-Bs'. The MiG-23ML was, in 1981 when production ended, the last major production MiG-23 fighter variant, although it served as the basis of the later MiG-23MLD conversion. 'Flogger-G' has also seen active service with the Soviet air force in Afghanistan. At least one regiment (with some 45 aircraft) was deployed to Kabul and later Bagram during 1986 and 1987. Used almost exclusively in their secondary ground-attack role, the MiG-23MLs were almost certainly conducting an operational evaluation of the variant's ground-attack capabilities. Many of the aircraft in Afghanistan received mission tallies in the form of small white stars under the nose, and one of the unit's pilots, Colonel Anatoly Levchenko, received a posthumous Hero of the Soviet Union award for an action in which he deliberately flew his crippled aircraft into an enemy AAA position.

While the MiG-23ML replaced MiG-23Ms in Frontal Aviation, a very similar aircraft, designated 23-14 by the OKB and MiG-23P by the Soviet air force, replaced some of the ageing 'Flogger-Bs' of the IA-PVO air defence force. Based on the airframe of the MiG-23ML, the MiG-23P featured a data link coupled to the autopilot, allowing the aircraft to be automatically guided to the most appropriate intercept point, with guidance about when to engage reheat and when to fire weapons being provided automatically to the pilot. No separate NATO reporting name has been given

Above: A JG 9 pilot clambers from the narrow cockpit of his MiG-23ML. The ground crew have already replaced all the safety pins and intake blanks. The rear view mirrors mounted on the canopy frame, and in the top of the canopy, can clearly be seen.

Right: A handful of JG 9 aircraft briefly wore a unit badge on their fins. This one was seen during a visit to Holzdorf, home to a MiG-21 interceptor wing.

Far right: A pair of MiG-23MLs have their landing gear extended. The heavy duty oleos and integral mudguards leave no room to doubt that this undercarriage was optimised for rough field operation.

o this variant, for which no first flight date is known.

The latest MiG-23 fighter variant is the 23-18 or MiG-23MLD (D standing for Dorabottanny, or manoeuvrability), not a production version at all, but a conversion based on the airframe of the MiG-23ML. The new variant has a number of features designed to improve high α capability, including vortex generators on the pitot probe and vestigial leading-edge root extensions. These are notched to generate powerful vortices at high angles of attack. With its increased α limits, the aircraft also features new leading-edge slats which deploy automatically to optimise handling and manoeuvrability at any given angle of attack. Dubbed 'Flogger-K' by NATO, the variant has a new chaff/flare dispenser with automatic actuation by a new RWR system, and a missile firing simulator system for economical missile training for the pilot, which does not involve launching a real missile. The aircraft also features new IFF equipment with a blade antenna replacing the old-style 'Odd Rods'.

Other reported improvements to the MiG-23MLD include the provision of swivelling pylons under the outer wing panels, allowing the wing to be swept even when these pylons are being used. On other variants, such pylons could be used to accommodate external fuel tanks, but these had to be jettisoned (with their pylons) before the wing could be pivoted. It has also been said that 'Flogger-K' is compatible with new Soviet missiles such as the AA-10 'Alamo' and AA-11 'Archer', and that the aircraft has a helmet-mounted sighting system similar to that used by the MiG-29 and Su-27.

Armament options

AA-11 'Archer' compatibility would mark a tremendous leap in capability for the MiG-23. With genuine all-aspect capability (e.g. able to home onto a head-on target), the 'Archer' has moving control fins fore and aft and has a vectoring rocket motor nozzle, making it incredibly agile. With a five-mile range and a 33-lb warhead, triggered by an active radar fuse, some analysts believe that the AA-11 is a better missile than the AIM-9 Sidewinder.

Hitherto, the 'Flogger's' Achilles Heel has always been its missile armament. The AA-2 had no all-aspect capability, while the AA-8 'Aphid' had a much-expanded launch en-

Above: Soviet combat aircraft types are rarely photographed with a full operational warload. This East German MiG-23ML seen on alert duty carries two R-23 AA-7 'Apex' missiles under the wing gloves, and two AA-8 'Aphids' under the port lower fuselage pylon.

Left: A Soviet MiG-23ML refuels before the last sortie of the day.

Above: The ultimate MiG-23 fighter variant was the MiG-23MLD, which featured minor aerodynamic improvements, an improved weapons system, and a lightened structure.

Below: The MiG-23MLD was dubbed 'Flogger-K' by NATO's Air Standards Co-ordinating Committee. It differed externally from the 'Flogger-G' in having small notches in the leading edge of each wing fillet and a small vortex generator on the pitot probe.

velope against manoeuvring targets, but only a minimal head-on capability. In terms of longer-range missiles, the AA-7 'Apex' was always bettered by the AIM-7 Sparrow in terms of range and head-on capability. It is no coincidence that most MiG-23 losses have been to missiles (mainly AIM-7s) in head-to-head engagements, where the reliability and extra reach of US missiles has been crucial. Over the Bekaa, for example, all but five of the 75 Israeli F-15 and F-16 kills were missile kills. The famous F-14 'Flogger' kills over the Mediterranean were another dramatic example of the superior reach and reliability of the AIM-7/AIM-9 being used to devastating effect.

If 'Flogger-K' can also carry the AA-10 'Alamo' this would mark an even greater increase in capability, since the IR-homing version of this weapon is a genuine BVR fire-and-forget missile. A passive radar-homing version may be under development, designed to home onto the radiation from enemy fighter radars. Even the standard semi-active, radar-

homing version is a major improvement over previous such missiles and may be better than the AIM-7 Sparrow. Such armament, if carried, would transform the MiG-23MLD into a fighter with much more modern capabilities, more like those enjoyed by the excellent MiG-29.

The number of aircraft converted to 'Flogger-K' standards is unknown, as is the current status of the conversion pro-

gramme. It may be offered to some export customers, and there may be scope for similar modifications to other variants, including the MiG-23M and MiG-23MF, and perhaps even the IA-PVOs MiG-23Ps. At least one MiG-23MLD regiment has been based at Cam Ranh Bay in Vietnam, another has been deployed to the disputed Etorofu Island in Japan's former northern territories, and another remains active at Jüterbog in what used to be East Germany. All other MiG-23 fighter units in that country converted to the MiG-29 before German re-unification in 1989.

'Flogger' improvements

The programme of improvements to 'fighter' MiG-23s is far from over, and is likely to continue as long as the aircraft remains in service. MiG-23MLDs in service in East Germany have recently started to receive huge chaff/flare dispensers (similar to those carried in the 'Fulcrum's' fin leading edge extensions) on the upper corners of the fuselage. A similar installation has also been seen on MiG-27s. One fuzzy photograph in the Soviet air force magazine 'Aviation and Kosmonautics' showed a 'Flogger-G' (perhaps a MiG-23P) with the

same blade antenna IFF as the MLD and with what appeared to be a new IRST (similar to that fitted to the MiG-29) above the nose.

Although most MiG-23 fighters were delivered to Frontal Aviation and have an important secondary ground-attack role, there are a number of dedicated ground-attack members of the 'Flogger' family. These latter derive from a 1969 Mikoyan OKB design study for a day or night 'jet Shturmovik' which would be both effective and cheap, rivalling Western types like the SEPECAT Jaguar and the Northrop F-5A. Supersonic performance was felt to be vital, in order that the aircraft would be able to escape from ground-based or airborne threats of any description, with minimum exposure. Originally, the Mikoyan OKB assumed that an all-new design would be necessary, but economic constraints forced it to look at a derivative of its MiG-23S fighter.

Deliberately attempting to emphasise that the new aircraft would be just that, despite its roots, Mikoyan assigned the project number 32. This did not stop the air force from using the same broad MiG-23 designation, perhaps feeling that funding would be easier for a new version of an existing de-

sign than for an entirely new aircraft. The new MiG–23B (32-24) was a minimum change version of the original production MiG–23S (and not the MiG–23M as has often been stated). The main area of change was the forward fuselage. Dispensing with the Sapphire radar, and replacing it with a less bulky PrNK 'Sokol' 23S navigation and attack system, Mikoyan designed a new, more-sloping nose allowing the pilot a much better view forwards and downwards. The new nose shape was distinctive, and quickly led to the new aircraft gaining the enduring nickname of 'Utkanos' (literally, Duck Nose).

Yet another new engine was selected, this time the 8000-kg (11500-kg with afterburner) Lyul'ka AL-21F-300. This led to the new ground-attack aircraft having rear fuselage contours similar to the MiG–23M, with the same short-

ened tailpipe and rear-located tailplane. The aircraft also featured the No. 2 (and later the No. 3) wing, as used on the MiG-23M and MiG-23UB.

Specific modifications for the low-level, ground-attack role included the provision of 'scabbed-on' armour-plate next to the cockpit, and a system whereby inert gas was pumped into fuel tanks as they emptied, displacing potentially explosive kerosene vapour. Other changes concerned the armament which the new variant could carry. The MiG-23B was designed to use a wide range of bombs (up to 18 100-kg bombs, eight 250-kg bombs or six 500-kg bombs), as well as rockets of various calibres, podded and unpodded, and various guided air-to-surface missiles.

The MiG-23B retained the twin-barrelled GSh-23L cannon pod of fighter variants under the fuselage, but could,

if necessary, augment this with two underwing UPK-23-250 cannon pods. Piotr Ostapenko flew the MiG-23B on its maiden flight on 20 August 1970, making the aircraft the third production variant to fly, after the MiG-23S and MiG-23UB. Only 24 production examples of the MiG-23B were completed, before production switched to the similar MiG-23BN. (The latter was confusingly given the earlier Bureau designation 32-23, perhaps indicating that it was intended to be the first ground-attack 'Flogger' but that it was delayed by equipment problems or engine availability.) The MiG-23BN differed in having an upgraded nav-attack system (the Sokol-23N) and the same 8000-kg (11500-kg with afterburner) Khatchatourov R-29B-300 engine as the MiG-23M, albeit slightly derated.

NATO assigned the MiG-23B and MiG-23BN the reporting names 'Flogger-F' and 'Flogger-H' respectively, the earlier code name indicating aircraft without the prominent lateral antenna fairings mounted on the lower corners of the forward fuselage, adjacent to the nose oleo. These were probably only the initial MiG-23Bs. The MiG-23BN introduced the leading-edge bullet fairings associated with the radio command guidance equipment required by the AS-7 'Kerry' ASM, and the transparent laser rangefinder window in the nose. The MiG-23BN proved disappointing in Frontal Aviation service, and consequently has been widely exported and even licence-built in India, where it equips some four squadrons. Some of these export aircraft went to Egypt, which passed most of them on to the USA (and two to China) after relations with the Soviet Union cooled.

'Flogger' fighter-bombers

Further variants of the basic MiG-23BN are also code-named 'Flogger-H', but were designated MiG-23BM (OKB Model 32-25) and MiG-23BK (OKB Model 32-26) by the Soviets. They proved rather more successful. They used the same systems as the early MiG-27 variants, and may have been produced as cheap 'Force Multipliers', perhaps even by conversion of MiG-23BNs. Some export aircraft, which have widely been assumed to be MiG-23BNs, may, in fact, have been MiG-23BMs or BKs (or at least have been upgraded to these standards) since they appear to share some of the same equipment. The MiG-23BK was basically equivalent to the MiG-27K, sharing the same basic nav-attack system and the same laser illuminator, while the MiG-23BM has many of the same avionics items as the original MiG-27. These later MiG-23s may have been compatible with some of the weapons more usually associated

59

Mikoyan-Gurevich MiG-23ML 'Flogger-G'

This MiG-23ML wears the colours of the Syrian air force, which has acquired the type in large numbers. The MiG-23ML was allocated the reporting name 'Flogger-G' by NATO's Air Standards Co-ordinating Committee. For many years the MiG-23ML was assumed to be broadly equivalent to the American F-4, but with vastly inferior weapons systems and no significant edge in performance when operationally configured. When the West finally managed to get its hands on an operational 'Flogger-C' (the first was this aircraft, which defected to Israel in the hands of a Syrian pilot, but more recently ex-East German MiG-23MLs have also been assessed) the results of the many evaluations came as something of a rude shock. The weapons system proved surprisingly effective and easy to use, and the aircraft's performance was staggering, with better acceleration than either the F-4 or the newer F-16. The MiG-23ML is now widely exported, and the top-of-the-line, much improved 'Flogger-K' (now the standard Soviet air force variant) remains something of an enigma.

Specification

Mikoyan-Gurevich MiG-23ML 'Flogger-G'

Fuselage length: 15.65 m/51.35 ft
Wingspan: fully swept 7.779 m/25.52 ft
Wheel track: 2.658 m/8.72 ft
Wheel base: 5.772 m/18.94 ft
Wing area: fully swept 34.16 m²/367.71 sq ft
Max take-off weight: 17800 kg/39,242 lb
Service load limits: 8.5 g up to Mach 0.85; 7.5 g above Mach 0.85
Maximum speed: high level Mach 2.35 (2500 km/h); unswept Mach 0.8; low level 1350 km/h
Service ceiling: 18500 m/60,696 ft
Range: 1950 km/1,211 miles; with external fuel 2820 km/1,752 miles

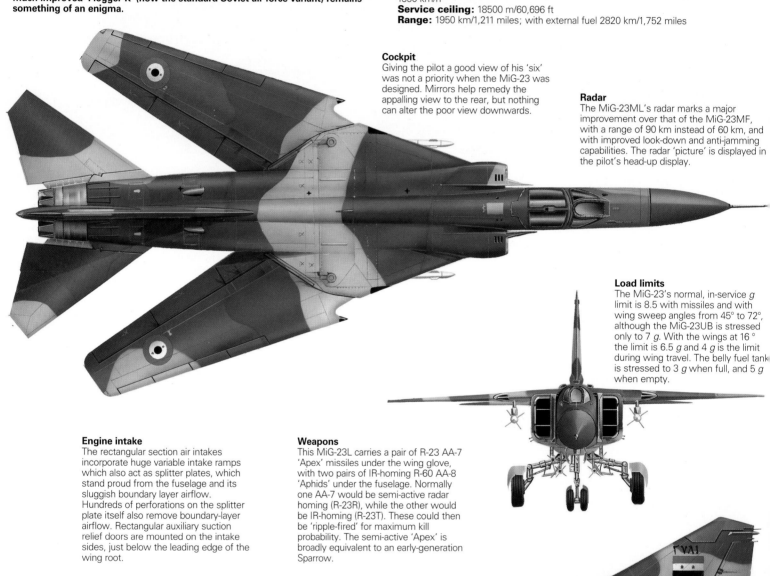

Cockpit
Giving the pilot a good view of his 'six' was not a priority when the MiG-23 was designed. Mirrors help remedy the appalling view to the rear, but nothing can alter the poor view downwards.

Radar
The MiG-23ML's radar marks a major improvement over that of the MiG-23MF, with a range of 90 km instead of 60 km, and with improved look-down and anti-jamming capabilities. The radar 'picture' is displayed in the pilot's head-up display.

Load limits
The MiG-23's normal, in-service g limit is 8.5 with missiles and with wing sweep angles from 45° to 72°, although the MiG-23UB is stressed only 7 g. With the wings at 16° the limit is 6.5 g and 4 g is the limit during wing travel. The belly fuel tank is stressed to 3 g when full, and 5 g when empty.

Engine intake
The rectangular section air intakes incorporate huge variable intake ramps which also act as splitter plates, which stand proud from the fuselage and its sluggish boundary layer airflow. Hundreds of perforations on the splitter plate itself also remove boundary-layer airflow. Rectangular auxiliary suction relief doors are mounted on the intake sides, just below the leading edge of the wing root.

Weapons
This MiG-23L carries a pair of R-23 AA-7 'Apex' missiles under the wing glove, with two pairs of IR-homing R-60 AA-8 'Aphids' under the fuselage. Normally one AA-7 would be semi-active radar homing (R-23R), while the other would be IR-homing (R-23T). These could then be 'ripple-fired' for maximum kill probability. The semi-active 'Apex' is broadly equivalent to an early-generation Sparrow.

Nosewheel
Like many Soviet tactical aircraft, the MiG-23 incorporates nosewheel braking, which helps to account for the very short landing distances that can be achieved. The nosewheel is hydraulically steerable.

Gun
The GSh-23L twin-barrelled cannon is housed in a GP-9 gun pack. This incorporates small ram air inlets which supply cooling air and ventilate the weapon, preventing the build-up of dangerous gases.

Airbrakes
Four hydraulically-actuated, externally-stiffened airbrakes are arranged around the rear fuselage, with the upper pair lying between the tailplane and tailfin, and the lower pair low on the fuselage sides.

Inside the Fighter 'Flogger'

Left: The instrument panel of a (Czech) MiG-23ML 'Flogger-G'. The turquoise paint is typical of 'Flogger' cockpits. Radar returns are projected directly on the HUD.

Above: The right-hand side panel of the same aircraft. The MiG-23 cockpit is typical of 1960s fighters, with a multitude of conventional analogue instruments.

Mikoyan-Gurevich MiG-23MLD 'Flogger-K'

1 Pitot head
2 Vortex generators
3 Radome
4 Radar scanner
5 Scanner tracking mechanism
6 'High-Lark 2' J-band pulse-Doppler radar equipment module
7 'Swift-Rod' ILS antenna
8 Radar mounting bulkhead
9 Cooling air scoop
10 Ventral Doppler navigation aerial
11 Weapons system avionics equipment
12 Nose compartment access doors
13 Yaw vane
14 Dynamic pressure probe [q-feel]
15 IFF aerial
16 Temperature probe
17 Cockpit front pressure bulkhead
18 Ventral laser rangefinder
19 Blade antenna
20 Nosewheel steering control
21 Torque scissor links
22 Pivoted axle beam
23 Twin aft-retracting nosewheels
24 Nosewheel spray/debris guards
25 Shock absorber strut
26 Nosewheel doors
27 Hydraulic retraction jack
28 Angle-of-attack transmitter
29 Rudder pedals
30 Control column
31 Three-position wing sweep control lever
32 Engine throttle lever
33 Cockpit section framing
34 Seat pan firing handles
35 Radar 'head-down' display
36 Instrument panel
37 Instrument panel shroud
38 Weapons sighting unit/head-up display
39 Armoured glass windscreen panel
40 AA-2 'Atoll' infra-red homing air-to-air missile

41 Missile launch rail
42 AA-2-2 'Advanced Atoll' radar homing air-to-air missile
43 Wing glove pylon
44 Upward-hinging cockpit canopy
45 Electrically heated rear view mirror
46 Pilot's K-36D 'zero-zero' ejection seat
47 Ejection seat headrest/drogue container
48 Canopy hinge point
49 Canopy hydraulic jack
50 Boundary layer splitter plate
51 Boundary layer ramp bleed air holes
52 Port engine air intake
53 Adjustable intake ramp screw jack control
54 Intake internal flow fences
55 Retractable landing/taxiing lamp, port and starboard [port only steerable]
56 Air data probes [automatic intake control system]
57 Variable-area intake ramp doors
58 Intake duct framing
59 Ventral cannon ammunition magazine, 200 rounds
60 Control rod linkages
61 Intake ramp bleed air ejector
62 Boundary layer spill duct
63 Avionics equipment
64 ADF sense aerial
65 Tailplane control rods
66 Forward fuselage fuel tanks
67 Notched wing glove fairing
68 Intake duct suction relief doors
69 Ground power and intercom sockets
70 Twin missile carrier/launch unit
71 Port fuselage stores pylon
72 Weapons system electronic control units
73 ECM equipment bay
74 Wing glove pylon attachment fitting
75 SOS-3-4 radar warning and suppression aerials

76 Wing sweep control horn
77 Screw jack wing sweep rotary actuator
78 Dual hydraulic accumulators
79 Central combining gearbox
80 Wing pivot box carry-through [welded steel construction]
81 Pivot box integral fuel tank
82 VHF aerial
83 Wing pivot bearing
84 Starboard SOS-3-4 radar warning and suppression aerials
85 Extended chord dog-tooth leading edge
86 Fixed portion of leading edge
87 Pivoting wing pylon
88 External fuel tank, 176-Imp gal [800-l] capacity
89 Nose section of MiG-23U 'Flogger C' tandem seat trainer
90 Student pilot's cockpit
91 Folding blind flying hood
92 Rear seat periscope, extended
93 Instructor's cockpit
94 MiG-23BN 'Flogger-F' dedicated ground-attack variant
95 Radar antenna fairing
96 Laser-ranging nose fairing
97 Raised cockpit canopy
98 Armoured fuselage side panels
99 Starboard wing leading-edge flap, down position
100 Leading-edge flap hydraulic actuator
101 Starboard wing integral fuel tank, maximum internal capacity 1265 Imp gal [5750 l]
102 Starboard navigation light
103 Wing full forward [16° sweep] position

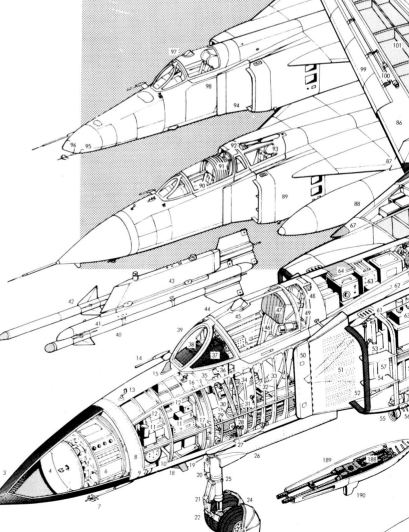

Wing sweep
The shoulder-mounted variable-geometry wing can be continuously swept or selected to any of three pre-set positions (known as 16°, 45° and 72°, but actually greater by some 2° and 40'). The wing is actuated by a pair of separately driven but interconnected hydraulic motors. Failure of one merely slows down the rate at which the wing transitions fore and aft. Early reliability and fatigue problems have now been overcome.

Stores pylons
The MiG-27L is generously endowed with hardpoints to allow the fitting of up to seven (or, exceptionally, nine) pylons. These are located on the fuselage centreline, under the engine intakes, under the wing gloves and on the 'shoulders' of the rear fuselage. A further two pylons can be carried under the outer wing panels, but these do not swivel and so can only be used with the wings swept forward for the whole flight. These latter pylons are thus seldom used except for the carriage of ferry tanks. The other pylons can be used for the carriage of a bewildering array of weapons, including guided and unguided bombs and missiles, and cannon, reconnaissance and EW pods. The rear fuselage pylons are seldom used, since they limit the amount of fuel that can be carried, due to centre of gravity considerations.

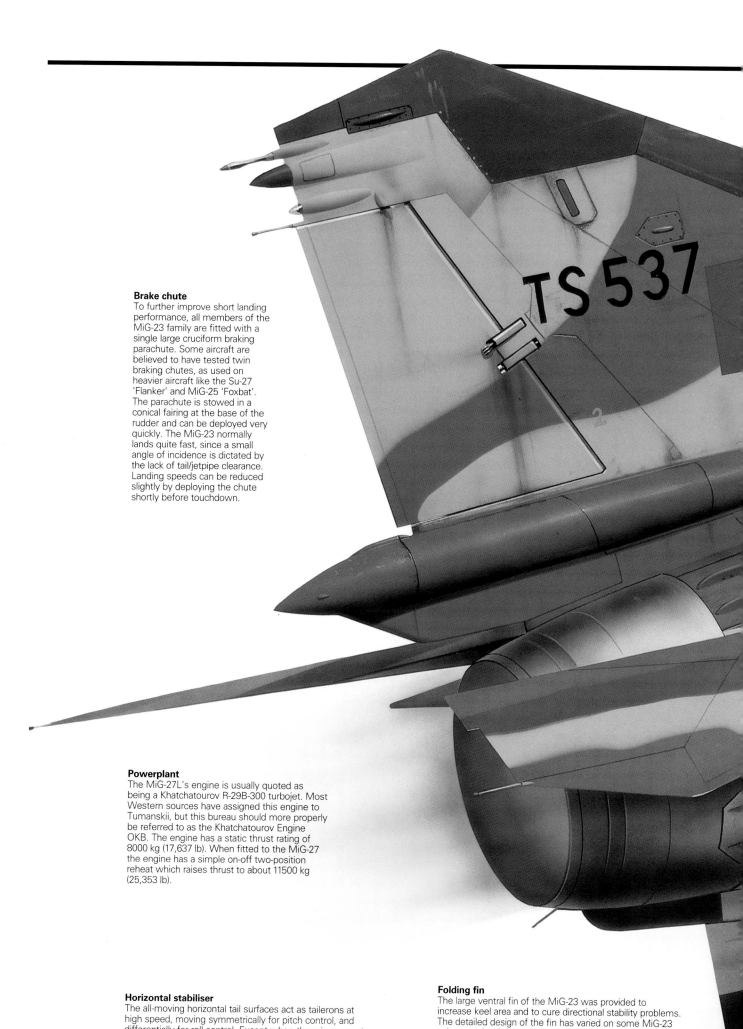

Brake chute
To further improve short landing performance, all members of the MiG-23 family are fitted with a single large cruciform braking parachute. Some aircraft are believed to have tested twin braking chutes, as used on heavier aircraft like the Su-27 'Flanker' and MiG-25 'Foxbat'. The parachute is stowed in a conical fairing at the base of the rudder and can be deployed very quickly. The MiG-23 normally lands quite fast, since a small angle of incidence is dictated by the lack of tail/jetpipe clearance. Landing speeds can be reduced slightly by deploying the chute shortly before touchdown.

Powerplant
The MiG-27L's engine is usually quoted as being a Khatchatourov R-29B-300 turbojet. Most Western sources have assigned this engine to Tumanskii, but this bureau should more properly be referred to as the Khatchatourov Engine OKB. The engine has a static thrust rating of 8000 kg (17,637 lb). When fitted to the MiG-27 the engine has a simple on-off two-position reheat which raises thrust to about 11500 kg (25,353 lb).

Horizontal stabiliser
The all-moving horizontal tail surfaces act as tailerons at high speed, moving symmetrically for pitch control, and differentially for roll control. Except when the wings are at maximum sweep, they are augmented by spoilers on the upper surfaces of the wings. No ailerons are fitted.

Folding fin
The large ventral fin of the MiG-23 was provided to increase keel area and to cure directional stability problems. The detailed design of the fin has varied on some MiG-23 sub-types, but it is present on all. It automatically folds up to starboard when the undercarriage is extended, to provide adequate ground clearance for the rear fuselage.

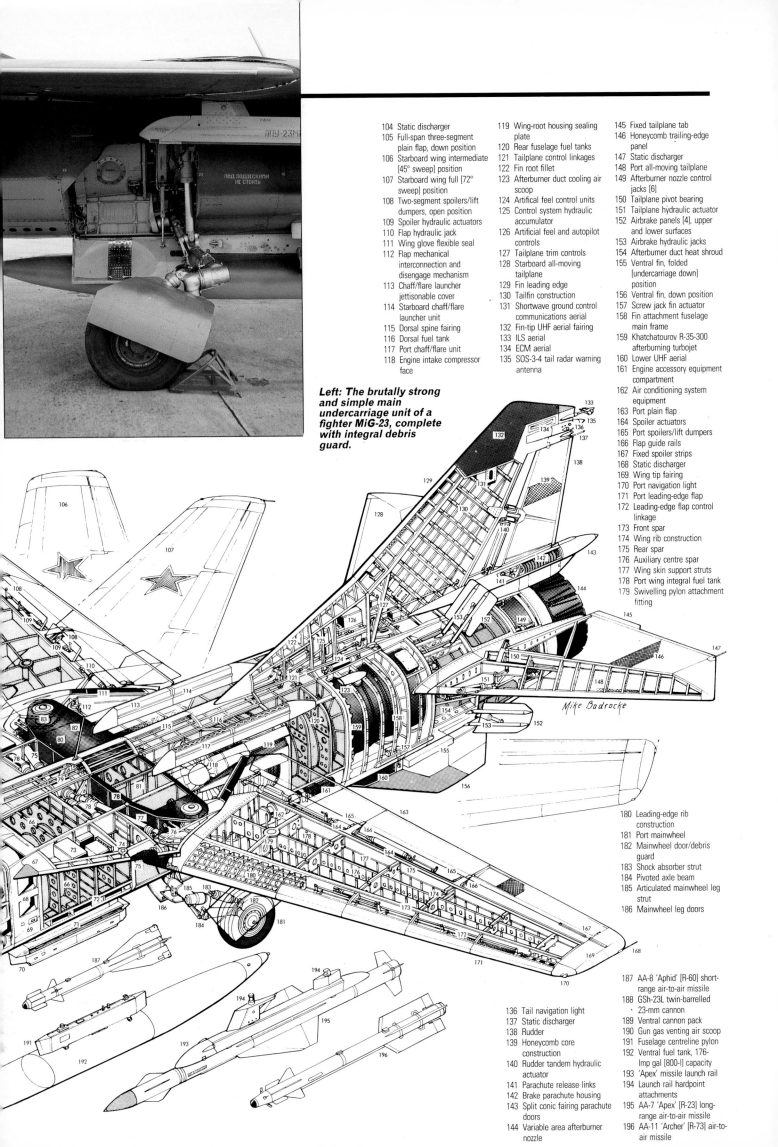

104 Static discharger
105 Full-span three-segment plain flap, down position
106 Starboard wing intermediate [45° sweep] position
107 Starboard wing full [72° sweep] position
108 Two-segment spoilers/lift dumpers, open position
109 Spoiler hydraulic actuators
110 Flap hydraulic jack
111 Wing glove flexible seal
112 Flap mechanical interconnection and disengage mechanism
113 Chaff/flare launcher jettisonable cover
114 Starboard chaff/flare launcher unit
115 Dorsal spine fairing
116 Dorsal fuel tank
117 Port chaff/flare unit
118 Engine intake compressor face

119 Wing-root housing sealing plate
120 Rear fuselage fuel tanks
121 Tailplane control linkages
122 Fin root fillet
123 Afterburner duct cooling air scoop
124 Artifical feel control units
125 Control system hydraulic accumulator
126 Artificial feel and autopilot controls
127 Tailplane trim controls
128 Starboard all-moving tailplane
129 Fin leading edge
130 Tailfin construction
131 Shortwave ground control communications aerial
132 Fin-tip UHF aerial fairing
133 ILS aerial
134 ECM aerial
135 SOS-3-4 tail radar warning antenna

Left: The brutally strong and simple main undercarriage unit of a fighter MiG-23, complete with integral debris guard.

136 Tail navigation light
137 Static discharger
138 Rudder
139 Honeycomb core construction
140 Rudder tandem hydraulic actuator
141 Parachute release links
142 Brake parachute housing
143 Split conic fairing parachute doors
144 Variable area afterburner nozzle

145 Fixed tailplane tab
146 Honeycomb trailing-edge panel
147 Static discharger
148 Port all-moving tailplane
149 Afterburner nozzle control jacks [6]
150 Tailplane pivot bearing
151 Tailplane hydraulic actuator
152 Airbrake panels [4], upper and lower surfaces
153 Airbrake hydraulic jacks
154 Afterburner duct heat shroud
155 Ventral fin, folded [undercarriage down] position
156 Ventral fin, down position
157 Screw jack fin actuator
158 Fin attachment fuselage main frame
159 Khatchatourov R-35-300 afterburning turbojet
160 Lower UHF aerial
161 Engine accessory equipment compartment
162 Air conditioning system equipment
163 Port plain flap
164 Spoiler actuators
165 Port spoilers/lift dumpers
166 Flap guide rails
167 Fixed spoiler strips
168 Static discharger
169 Wing tip fairing
170 Port navigation light
171 Port leading-edge flap
172 Leading-edge flap control linkage
173 Front spar
174 Wing rib construction
175 Rear spar
176 Auxiliary centre spar
177 Wing skin support struts
178 Port wing integral fuel tank
179 Swivelling pylon attachment fitting

Mike Badrocke

180 Leading-edge rib construction
181 Port mainwheel
182 Mainwheel door/debris guard
183 Shock absorber strut
184 Pivoted axle beam
185 Articulated mainwheel leg strut
186 Mainwheel leg doors

187 AA-8 'Aphid' [R-60] short-range air-to-air missile
188 GSh-23L twin-barrelled 23-mm cannon
189 Ventral cannon pack
190 Gun gas venting air scoop
191 Fuselage centreline pylon
192 Ventral fuel tank, 176-Imp gal [800-l] capacity
193 'Apex' missile launch rail
194 Launch rail hardpoint attachments
195 AA-7 'Apex' [R-23] long-range air-to-air missile
196 AA-11 'Archer' [R-73] air-to-air missile

Inside the Attack 'Flogger'

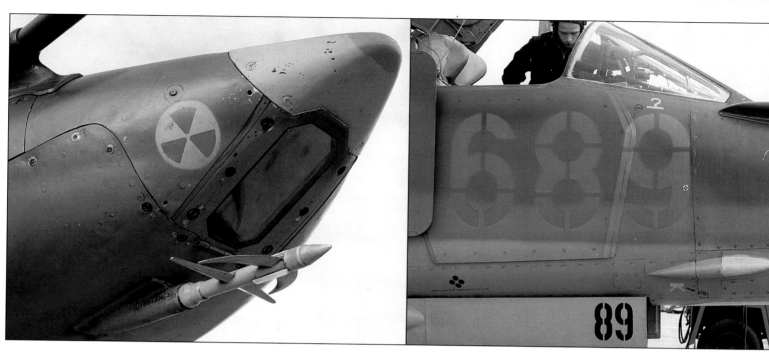

Mikoyan-Gurevich MiG-27 'Flogger-J, Variant 2'

1 Pitot head
2 Ranging radar antenna fairing
3 Nose aperture glazing
4 'Swift Rod' ILS aerial
5 Laser ranger
6 Ventral laser target designator
7 Nose compartment bulkhead
8 Radar altimeters
9 Lower IFF aerial
10 Temperature probe
11 Navigation and weapons system electronics equipment
12 Nose compartment construction
13 Avionics equipment access doors, port and starboard
14 Dynamic pressure probe [q-feel]
15 Instrument access panel
16 Forward pressure bulkhead, armoured
17 Ventral Doppler antenna
18 Blade antenna
19 Lateral ECM antenna, port and starboard
20 Nosewheel steering mechanism
21 Levered axle beam shock absorber
22 Twin nosewheels
23 Nose undercarriage leg strut
24 Nosewheel doors
25 Hydraulic retraction jack
26 Armoured cockpit pressure floor
27 Angle-of-attack transmitter
28 Rudder pedals
29 Instrument panel
30 Control column
31 Instrument panel shroud
32 Armoured glass windscreen panels
33 Pilot's head-up display
34 57-mm rocket
35 UB-16 rocket pack
36 Upward-hinging cockpit canopy

37 Electrically heated rear view mirror
38 Ejection seat headrest
39 Pilot's K-36D 'zero-zero' ejection seat
40 Canopy external latch
41 Seat pan firing handles
42 Engine throttle and wing sweep control levers
43 Port side console
44 Cockpit section framing [integrally armoured skin panelling]
45 Armoured rear pressure bulkhead
46 Ground test panel
47 Nose undercarriage wheel bay
48 Electrical system equipment
49 Canopy hydraulic jack
50 Canopy hinge point
51 Starboard engine air intake
52 ECM antenna
53 ADF sense aerial

54 Avionics equipment [navigation and communications]
55 Boundary layer spill duct
56 Boundary layer splitter plate
57 Avionics equipment cooling air intake
58 Fixed-geometry engine air intake
59 Retractable landing/taxiing lamp, port and starboard [port only steerable]
60 Intake duct framing
61 Control rod runs
62 Ventral cannon ammunition magazine, 260 rounds

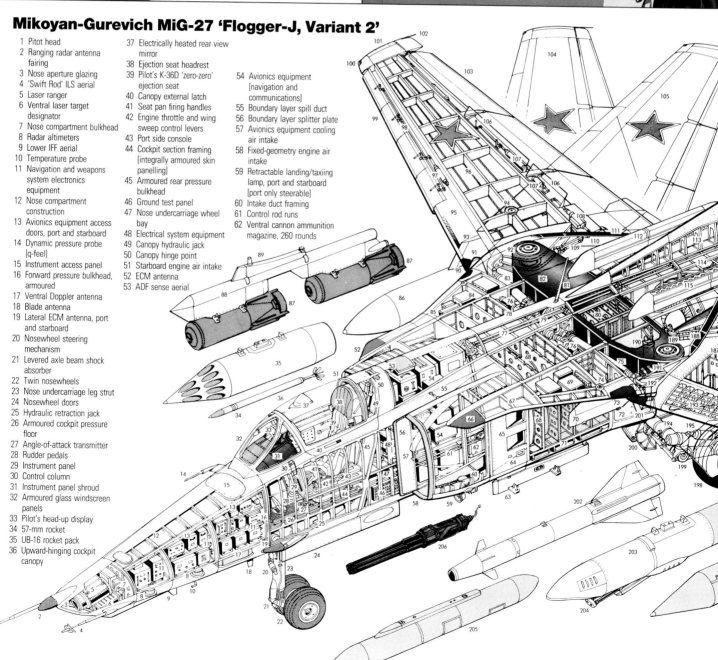

67

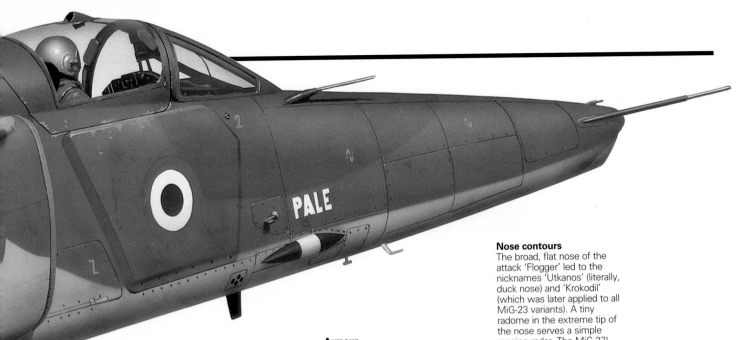

Nosewheel bay
The bulged nosewheel doors cover the twin-wheel nose undercarriage unit. This is fitted with large low-pressure tyres and used to incorporate a built-in mud/debris deflector for operations from rough/semi-prepared airfields, although this seems to be deleted on all Indian and many other late-mark MiG-27s.

Armour
Huge armoured panels, like those fitted to the MiG-23BN, are crudely 'scabbed-on' to the cockpit sides of most, but not all, MiG-27s. These protect the pilot from small arms fire and sometimes mount tiny vortex generators. On Soviet aircraft they normally act as the 'canvas' for the huge two-digit tactical codes. Angle-of-attack indicator vanes are mounted on each side of the lower forward fuselage immediately ahead of the armour.

Nose contours
The broad, flat nose of the attack 'Flogger' led to the nicknames 'Utkanos' (literally, duck nose) and 'Krokodil' (which was later applied to all MiG-23 variants). A tiny radome in the extreme tip of the nose serves a simple ranging radar. The MiG-27L lacks the small dielectric 'pimple' fitted to many current Soviet MiG-27s. A laser rangefinder, which almost certainly also has the ability to 'lock on' to laser energy radiated by a marked target, is housed behind an optically-flat laser-transparent glass panel at the front of the bulge below the nose. Twin probes are mounted on each side of the top of the nose, unlike the MiG-27M, where these probes are mounted lower on the nose. To starboard is a simple air data/pitot probe, while to port is the rather shorter RSBN 'Swift Rod' ILS and TACAN antenna. MiG-27s and MiG-27Ks, and the earlier MiG-23s, had the 'Swift Rod' antenna mounted below the nose.

Intake
The MiG-27 has simple fixed-geometry air intakes, without the moveable intake ramps and boundary layer extraction holes fitted to other MiG-23 variants' intakes. This is lighter and more reliable than the original 'Flogger' intake, and is no less efficient at subsonic and low supersonic speeds.

Cockpit
By comparison with the standard 'fighter' MiG-23, the pilot's ejection seat is raised and the armoured windscreen is less steeply raked. These improvements give a better view downwards and forwards over the nose. This necessitated a new rearward-hinging canopy. The view aft from the narrow cockpit is atrocious, and needs to be augmented by mirrors. One is faired into the top of the canopy, and others are mounted on the frame.

Mikoyan/HAL MiG-27L 'Flogger-J' No. 9 Squadron, 'The Wolfpack' Indian Air Force Hindan, 1990

India's MiG-27s are designated MiG-27 (Model 32-29L) by Mikoyan themselves, although they are acknowledged to be an export version of the MiG-27M (Model 32-29) 'Flogger-J2'. In fact, so much equipment is missing (by comparison with full-standard Soviet MiG-27Ms) that the aircraft is effectively equivalent to the earlier MiG-27D (Model 32-27) 'Flogger-J'. A planned mid-life avionics upgrade will dramatically increase the capability of these aircraft, adding a similar Smiths/Sagem DARIN nav/attack system to that currently fitted to Indian Jaguars. Indian participation in the MiG-27L programme has been significant; the first aircraft were assembled from Soviet-supplied kits at HAL's Nasik plant, but under Phase Two of the programme major Indian sub-assemblies were incorporated, with more, smaller components added during Phase Three. Phase Four introduced local airframe manufacture, with locally built engines and some indigenous systems. The Indian name 'Bahadur' (Valiant) was allocated during a period when virtually all aircraft were given local names, under the direction of a particular Chief of the Air Staff. It is now seldom used.

Gun

Affixed to the belly of the MiG-27 is a single six-barrelled 30-mm GSh-6-30 cannon, with stowage for some 250 rounds of ammunition. This powerful weapon replaced the twin-barrelled 23-mm GSh-23L cannon gondola used by fighter MiG-23s and by the MiG-23BN series, and which proved inadequate for most air-to-ground uses, but especially against hard or armoured targets. The introduction of a 30-mm cannon dramatically increased the destructive potential of the shells fired, and rate of fire was kept within acceptable limits by adopting a 'Gatling-type' multi-barrel gun. Weight of fire can easily be further increased by the carriage of twin-barrelled 23-mm gun pods underwing. These pods include one which has barrels that can be depressed for strafing ground targets.

Specification

Mikoyan-Hindustan Aeronautics MiG-27L 'Flogger-J'

Overall length: 17.076 m/56.02 ft
Fuselage length: 15.485 m/50.82 ft
Wingspan: swept forward 13.965 m/45.82 ft
Wheel track: 2.728 m/8.95 ft
Wheel base: 5.991 m/19.66 ft
Wing area: fully swept excluding LERX 34.16 m²/367.70 sq ft; swept forward excluding LERX 37.35 m²/402.04 sq ft
Max take-off weight: 20670 kg/45,569 lb; semi-prepared strip 18100 kg/39,903 lb
Take-off run: 950 m/3,117 ft
Landing run: with chute 900 m/2,953 ft; without chute 1300 m/4,265 ft
Service load limits: 7 g up to Mach 0.8; 6 g above Mach 0.8
Maximum speed: high level Mach 1.7 (1885 km/h)
Radius: lo-lo-lo, 5 mins over target 225 km/140 miles with two Kh-29 missiles; 540 km/336 miles with two Kh-29 missiles and three external fuel tanks

Leading edge root extensions

The MiG-27D, MiG-27M and MiG-27L all have prominent strakes leading forward from the leading edge of the wing glove along the 'shoulder' of the air intake. These were added to provide a location for new forward hemisphere RWR/ESM equipment, but also improve handling at high angles of attack and increase instantaneous turn rates.

Colour scheme

Indian MiG-27Ls wear a variety of colour schemes, all designed primarily as desert-type camouflage. Some aircraft have a glossy finish, but most are matt, and a handful of the glossy aircraft have large areas of dark green and a rich, dark chocolate colour. Like all Indian Air Force aircraft, the MiG-27Ls wear green, white and saffron roundels and fin flashes, with two-letter, three-digit RAF-type serial numbers. Squadron badges are fairly common on the MiG-27s.

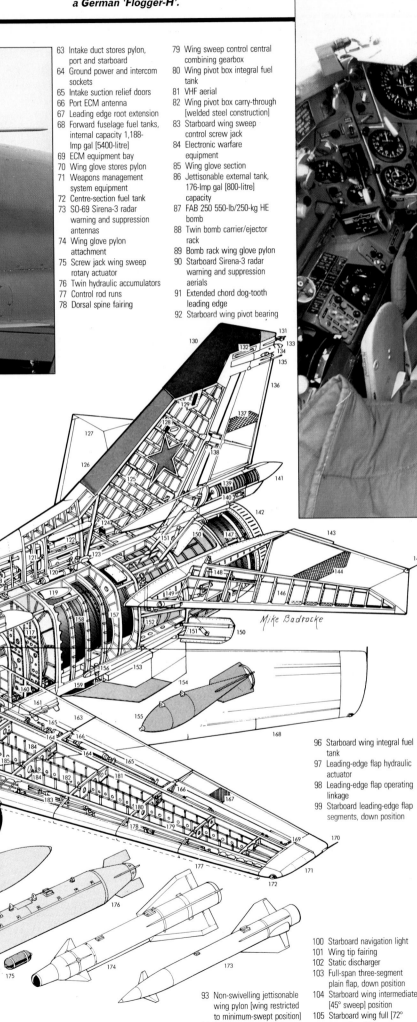

63 Intake duct stores pylon, port and starboard
64 Ground power and intercom sockets
65 Intake suction relief doors
66 Port ECM antenna
67 Leading edge root extension
68 Forward fuselage fuel tanks, internal capacity 1,188-Imp gal [5400-litre]
69 ECM equipment bay
70 Wing glove stores pylon
71 Weapons management system equipment
72 Centre-section fuel tank
73 SO-69 Sirena-3 radar warning and suppression antennas
74 Wing glove pylon attachment
75 Screw jack wing sweep rotary actuator
76 Twin hydraulic accumulators
77 Control rod runs
78 Dorsal spine fairing

79 Wing sweep control central combining gearbox
80 Wing pivot box integral fuel tank
81 VHF aerial
82 Wing pivot box carry-through [welded steel construction]
83 Starboard wing sweep control screw jack
84 Electronic warfare equipment
85 Wing glove section
86 Jettisonable external tank, 176-Imp gal [800-litre] capacity
87 FAB 250 550-lb/250-kg HE bomb
88 Twin bomb carrier/ejector rack
89 Bomb rack wing glove pylon
90 Starboard Sirena-3 radar warning and suppression aerials
91 Extended chord dog-tooth leading edge
92 Starboard wing pivot bearing

93 Non-swivelling jettisonable wing pylon [wing restricted to minimum-swept position]
94 Pylon attachment joint
95 Fixed portion of leading edge

96 Starboard wing integral fuel tank
97 Leading-edge flap hydraulic actuator
98 Leading-edge flap operating linkage
99 Starboard leading-edge flap segments, down position

100 Starboard navigation light
101 Wing tip fairing
102 Static discharger
103 Full-span three-segment plain flap, down position
104 Starboard wing intermediate [45° sweep] position
105 Starboard wing full [72° sweep] position
106 Two segment spoilers/lift dumpers, open position

107 Spoiler hydraulic actuators
108 Flap hydraulic jack
109 Flap mechanical interconnect and disengage mechanism
110 Wing root housing
111 Wing glove flexible seal
112 Chaff/flare launcher jettisonable cover
113 Fin root fillet construction
114 Dorsal fuel tank
115 Port chaff/flare launcher
116 Wing root housing sealing plates
117 Rear fuselage fuel tankage
118 Afterburner duct cooling air scoop
119 Tailplane control spring linkages
120 Artificial feel control units
121 Control system hydraulic accumulators
122 Artificial feel and autopilot controls
123 Fin spar attachment joint
124 Tailplane trim controls
125 Tailfin construction
126 Leading edge HF aerial
127 Starboard all-moving tailplane
128 Remote compass transmitter
129 Shortwave ground control communications aerial
130 Fin-tip UHF aerial fairing
131 ILS aerial
132 ECM aerial
133 Sirena-3 tail warning radar antenna
134 Tail navigation light
135 Static discharger
136 Rudder
137 Honeycomb core construction
138 Tandem rudder hydraulic actuators
139 Brake parachute housing
140 Parachute release linkage

141 Split conic fairing parachute doors
142 Two-position on/off afterburner nozzle
143 Fixed tailplane tab
144 Honeycomb core trailing-edge panel
145 Static discharger
146 Port all-moving tailplane
147 Afterburner nozzle pneumatic control jacks [6]
148 Tailplane pivot bearing
149 Tailplane hydraulic actuator
150 Airbrake [four] upper and lower surfaces
151 Airbrake hydraulic jacks
152 Afterburner duct head shroud
153 Ventral fin folded [undercarriage down] position
154 Ventral fin down position
155 FAB 250 550-lb/250-kg low-drag HE bomb
156 Screw jack ventral fin actuator
157 Fin attachment fuselage main frame
158 Khatchatourov R-29B-300 afterburning turbojet engine
159 Lower VHF aerial
160 Engine accessory equipment gearbox
161 Rear fuselage stores pylon
162 Port flap hydraulic actuator
163 Port plain flap
164 Spoiler hydraulic actuators
165 Port spoilers/lift dumpers
166 Flap guide rails
167 Flap honeycomb core construction
168 Port wing fully swept [72°] position
169 Fixed spoiler strips
170 Static discharger
171 Wing tip fairing
172 Port navigation light
173 AS-7 'Kerry' air-to-surface missile

174 AS-14 'Kedge' air-to-surface missile
175 AO-2.5 5.5-lb/2.5-kg bomblets [48]
176 KMG-U bomblet dispenser
177 Port leading-edge flap
178 Leading-edge flap control linkage
179 Front spar
180 Wing rib construction
181 Rear spar
182 Auxiliary centre spar
183 Leading-edge flap hydraulic actuator
184 Wing skin support posts
185 Port wing integral fuel tank
186 Wing pylon attachment joint
187 Wing skin panelling
188 Wing glove flexible seal
189 Port wing pivot bearing
190 Main undercarriage hydraulic retraction jack
191 Telescopic fuel connection to wing tank
192 Wing sweep control horn
193 Leading-edge rib construction
194 Articulated main undercarriage leg strut
195 Shock absorber strut
196 Mainwheel door/debris shield
197 Port mainwheel
198 Low-pressure rough-field-capable tyres
199 Pivoted axle beam
200 Mainwheel leg doors
201 Bulged fuselage fairing, low pressure tyre stowage
202 AS-10 'Karen' air-to-surface missile
203 SPPU-22 23-mm cannon pack with 260 rounds
204 Depressable twin cannon barrels
205 Elint recce pod
206 GSh-6-30 six-barrelled 30-mm cannon

Mike Badrocke

Mikoyan-Gurevich MiG-23BN (?) 'Flogger-H'

This MiG-23BN (which may actually be a MiG-23BK or BM) wears the distinctive insignia of the Czech and Slovak air force, with an unidentified unit badge on the nose. All MiG-23 fighter-bombers, apart from the initial handful of pre-series MiG-23Bs (known to NATO as 'Flogger-Fs'), share the common 'Flogger-H' reporting name. The MiG-23B and MiG-23BN proved disappointing, and never reached front-line Soviet units. Instead they were largely sent for export, and the MiG-27 was developed for the Soviet air forces. Because this entered service with the Soviet Group of Forces in Germany, it was 'spotted' by the West before any of the MiG-23 fighter-bombers, and received an 'earlier' reporting name. Later, Mikoyan developed two new MiG-23 fighter-bomber variants, the MiG-23BM and BK, using various MiG-27 sensors and systems, and some of these aircraft were also exported. It is extremely difficult to tell the three 'Flogger-H' variants apart, and many aircraft traditionally described as MiG-23BNs may be no such thing.

Specification

Mikoyan-Gurevich MiG-23BN/BM/BK 'Flogger-H'

Fuselage length: 15.349 m/50.36 ft
Wingspan: fully swept 7.779 m/25.52 ft; swept forward 13.965 m/45.82 ft
Wheel track: 2.728 m/8.95 ft
Wheel base: 5.991 m/19.66 ft
Wing area: fully swept 34.16 m²/367.71 sq ft; swept forward 37.35 m²/402.05 sq ft
Max take-off weight: 18900 kg/41,667 lb
Max landing weight: 15200 kg/33,510 lb
Service load limits: 7 g up to Mach 0.8; 6 g above Mach 0.8
Maximum speed: low level 1350 km/h (Mach 1.7)
Service ceiling: 18500 m/60,696 ft
Radius: lo-lo-lo, 5 mins over target 400 km/249 miles with six 500-kg/1,102-lb bombs; 600 km/373 miles with four 250-kg/551-lb bombs

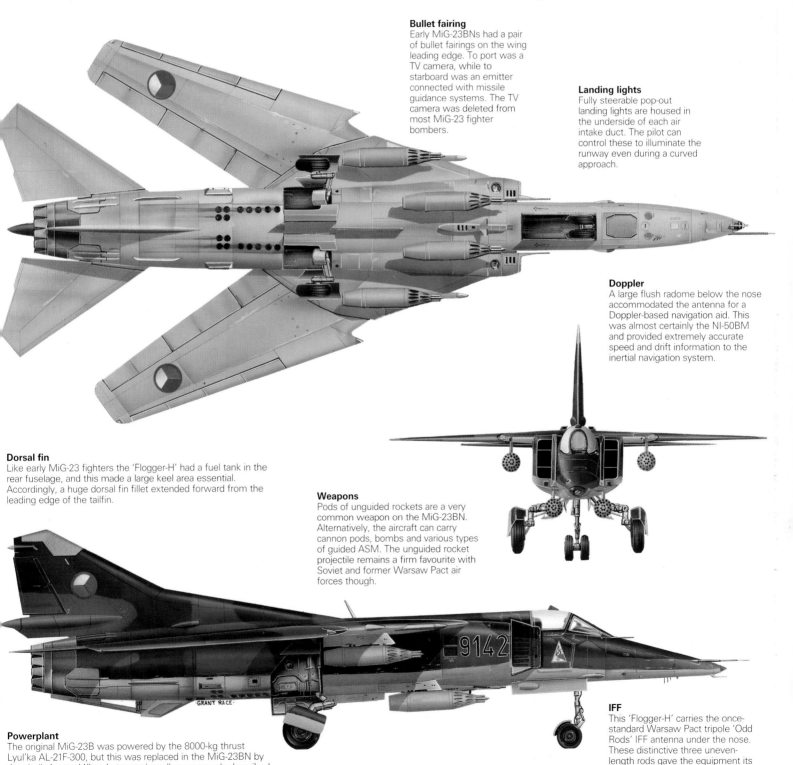

Bullet fairing
Early MiG-23BNs had a pair of bullet fairings on the wing leading edge. To port was a TV camera, while to starboard was an emitter connected with missile guidance systems. The TV camera was deleted from most MiG-23 fighter bombers.

Landing lights
Fully steerable pop-out landing lights are housed in the underside of each air intake duct. The pilot can control these to illuminate the runway even during a curved approach.

Doppler
A large flush radome below the nose accommodated the antenna for a Doppler-based navigation aid. This was almost certainly the NI-50BM and provided extremely accurate speed and drift information to the inertial navigation system.

Dorsal fin
Like early MiG-23 fighters the 'Flogger-H' had a fuel tank in the rear fuselage, and this made a large keel area essential. Accordingly, a huge dorsal fin fillet extended forward from the leading edge of the tailfin.

Weapons
Pods of unguided rockets are a very common weapon on the MiG-23BN. Alternatively, the aircraft can carry cannon pods, bombs and various types of guided ASM. The unguided rocket projectile remains a firm favourite with Soviet and former Warsaw Pact air forces though.

Powerplant
The original MiG-23B was powered by the 8000-kg thrust Lyul'ka AL-21F-300, but this was replaced in the MiG-23BN by the similarly-rated Khatchatourov (usually erroneously described as Tumanskii) R-29B-300.

IFF
This 'Flogger-H' carries the once-standard Warsaw Pact tripole 'Odd Rods' IFF antenna under the nose. These distinctive three uneven-length rods gave the equipment its NATO reporting name.

with the MiG-27, including missiles like the AS-10 'Karen', the AS-12 'Kegler' and the AS-14 'Kedge', and various gun pods developed for the MiG-27.

Because it was noticed by the West before the MiG-23B family, it was always assumed that the MiG-27 was the first ground-attack derivative of the MiG-23 family, and that the MiG-23B, BN, BM and BK were later versions, less sophisticated and less expensive to produce because of their commonality with the MiG-23 fighter. In fact, the MiG-27 was developed from the MiG-23B in order to remedy some of the deficiencies of the earlier aircraft, and it was seen first because the disappointing MiG-23B/BN never reached squadron service in the Group of Soviet Forces in Germany, where Soviet tactical aircraft were usually 'first spotted'.

The original MiG-27, and the similar MiG-27K, were ordered into production off their drawing board, before Mikoyan OKB designations could be applied. Consequently, they are known to the Bureau and air force alike as the MiG-27. The aircraft first flew in the hands of Valery Menitsky, now the chief test pilot at Mikoyan. The MiG-27 differs from the earlier attack 'Floggers' in having new avionics and a revised powerplant.

Externally, the MiG-27 is distinguishable by its simplified engine intakes, which lack moveable splitter plates, and by its simple afterburner nozzle. These have a detrimental effect on maximum speed, but have improved fuel consumption and

reliability. The powerplant itself is the same R-29B-300 as is fitted to the MiG-23BN.

Most importantly, the MiG-27 was given a new nav-attack system, loosely based on that of the MiG-23BM, but with a new version of the PrNK-23 navigation and weapons aiming system incorporating a navigation computer, a new automatic flight planning system, a thermal jammer and a new laser rangefinder.

The MiG-27 also gained an extra hardpoint, bringing war-load capacity to 4000 kg on its seven pylons. More importantly, the 23-mm cannon, often criticised for being of in-adequate calibre, was replaced by a new six-barrelled GSh-6-30 30-mm Gatling gun, with 260 rounds of ammunition. Further gun armament could be carried in the form of underwing cannon pods.

Guns for ground attack

Such gun pods include the UPK-23, which contains a pair of forward-firing 23-mm cannon, or perhaps more probably a single twin-barrelled GSh-23L 23-mm cannon, and about 250 rounds of ammunition. Another more unusual cannon pod is the SPPU-22, which contains the same basic weapon, with 260 rounds of ammunition, but fitted with barrels which can be depressed to allow strafing in level flight.

Like the MiG-23BN, the MiG-27 can carry the full range of podded and unpodded rockets (the 57-mm UV-32-57 being a favourite pod and the 240-mm S-24 being a favourite HVAR), as well as 50-kg, 100-kg, 250-kg and 500-kg bombs. Cluster and dispenser weapons include the relatively new KMG-U bomblet dispenser, which contains 48 AO-2.5

Above: The original MiG-27 lacked a laser rangefinder but was otherwise similar to the MiG-27K. This aircraft (again seen at Frunze) was probably the first prototype. The MiG-27 introduced simple fixed-geometry air intakes and a simplified afterburner nozzle, which improve fuel consumption and reliability. Later MiG-27 variants were significantly more capable, with much improved avionics systems.

Top: The Indian Air Force version of the 'Flogger-J' is known locally as the Bahadur ('Valiant') and is designated MiG-27L by Mikoyan. Said to be an export version of the definitive MiG-27M, it looks more like the earlier MiG-27D. All three variants share the 'Flogger-J' reporting name.

Above: A MiG-27D 'Flogger-J' is seen landing at Kabul during the type's brief combat deployment to Afghanistan. The MiG-27 was too sophisticated an aircraft to be used effectively in Afghanistan, where it made better sense to use cheaper ground attack types.

bomblets (each of about 7.5 kg weight) in eight six-bomb drums. These dispense their bomblets either downwards or outwards, and a MiG-27 with four such weapons could cover a wide swathe of ground. The needle-nosed dispensers themselves can be carried on any pylon stressed for a 500-kg bomb, and can be jettisoned after the bomblets have been dispensed. The aircraft can also carry IR-homing air-to-air missiles for self-defence, and a variety of guided air-to-surface missiles.

The MiG-27 is also believed to have an important tactical nuclear-strike role. Mikoyan has confirmed that the aircraft has nuclear weapons delivery systems, listing this weapon option casually between references to 500-kg bombs and napalm tanks!

As the heaviest 'Flogger' variant to date, the MiG-27 also gained a redesigned undercarriage, with huge low-pressure tyres, which may also have been fitted to later MiG-23B variants. Despite the effectiveness of this energy-absorbing undercarriage, take-off and landing performance of the MiG-27 remain the worst of any 'Flogger' variant.

Like earlier 'Flogger' variants, the MiG-27 has spawned a number of sub-variants. The first of these was the MiG-27K (no OKB designation was allocated), which had a weapons

system based on that of the MiG-23BK, with provision for night or bad weather blind-bombing with a very high degree of accuracy, and with provision for firing laser-guided ASMs. RWR and countermeasures systems were more highly automated, and a new weapons management system allowed the pilot greater flexibility in selecting and using the various stores, simultaneously when necessary. Externally, the MiG-27K could be identified by the laser 'window' in the nose forward of the 'Swift Rod' ILS antenna.

The final three versions of the MiG-27 did receive OKB model numbers, and consist of the MiG-27D (32-27), the MiG-27M (32-29) and the MiG-27L (32-29L). All three are fitted with a revised PrNK-23M nav-attack system with more flexible and numerous operating modes, and all were equipped with a new Klen laser rangefinder in place of the Fone unit fitted to earlier MiG-27s. Equipment includes a new photo-reconnaissance pod with three optical cameras and various other sensors, and various new types of gun pod.

The MiG-27M can be distinguished from the other late MiG-27s by the wider aperture for its laser rangefinder, fitted in the flattened underside of the nose instead of in a bulged narrow fairing. A much larger fairing further aft accommodates the combined TV tracker and laser designator. Pitot probes and 'Swift Rod' antenna are carried low on the nose, with a dielectric pimple above the laser rangefinder, while the MiG-27D and MiG-27L have these higher, and have a faired-in dielectric radome following the nose contours. All three aircraft types have extended wing-root leading-edge fairings and lack the conical fairings, usually ascribed as being missile-guidance antennas, on the leading edges of the wing gloves.

The 'Valiant' MiG

The MiG-27L is described by Mikoyan as the export version of the MiG-27M for India, where it is built under licence as the HAL Bahadur ('Valiant'). In fact, the aircraft could more accurately be described as an export version of the MiG-27D, which it resembles more closely. Politically, however, India just had to have the full standard, very latest MiG-27 version. It does lack certain more-sensitive equipment items, and may not have nuclear weapons delivery systems fitted, though this is uncertain. The nose contours follow those of the MiG-27D, with only a single laser designator window in a fairing under the nose. The Indian Air Force has been very happy with its MiG-27s, whether or not they are MiG-27Ms as advertised, and the aircraft already equip five front-line squadrons.

Above: The nose 'pimple', bulged undernose fairing and low-mounted pitots identify this aircraft as a MiG-27M 'Flogger-J2'. The aircraft shows obvious signs of having been recently re-coded, with bright green paint covering the 'scabbed-on' armour on which the code is painted. This aircraft serves with the 116th Fighter Bomber Regiment at Brand (part of the Grossenhain-headquartered 105th Fighter Bomber Division).

The older MiG-27D 'Flogger-J' is also in service in what used to be East Germany. This aircraft wears the yellow codes of the Mirow-Larz-based 19th Fighter Bomber Regiment (part of the 125th Fighter Bomber Division), and carries what appears to be a reconnaissance pod under the intake.

Mikoyan MiG-23/-27 'Flogger'

MiG-27s of unknown sub-type were sent to Afghanistan in 1988, where they operated from Shindand until the final Soviet pull-out in February 1989. Their use in Afghanistan was probably more for operational trials than for their usefulness in direct operations against the Mujahideen. More useful in-theatre was the slower and more nimble Su-25, and numbers were made up by Su-22s. This latter type has always tended to have a broader conventional role, and was easier to fly, and was thus presumably felt to be more suitable for the Afghan air force. For commonality, Soviet fighter-bomber regiments deployed to Afghanistan tended to use the same aircraft types as Afghan units, and the presence of the MiG-27 (with its important nuclear-strike role) in the country was thus unusual. The MiG-27s flew their first operational mission against positions south of Kandahar on 31 October 1988, and operated quite intensively for four months, until they were withdrawn. No losses were reported during the period, but this was hardly surprising since these sophisticated low-level strike aircraft were mainly being misused in medium-level, level-bombing attacks.

Today, the MiG-23 is a mature design, and the aircraft's many weaknesses and problems have largely been overcome. Reliability and handling difficulties are now a matter of history, although it will take longer for the 'Flogger' to live down its unfortunate reputation. In the shape of the MiG-23MLD and MiG-27M (the ultimate fighter and fighter-bomber variants) the aircraft has become a fully viable front-line aircraft for the 1990s, capable of holding its own against all but the very latest Western types, and able to fulfil its mission over the modern battlefield.

Despite the widespread introduction of later aircraft types, the MiG-23 still has a long front-line career ahead of it, both in Soviet service and with a host of export customers. For many years to come the most common posting for a newly trained Soviet pilot will be to a MiG-23 or MiG-27 regiment, and the same will be true in many other air arms. As a second-line hack and trainer, the MiG-23's life will be limited only by airframe fatigue, and it seems that Mikoyan built its 'Swinger' good and strong, so MiG-23UBs may yet turn out to be the MiG-15UTIs or T-33s of tomorrow.

Below: Although largely replaced by the MiG-29 in most front-line Soviet air force regiments, large numbers of MiG-23s remain in use in less important regions. In many former Soviet client states the MiG-23 represents the most important type in service, and seems assured of a long and fruitful career probably stretching into the next century. Here a German MiG-23ML flies into the sunset.

Left: The rare sight of the MiG-23 and its successor, the MiG-29 'Fulcrum', taking off together. In this case both aircraft are from the Czech and Slovak air force. The outbreak of peace in Europe seems certain to cut short MiG-29 production, making it unlikely that the remaining MiG-23s will be replaced by the newer type.

MiG-23/-27 'Flogger' Operators

Soviet Union

Even in post-Cold War Europe, with *glasnost* (literally 'openness') at its height, it is impossible to gain access to a detailed order of battle of the Soviet air forces. Such listings do exist, even in the West, but they lie deep in the more highly classified files of the more efficient intelligence agencies, and perhaps in the offices of the government officials in charge of arms control negotiations. It is thus impossible to give a detailed listing of Soviet MiG-23/-27 units, or even to give an accurate figure of the total number left in service.

All that can be said with certainty is that while the early 'Flogger' variants have been retired, or re-assigned to training duties, large numbers of 'Flogger-Gs', 'Flogger-Ks' and 'Flogger-Js' remain in front-line service. It is misleading to speak of a single Soviet air force, since there is no such thing.

Basically there are two separate air arms, comprising those units assigned to support of the army, and those assigned to defence of the homeland. The army-support units range from light helicopters to heavy transports, and from jet fighters to strategic bombers, and are assigned either to the Air Armies of the Supreme Command (VGK), or to the Air Armies of the Military Districts or Groups of Forces; the latter is known generically as Frontal Aviation. There is also a separate Military Transport air force.

Air defence units are assigned to the Troops of the Air Defence (IA-PVO), although the distinctions are sometimes blurred in that in some border regions a PVO unit might come under the operational control of the local Frontal Aviation commander. Finally, it must be remembered that the Navy also has its own independent air arm, and this is growing in size and importance as aircraft are transferred to it to avoid being counted in CFE (Conventional Forces in Europe) arms control limits.

Still the biggest operator of the 'Flogger' is Frontal Aviation. Though a complex organisation, Frontal Aviation has a single broad role, to win and exploit local air supremacy. The winning of air supremacy over the battlefield necessitates the employment of huge numbers of fighter aircraft, while to exploit it, fighter-bombers are employed. The 'Flogger' was at one time the most important aircraft in service in both roles. Today, even though many MiG-23 fighter units have now been re-equipped with the MiG-29, large numbers of MiG-23MLs and MiG-23MLDs remain in service. Known operators include a regiment at Cam Ranh Bay in Vietnam (these aircraft carry a dolphin badge on the fin) and the 833rd Fighter Regiment based at Jüterbog, near Berlin. 'Flogger-G' units based at Finow, Falkenburg and Altenburg converted to the MiG-29 sometime after 1987. In Poland, MiG-23 regiments are based at Brzeg and Kolobrzeg, but in Czechoslovakia the last MiG-23 regiment (which included a single MiG-29 squadron) at Milovice returned to the USSR in early 1991. Other MiG-23 fighter units have been provisionally identified at Dushanbe-Gissar and Khanabad in the Turkestan Military District and at Burevestnik/Iturup in the Middle Eastern Military District. This represents only the tip of a very large iceberg.

No current MiG-27 or MiG-23BN bases inside the Soviet Union are definitely identified. In the 16th Air Army in what used to be East Germany, however, things are different, with four MiG-27D and MiG-27M regiments identified. These are the 19th Fighter Bomber Regiment (part of the 125th Fighter Bomber Division) at Mirow-Larz, and the three Fighter Bomber Regiments (the 116th at Brand, the 296th at Grossenhain and the 339th at Finsterwalde) of the 105th Fighter Bomber Division.

In the PVO, more MiG-23 bases have been identified. These consist of Kursk East, Smolensk North, Tunoshnoye-Yaroslavl and Yefremov (all in the Moscow Military District of the Moscow TVD), and at Alakurtti and Malyavr (both in the Leningrad Military District, North West TVD), and finally at Khrabrovo (in the Baltic Military District of the Western TVD). The identified bases represent only a tiny fraction of the actual total.

Arms control negotiations have led to a major strengthening of the Aviatsiya Voyenno – Morskove Flota (Naval Air Arm) and large numbers of interdictors have been transferred from the air forces to escape inclusion in the CFE limits. These aircraft have included large numbers of Su-24 'Fencers' and MiG-27 'Floggers', giving the Navy control of one of the most advanced overland nuclear strike forces in existence. Some of the naval MiG-27s are based at Ki Yavr (Leningrad Military District, Atlantic Fleet), while others have undergone trials on the dummy carrier deck at Saki in the Crimea.

The large two-digit codes carried by Soviet tactical aircraft are a regimental identification number only, and change when an aircraft moves unit. A pair of Mikoyan c/ns has been identified, however, and these are noted below:

MiG-23MF: 4602
MiG-23UB: 0904106

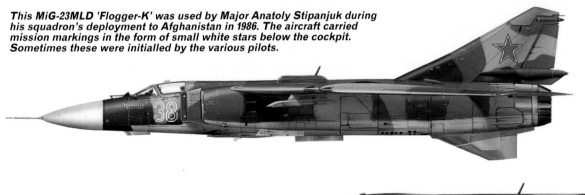

This MiG-23MLD 'Flogger-K' was used by Major Anatoly Stipanjuk during his squadron's deployment to Afghanistan in 1986. The aircraft carried mission markings in the form of small white stars below the cockpit. Sometimes these were initialled by the various pilots.

Below: This MiG-23MLD 'Flogger-K' was based at Cam Ranh Bay, Vietnam, during the late 1980s. It was one of the first Soviet aircraft seen wearing a squadron badge, in this case a Disney-like dolphin.

Below: This MiG-23MF, retired to the museum at Frunze, retains the original overall grey colour scheme applied to many IA-PVO 'Floggers'. The aircraft also carries an outstanding maintenance award on the nose.

Above: MiG-23UBs serve with every MiG-23 and MiG-27 unit in the Soviet air forces (including those in the IA-PVO), and with most MiG-29 and Su-27 regiments too. In many respects, the MiG-23UB has become the MiG-15UTI 'Midget' of the 1980s and 1990s, having become a great all-round hack and trainer. Most wear standard green and brown Frontal Aviation camouflage.

above: *This desert-camouflaged MiG-23ML 'Flogger-G' served with a demonstration squadron of the Proskurovskii Regiment at Kubinka during the late 1980s. Another squadron at Kubinka (probably belonging to one of the other two regiments at this huge base) still operates MiG-23MLs in the air-defence role.*

Right: *This red-coded MiG-27M 'Flogger-J2' serves with the 116th Fighter Bomber Regiment at Brand, as part of the 125th Fighter Bomber Division.*

Above: *This 833rd Fighter Regiment MiG-23MLD 'Flogger-K' is fitted with overwing chaff/flare dispensers. It was photographed on approach to its base at Jüterbog, south of Berlin.*

Below: *A high-vis orange and white brake chute bobs behind a taxiing MiG-27D 'Flogger-J' of the Mirow-based 19th Fighter Bomber Squadron. A Guards badge is worn on the intake.*

Afghanistan
Afghan Republic Air Force

Unconfirmed reports suggest that Afghanistan received up to 45 MiG-23 'Floggers', though the presence of Soviet MiG-23s in-country, and the practice of painting Afghan markings on Soviet tactical aircraft, may explain away these reports. Two were claimed as shot down by the Pakistan air force during airspace violations in October and November 1988.

Algeria
Armée de l'Air Algérienne/Al Quwwat al Jawwiya al Jaza'eriya

Two squadrons are equipped with about 40 MiG-23BNs, which operate alongside Su-20 'Fitters'. An unknown number of 'Flogger-E' fighters have also been delivered, and these equip at least one air defence regiment, augmenting ageing MiG-21s.

Known serials include:
MiG-23BN: 383, 388, 389

Angola
Força Aérea Popular de Angola e Defesa Anti Avioes

Angola received the first of about 50 MiG-23s during 1985. These have included MiG-23MFs (MiG-23MS would seem more likely), MiG-23BNs and MiG-23UBs. Cuban personnel flew and maintained these and other Força Aérea Angola aircraft until January 1989, when Cuba and South Africa withdrew from direct participation in the long-running civil war. A Cuban-flown single-seat 'Flogger' was shot down by the South African Air Force in 1985, and other losses included two destroyed by UNITA sabotage and a 'Flogger-C' shot down by UNITA on 28 October 1987. The Cuban crew was captured. Angolan MiG-23s are based at Menongue, but frequently operate from Langongo in the South.

Below: *This MiG-23BN (possibly a BM or BK) serves with Bulgaria's 25th Bomber Regiment at Sadovo. The yellow eye device on the nose is not a unit badge, but a bird-scaring measure! Bulgaria also operates small numbers of MiG-23MF and ML fighters.*

Bulgaria
Bulgarski Vozdushni Voiski

Bulgaria operates some 39-48 single-seat MiG-23s, comprising MiG-23MFs, MLs and reportedly MLDs, as well as MiG-23BNs. These are backed up by nine to 12 MiG-23UBs. The MiG-23BNs, delivered in 1977 to replace ageing MiG-17s, are based at Sadovo with the 25th Bomber Regiment. Two-digit tactical codes are applied in white.

A yellow eye carried on the forward fuselage is not a unit insignia, but a method of keeping birds away on the ground! A second batch of MiG-23BNs was delivered in 1980. The MiG-23BN unit has a full complement of pilots, unusual in the Bulgarian air force, where pilots have had to resign from membership of any political party or lose their jobs, and where lack of flying pay (due to fuel shortages) has sent wages plummeting to below the level of those of bus drivers.

A number of MiG-23MFs, and later a small batch of MLs, have also been delivered. These replaced MiG-21s with the fighter regiment at Dobroslavcy, tasked with the air defence of Sofia. The MiG-23MFs, delivered in 1978, were the first export 'Flogger-Bs'. Some MiG-23UBs used for advanced training operate from Dolna Metropolija, and others with the aviation academy at Pleven.

MiG-23MF: 647
MiG-23BN: 21, 50, 57, 60, 61, 66
MiG-23UB: 25, 040

China

People's Liberation Army Air Force

At least two, and perhaps as many as four, ex-Egyptian MiG-23s (sub-type unknown) were delivered to China after Egypt's break with Moscow. Details of their use and fate are unknown.

Cuba

Força Aérea Revolucionara

About 20 MiG-23MS 'Flogger-Es' delivered in 1977 operate from San Julian in the air-defence role, reportedly augmented by a handful of 'Flogger-Bs'. A similar number of MiG-23BNs equip two fighter-bomber squadrons at Guines and a third at Santa Clara. One of these aircraft defected to the US Navy Air Station at Key West in 1991, and was returned, without pilot, a few days later. Persistent rumours suggest that MiG-27s may also have been delivered.

Egypt

Al Quwwat al Jawwiya il Misriy

Egypt was an early export customer for the MiG-23, receiving some 16 MiG-23MS 'Flogger-Es' and MiG-23BNs in 1974. The MiG-23 was too advanced to be kept in service in such small numbers after the bre with the USSR in the mid-1970s; the aircra were placed in storage, and then later sold the USA and China. Other equipment of Soviet origin fared better, with China, Iraq a other friendly states providing support.

Ethiopia

Ethiopian air force

MiG-23BNs were first delivered in 1977, following the Somali invasion of the Ogade more were delivered in 1985. Until the fall c the Mengistu regime in early 1991 the survivors (around 36 aircraft) were based at Dire Dawa with the 3rd Air Regiment, and a Debre Zeit.

Above and below: This MiG-23BN hit the headlines on 20 March 1991, when it was flown by a defecting pilot, Major Orestes Lorenzo Perez, to the US Naval Air Station at Key West, Florida. The 38-year-old defector was a veteran MiG-21 pilot, but was making his first solo MiG-23 flight.

Below: Czechoslovakia's air arm undergoing a major organisation. change, adopting some wartime RAF (Free Czech) squadron identities and becoming widely known as the Czech and Slovak a force. The country's liberalisatior was also accompanied by the strengthening of links with other European air arms. Here Major Josef Milar brings his MiG-23ML t land at Fairford during a goodwill visit to Britain.

Czechoslovakia

Ceskoslovenske Letectvo

Czechoslovakia has received some 105 MiG-23MFs since 1978, paying a reported $6.6 million per aircraft (albeit not in hard currency). These serve with the 1st Fighter Regiment at Ceske Budejovice, home of the famous Budweiser brewery! Detached flights operate from Bechyne, Plzen and Zatec as part of the 3rd Air Defence Division. A top-up attrition purchase of about 45 MiG-23MLs was made in 1985.

The 140 MiG-23BNs were delivered from 1979 and serve with the 28th Fighter Bomber Regiment at Caslav, HQ unit of the 34th Fighter Bomber Division. This unit also

includes two Su-22 and one Su-25 regiments. The MiG-23BNs frequently operate with detached flights, at Bechyne, Hradec-Kralove, Pardubice and Namesti. They come under the control of the 10th Air Army, headquartered at Hradec-Kralove.

The MiG-23UBs serve with the front-line units, and with training units at Kosice and Prerov.

MiG-23ML: 2406, 4644 (*24644*)
MiG-23MF: 2409, 3924, 7182
MiG-23BN: 5741, 9142, 9549, 9550, 9829, 9831, 9849
MiG-23UB: 7721, 7907, 8109, 8325

Below: Czech MiG-23s, like this MiG-23ML, wear a four-digit tactical code based on the last four numerals of their construction number. About 45 MiG-23MLs were delivered to Czechoslovakia.

Above: The devil insignia of the Czech MiG-23 fighter regiment, normally worn as a flying suit patch, but also applied to a handf of the unit's aircraft.

Left: This MiG-23BN wears a triangular unit badge on the forward fuselage.

Germany

...ftstreitkräfte und ...ftverteidigung der National ...lksarmee and Federal German ...ftwaffe

...st Germany, for many years the USSR's ...st loyal WarPac ally, received a reported ...al of 45 MiG-23MFs, at a reported coat of ...6 million each. These served with ...gdfliegergeschwader 9 'Heinrich Rau' at ...enemünde from about 1978. An unknown ...antity of MiG-23ML 'Flogger-Gs' (probably ...) were delivered from 1985, augmenting ...t never completely replacing the older ...G-23MFs. Some of the MiG-23MFs were ...urned to the Soviet Union, others had ...en written off in service, and some may ...ve been relegated to ground instructional ...e. In the latter role, there is some ...dence that East Germany used at least ...e non-flyable MiG-23S, painted in East ...rman markings. By 1991 JFG 9 had two ...G-23ML Staffeln (with 28 surviving ...craft), and one Staffel equipped with the ...ler variants (nine MiG-23MFs and five ...s). The Federal Luftwaffe evaluated both ...pes.

...East Germany also took delivery of ...tween 20 and 24 'Flogger-Hs' from 1981, ...ich apparently bear the export ...signation MiG-24BN. These served with ...e two Staffeln of Jagdbombernflieger-...schwader 37 'Klement Gottwald' at ...ewitz. Grounded and placed in storage ...er re-unification, a handful of the 18 ...rvivors has been evaluated at Manching. ...e Federal Luftwaffe never had any plans ...integrate them and a foreign sale of these ...ertly offensive aircraft is unlikely. Their ...ost probable fate is scrapping or ...signment to museums. Between 10 and ...MiG-23UBs were shared by the fighter ...d fighter-bomber wings, and eight of ...ese remained in use by

re-unification, three with JBG 37.

German MiG-23s were all painted in a three- or four-tone brown and green camouflage, with duck-egg blue and grey (rear fuselage) undersides. Three-digit tactical codes were applied in red (fighters) or black (trainers). Codes were sometimes shortened or extended to confuse the West, especially for photographic sorties.

Squadron markings were eventually applied to some of JFG 9's aircraft, while some 'Floggers' gained the winged 'Q' insignia denoting excellence of maintenance. West German markings were applied in black and white. In the list below (which is incomplete), East German tactical codes are given first, followed by c/n in brackets, followed by the West German serial.

MiG-23MF: 395 *(13364)*, 564, 567, 568 *(13095)* 20+01, 577 *(13299)* 20+02, 584 *(13098)* 20+04, 585 *(13100)* 20+05, 586 *( )* 20+06, 591 *(13300)* 20+07, 592 *(13897)* 20+08, 593 *(13352)* 20+09

MiG-23ML: 329 *(24623)* 20+10, 330 *( )* 20+11, 331 *(24621)* 20+12, 332 *(24625) written off, 333 (24624)* 20+13, 336 *(24627)* 20+14, 337?, 338 *(24630)* 20+15, 339 *20+16, 340 (24636)* 20+17, 341 *(24637)* 20+18, 343 *(24617)* 20+19, 345 *(24618)* 20+20, 349 *( )* 20+21, 350 *(24639)* 20+22, 353 *( )* 20+23, 471 *(24250)* 20+24, 475 *(24254)* 20+25, 488 *(24255)* 20+26, 519?, 550 *(24018)* 20+27, 551 *( )* 20+28, 554 *(24027)* 20+29, 558 *( )* 20+30, 563 *(24031)* 20+31, 567 *( )* 20+32, 569 *(24038)* 20+33, 576 *( )* 20+34, 601 *(24050)* 20+35, 606 *(24051)* 20+36, 610 *(24249)* 20+37,

MiG-23BN/-24BN: 689 *(11085)* 20+38, 690 *(11087)* 20+39, 691 *(11088)* 20+40, 692 *(14101)* 20+41, 694 *(14210)* 20+42, 695 *(14211)* 20+43, 696 *(14212)* 20+44, 697 *(14213)* 20+45, 698 *( )* 20+46, 701 *(14217)* 20+47, 702 *(14218)* 20+48, 704, 705 *(22830)* 20+49, 707 *(14220)* 20+50, 710 *(14225)* 20+51, 712 *(15600)* 20+52, 715 *(15721)* 20+53, 718 *(15729)* 20+54, 720 *( )* 20+55

MiG-23UB: 100 *(A1038504)* 20+56, 101, 102 *( )* 20+61, 103 *(A1038506)* 20+57, 104 *( )* 20+62, 105 *( )* 20+63, 106 *(A1038034)* 20+58, 107 *(A1038221)* 20+59, 108, 109 *( )* 20+60

Above: Some German MiG-23MLs may be traded for Czechoslovakian MiG-29s, since Germany needs more of these aircraft, and Czechoslovakia is eager to reduce the number of types in service.

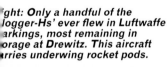

Left: The MiG-23ML 'Flogger-G' (seen here) never entirely replaced the older MiG-23MF 'Flogger-B' in German service.

...ght: Only a handful of the ...logger-Hs' ever flew in Luftwaffe ...arkings, most remaining in ...orage at Drewitz. This aircraft ...rries underwing rocket pods.

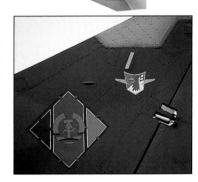

Above: The regimental badge of JFG 9 was briefly carried on the tailfins of some JFG 9 MiG-23MLs, alongside the German Democratic Republic insignia.

Left: An armed MiG-23ML of Peenemünde-based JFG 9. Live firing exercises were conducted against drones over the Baltic.

Above: The East German MiG-24BNs were operated by JBG 37 'Klement Gottwald' based at Drewitz in the south-east of the country, quite close to the Polish border. Most East German air force bases were located well to the east, far from the inner German border.

Below: This MiG-23ML was painted up in special wing colours, with the griffon badge on the nose, just before the LSK/LV disbanded. The aircraft later received a Luftwaffe serial and national markings, as seen here.

Above: One of the MiG-23UBs assigned to JBG 37, the attack 'Flogger' unit.

Left: The tail-down stance of a taxiing MiG-24BN is clearly evident in this view of a JBG 37 aircraft.

Below: One of the MiG-24BNs at Manching is seen prior to application of a 98+ series experimental serial number.

Hungary
Magyar Legiero

Twelve single-seat MiG-23MFs were delivered to Hungary, last WarPac recipient of the type. They made their public debut during the annual air day parade over Budapest on 4 April 1980. They are based at Papa with the Saman Squadron of the 'Stromfeld' Regiment. Four 'Flogger-Cs' were transferred directly from Frontal Aviation, and thus wore standard WarPac camouflage, whereas the MiG-23MFs initially wore an overall grey colour scheme. The aircraft have recently been repainted with Hungary's new 'arrowhead' national insignia replacing the Communist star. Hungary has lost three MiG-23MFs, one of them in a spectacular air show accident, and a single two-seater.

MiG-23MF: 01 (*12310*), 02 (*12401*), 03 (*12402*), 04 (   ) written off 1989, 05 (   ) written off 1988?, 06 (*12405*), 07 (*12406*), 08 (   ), 09 (   ) written off 1990, 10 (   ), 11 (   ), 12 (*12501*)

MiG-23UM: 14 (   ), 15 (*1250038*), 16 (   ) written off 1990, 20 (*19015091*)

Below: This MiG-23MF wears the old WarPac-style national markings. It survives to this day, but now wears the new air force chevron insignia.

Above: This smart-looking Hungarian MiG-23MF 'Flogger-B' was the aircraft lost in a spectacular crash at the first Papa airshow while being flown by the deputy squadron commander. Hungarian MiG-23s carry a two-digit sequential tactical code in red, outlined thinly in white.

bove: Hungary's MiG-23MFs were elivered in an overall grey colour cheme, and this sand and drab amouflage was applied locally. It as proved extremely successful in ervice. For many years, the Soviet r force in Hungary also operated vo MiG-23 regiments, but these ere eventually replaced by iG-29s.

ight: The 12th and final MiG-23MF elivered to the Hungarian air rce. This particular aircraft is one f nine surviving single-seaters still perating from Papa air base with e Saman squadron of the tromfeld regiment.

Above: The end of the Warsaw Pact led to the abandonment of the old Communist-style red star and its replacement by a new national marking. The arrowhead design seen here was one of three designs considered, the others being based on a green roundel or disc with a red and white chevron superimposed.

Below: This MiG-27L 'Bahadur' wears the characteristic badge of No. 9 'Wolfpack' Squadron. Indian MiG-27s wear a highly effective disruptive camouflage scheme and a three digit RAF-style serial number. Most units wear badges.

ndia

dian Air Force

dia is one of the most important export stomers for the 'Flogger', representing as it es a genuinely non-aligned power with no s to force it to 'buy Soviet'. A long and ppy experience with the MiG-21, together th a desire to keep procuring aircraft from th East and West, made it inevitable that e Indian Air Force would consider the iG-23 for service. Having fulfilled its deep netration strike aircraft requirement with e SEPECAT Jaguar, India chose the iG-23BN 'Flogger-H' to meet its TASA actical Air Strike Aircraft) requirement for a AL Marut/Ajeet and Su-7 replacement. elivery of 95 MiG-23BNs and 15 MiG-23UB ainers began in December 1980. These craft re-equipped Nos 10, 31, 220 and 221 quadrons, allowing the final retirement of the arut in 1985. Today the MiG-23BNs serve ith No. 10 'Winged Dagger' Squadron and . 221 'Valiants' Squadron at Jodhpur, and ith No. 31 'Ocelot' Squadron and No. 220 esert Tigers' Squadron at Halwara.

Above: No. 9 Squadron's badge is seen in close-up. It consists of three wolves' heads in a stylised roundel, with the squadron number and nickname superimposed in black.

Left: These rocket-armed MiG-23BNs serve with No. 10 'Winged Dagger' Squadron, which is normally based at Jodhpur. The second aircraft is unusual in that it wears a European-style camouflage scheme. The nearest aircraft has a yellow disc on the nose, on which the squadron insignia is usually painted. The finished badge can be seen on the intake of the aircraft pictured above. No. 10 Squadron was the Indian Air Force's first MiG-23 unit, and was followed by three more MiG-23BN units before the adoption of the MiG-27L.

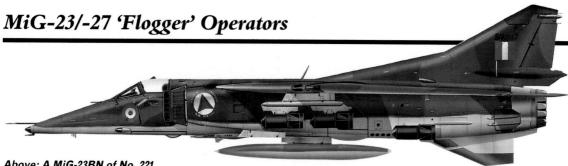

Above: A MiG-23BN of No. 221 Squadron, the 'Valiants', which is based alongside No. 10 at Jodhpur.

As early as 1982, India confirmed its requirement for more 'Floggers', to equip an eventual six further squadrons. It was decided to licence-build 165 examples of the MiG-27M variant at the Nasik plant of Hindustan Aeronautics. Phase 1 of this ambitious programme involved merely the assembly of Soviet-built components, and this commenced in 1984, with the first aircraft being rolled out in October of that year. Phase 2 used major sub-assemblies built by HAL, and Phase 3 brought in smaller HAL-built components. The final phase introduced local airframe manufacture, with some indigenous systems, including licence-built engines. The MiG-27 was initially given the local name Bahadur ('Valiant'). MiG-27Ms serve with No. 2 'Winged Arrow' Squadron at Kailakunda, Nos 9 ('Wolf Pack') and 18 ('Flying Bullets') Squadrons at Hindan, and with Nos 22 and 222 ('Tigersharks') Squadrons at Hashimara. The last MiG-27 unit will be No. 20 Squadron, currently the last Hawker Hunter squadron.

In the air defence role, India procured 40 MiG-23MFs (known locally as the Rakshak, or 'Guardian') as an interim air defence fighter to counter Pakistan's acquisition of the F-16. They equipped Nos 223 and 224 Squadrons from 1982, No. 223 converting to the MiG-29 in 1989. The survivors still serve with No. 224 Squadron at Adampur.

Above and left: No. 18 Squadron, Indian Air Force, operates the MiG-27M and is based alongside No. 9 (the 'Wolfpack') at Hindan. Its aircraft carry a pale blue badge on the engine intake, and some carry names or slogans in small white letters on the forward fuselage.

Right: A MiG-23BN armed with four rocket pods peels away from the camera ship. The tiger's head badge on the air intake identifies the aircraft as belonging to No. 220 Squadron, which is nicknamed the 'Desert Tigers'.

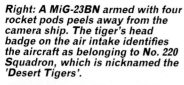

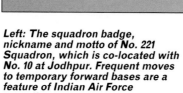

Left: The squadron badge, nickname and motto of No. 221 Squadron, which is co-located with No. 10 at Jodhpur. Frequent moves to temporary forward bases are a feature of Indian Air Force operations.

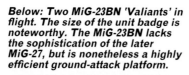

Below: Two MiG-23BN 'Valiants' in flight. The size of the unit badge is noteworthy. The MiG-23BN lacks the sophistication of the later MiG-27, but is nonetheless a highly efficient ground-attack platform.

Above: Four MiG-23MFs of the Adampur-based No. 224 Squadron. When No. 223 converted to the MiG-29, No. 224 received most of i aircraft, growing in size.

Left: India procured the 'Flogger-L purely as a stopgap, pending the delivery of the Mirage 2000 and th MiG-29.

Iraq
Al Quwwat al Jawwiya al Iraqiya

Iraq received its first MiG-23s, actually 'Flogger-Es', in 1976, replacing a regiment of MiG-19s. About 70 MiG-23BNs were delivered for ground-attack duties from the late 1980s. Iraqi MiG-23BNs have been equipped with Mirage F1-style inflight-refuelling probes, possibly as part of the same programme under which Libyan MiG-23s were similarly equipped. MiG-23 strength was seriously depleted by the Gulf War. An unknown number were destroyed on the ground, eight more were shot down, and nine fled to Iran. (The latter consisted of one MiG-23UB, four MiG-23MLs and four MiG-23BNs.)

Libya
Libyan Arab Jamahiriya Air Force/Al Quwwat al Jawwiya al Jamahiriya al Arabiya al Libyya

The MiG-23MS was first seen in Libya during 1974, perhaps indicating that Libya was the first export customer for this variant. Some reports, however, suggest that the initial batch of eight (with five trainers) was delivered in May 1975. Some 30 were delivered, with 35 MiG-23BN fighter-bombers. The Libyan 'Floggers' have been active service in Chad and in clashes with Egypt. Two were shot down by US Navy Tomcats on 4 January 1989, and others were destroyed on the ground during the earlier Operation El Dorado Canyon. At least two Libyan 'Floggers' have been used in defection attempts, one crashing in Italy and the other on Crete. Four more landed in

Left: A mixed formation of Iraqi 'Floggers' is seen during a pre-Gulf war military parade. Most of Iraq's MiG-23MS and MiG-23BN aircraft were destroyed in air combat or allied bombing.

Below: The fate of this Iraqi MiG-23BN is unknown. Iraq probably lost at least half of its MiG-23 force, most of them to allied air attacks which destroyed the aircraft in their shelters.

Egypt on 1 March 1988, due to a 'fuel shortage', and returned to Libya the next morning. The original Libyan air force roundel insignia was replaced by a plain Islamic green disc on the orders of Colonel Khadaffi. Some Libyan MiG-23s are said to have been fitted with Mirage F1-style inflight-refuelling probes by a German company, Intec Technical Trade and Logistik, who have also helped modify C-130

(and perhaps Il-76) transports for inflight-refuelling duties. MiG-23BNs are based at Gamal Abdel Nasser (formerly El Adem), with 'Flogger-Es' at al Bumbah (Okba bin Nafa), and Benghazi-Benina.

MiG-23MS: 4714, 6916, 9082
MiG-23UB: 23022

Right: Libyan MiG-23MS 'Flogger-Es' were delivered wearing red, white and black UAR-style roundels, but Colonel Khadaffi replaced these with plain green discs and fin flashes.

Left: Snapped by a US Navy jet, this MiG-23MS is a Libyan 'Flogger-E'. These aircraft are frequently encountered by Sixth Fleet aircraft operating in the southern Mediterranean.

Below: Most Polish air force 'Floggers', like this two-seat MiG-23UB, now wear camouflage. The '1000' on the nose indicates 1,000 hours, and was applied to celebrate a pilot achieving that total on the MiG-23.

Nigeria
Federal Nigerian air force

Nigeria has reportedly received about 40 MiG-23BNs and some 10 MiG-23UBs.

North Korea
Korean People's army air force

North Korea received a first batch of eight MiG-23MLs (the first of this variant to be exported) in September 1984, reportedly as payment for overflight rights by Soviet maritime reconnaissance aircraft. Two of this initial batch were lost in a collision on 8 May 1985. The number of aircraft on charge is thought to have risen to about 46, plus an unknown number of trainers.

Poland
Polskie Lotnictwo Wojskowe

Forty-five MiG-23MFs have been delivered to Poland since 1981 and these serve with No. 28 PLM at Slupsk. The aircraft wear a squadron badge, and the coat of arms of the city of Slupsk.

MiG-23MF: 001 *(0390221001)*, 007, 010 *(0390221010)*, 021 *(0390224121)*, 050, 062 *(0390224062)*, 065 *(0390224065)*, 101 *(0390224101)*, 110, 115 *(0390224115)*, 117(*) *(0390224117)*, 120, 139, 147 *(03902217147)*, 148* *(0390217148)*, 149 *(0390217149)*, 152(*) *(0390224152)*, 153 *(0390224153)*, 455*, 456* *(0390220456)*, 458* *(0390220459)*, 460, 461 *(0390224461)*

MiG-23UM: 831,
842*, 844, 845, 846 (*A1037846*), 950
*grey colour scheme

Right: A handful of Polish MiG-23s, like this two-seater, still wear an overall air defence grey colour scheme.

Above: A small American Indian's head badge can just be discerned on this Polish MiG-23MF 'Flogger-B'.

Right: This 'Flogger-B' carries the griffon badge of the city of Slupsk, and a bumblebee and Indian's head as flight and squadron badges.

Romania

Aviatiei Militare Romane

One regiment, with between 12 and 16 MiG-23MFs and a pair of UBs, is based at Giarmata. Another two regiments, Nos 1 and 3 (perhaps with as many as 32 aircraft), are based at Mihail Kogalniceanu.

MiG-23MF: 174 (*17174*), 192, 193, 194, 195 (*17195*), 222, 243, 259, 261, 274, 406
MiG-23UB: 111, 135, 137 (*B1038437*)

Right: Romanian MiG-23s wear a huge variety of colour schemes. This one wears a green/brown disruptive camouflage similar to that applied to current Soviet 'Floggers', with its three-digit code applied in red.

Above: This Romanian 'Flogger-B' has an over-painted radome and white code letters. The camouflage pattern is random.

Below: Another Romanian 'Flogger-B', this one in the original air-defence grey and still with traces of the old-style star marking on the tail.

Above: Ceasescu ordered the replacement of the old-style Communist star by a roundel in the national colours long before the break-up of the Warsaw Pact.

Below: One of the MiG-23UBs delivered to Romania. These aircraft display as many different schemes as the single-seaters.

Left: This Romanian MiG-23MF 'Flogger-B' wears an unusual 'tiger-stripe' camouflage pattern. Romanian MiG-23s have recently been augmented by MiG-29s, but further deliveries of the more advanced fighter seem unlikely.

Sudan

Silakh al Jawwiya as Sudaniya/ Sudanese air force

Some sources suggest that Sudan has taken delivery of the MiG-23BN. The aircraft came from Libya in several small batches, beginning in 1987, and around a dozen are thought to be in service. At least seven have been lost, three of them shot down by SPLA guerrillas.

Syria

Syrian air force and air defence command

Many of the initial batch of MiG-23MSs were destroyed by the Israeli air force in the frantic air battles over the Bekaa in 1982. Attrition was made up by initial deliveries from Arab allies, notably Libya, and the 'Flogger' fleet has since been further strengthened by deliveries of newer aircraft, including MiG-23MLs and MiG-23MFs. Two more MiG-23s were shot down by Israel in 1985, and another aircraft defected. About 80 MiG-23s remain in service.

Above: This Syrian 'Flogger-G' was extensively evaluated by Israel after its pilot defected. It is seen here in joint Israeli and Syrian markings.

USA

US Air Force

The USAF received a number of MiG-23MS and MiG-23BN airframes and engines from Egypt in the late 1970s. These were refurbished and restored to flying condition, and were operated under a veil of secrecy. One of these crashed, killing USAF General Robert S. Bond on his last flight before retirement. No photos of US MiG-23s have emerged, and their current status is uncertain, although some at least are understood to have been grounded. Top-ups were received in the form of ex-German MiG-23MLs 20+15, 20+32 and 20+36, which flew into Ramstein on 26 March 1991 (along with two Su-22s) for onward shipment to the USA.

Vietnam

Vietnamese People's Army Air Force

The number of MiG-23s delivered to Vietnam is unknown, reports varying from 30 to 100 aircraft. Local pilots underwent training in 1985, and deliveries followed soon after. Serials include 5209, 5277 and 5280, which may be the 'last four' of their construction numbers. One known MiG–23 base is Hanoi.

Yemen

Yemen air force

The amalgamation of the two Yemens has produced a single air force. This has 25 MiG-23MLs on charge, inherited from the South Yemen (People's Democratic Republic of Yemen) air force.

Right: The MiG-23 looks set to enjoy several more years of productive service, under a number of different flags.

Above: The Greek air force obtained its C-47s from various sources, and more than a dozen still serve with 355 'Ifestos' Mira (squadron) at Elefsina. This Dakota betrays its ancestry (and its age!) by carrying its former RAF serial.

Left: After dealing with cast-off equipment for too long, a handful of current air force pilots get to fly more modern types, such as this Mirage 2000.

Aeroporia

Main picture: McDonnell Douglas F-4E Phantoms have carried the blue and white Greek roundel for many years and are only now starting to be replaced as front-line combat aircraft. Despite this, the three remaining squadrons will be active for several years yet.

Greek warplanes

photographed by
Hans Nijhuis and Peter Steinemann

Left: Twenty-nine of the 40 Dassault Mirage F1CGs delivered survive to fulfil an air-defence role with 342 'Sparta' Mira at Larissa and 334 'Thalos' Mira based at Iraklion, Crete. The F1s are unique in Elliniki Aeroporia service in carrying the name of a Greek island in Hellenic script under the cockpits.

Above: When deciding on which aircraft should defend its skies into the next century, the Elliniki Aeroporia was constrained by financial considerations. This resulted in a 'second-choice' combined buy of 40 Mirage 2000s and a further 40 F-16s. Mirage deliveries began in 1988, these multi-role aircraft being designated Mirage 2000EG. A number of two-seat Mirage 2000BGs are also allotted to each squadron.

Left: The all-weather air defence wing at Nea Ankhialos, 111 Pterix, is now operational with two squadrons of General Electric-powered F-16CG Fighting Falcons. These aircraft are operated by 330 'Keraunos' Mira and 346 'Jason' Mira. The latter unit also includes the type's conversion unit, with five F-16DGs. A follow-on order for a further 20 aircraft may go to form an anti-shipping squadron.

Left: This Mirage 2000EG was serving as one of the alert aircraft of the 114 Pterix (wing) at Tanagra. Standing with canopy open and live MATRA 550 Magic AAMs on its missile rails, it can be airborne in minutes. Tanagra is close to Athens but central enough to enable aircraft to meet intruders approaching Greek territory from any direction.

Right: Two of the three F-4E squadrons are tasked with ground attack. This aircraft, while nominally based with 337 'Fantasma' Mira in an air-defence role, is seen here carrying an SUU-20 practice bomb dispenser. The first Phantoms to be delivered were from USAF stocks and arrived in 1974, while further batches were delivered in 1991.

Left: This proud young Mirage 2000 pilot is wearing a blue and white Dassault users' badge akin to the more familiar Fighting Falcon emblem worn by F-16 pilots. All the Mirage 2000 pilots already had extensive fast-jet experience before undergoing their type conversion course, many transitioning from the immortal Starfighter.

Left: A pair of 330 'Keraunos' Mira F-16CGs hold at the end of the runway at Nea Ankhialos, their home base. This was the first of the Elliniki Aeroporia's Fighting Falcon squadrons, which began the displacement of the F-5A Freedom Fighters on which the air force had previously relied for air defence. The Fighting Falcons are armed with the AIM-9L version of the Sidewinder AAM. Each unit also operates a number of two-seat F-16DGs for training.

Above: Three squadrons of F-5s still serve, including one of RF-5As. More NF-5As may still be delivered. Their origins are varied, as evidenced by this pair; the F-5A in air superiority grey came from the Imperial Iranian Air Force, while the camouflage on the aircraft in the foreground betrays its Royal Jordanian Air Force origins.

Right: Nearly 100 F-5s carry Greek markings, but many of these are held in storage at any one time. This Sidewinder-equipped Freedom Fighter continues to provide air-defence capability with 341 'Assos' Mira.

Below: Training for the F-5s was initially provided by 10 new-build F-5Bs received from the USA. However, this was one of six delivered from Jordan.

Right: Excessive weathering on this F-5B trainer reveals it to be one of the Jordanian aircraft delivered in two batches in 1983 and 1989.

Left: The 337 'Fantasma' Mira Dioxeos Vomvardismou (fighter-bomber squadron) operates air-defence Phantoms from Larissa air force base. The large base at Larissa is home to four squadrons and is also the headquarters of NATOs 28th Tactical Air Force, which controls seven combat wings. Instead of its normal complement of AIM-9P Sidewinders on its inboard pylon, the F-4E carries an A/A37U towed target. The brightly painted drogue will serve as a gunnery target for the remainder of the M61 Vulcan cannon-armed Phantoms of the squadron.

Right: The Phantom has had a long life with the Elliniki Aeroporia, with no prospect of it leaving Greek skies. Throughout their service careers the F-4Es have been modernised and re-equipped, as evidenced by the ALR-45 radar warning receivers that have been retro-fitted on the intakes.

Below: All Hellenic air force aircraft carry the Greek characters 'Pi Alpha', the initials for Polemiki Aeroporia – literally 'War Aviation'. For this Sidewinder-armed Phantom, it is an apt title.

Above: At one time 36 Republic RF-84F Thunderflashes graced Greek skies, and even when the type was extinct elsewhere a handful lived on, performing vital 'Tac R' missions, pleasing intrepid aircraft photographers and irritating the populace with the thunder of their Wright J65 engines as they screeched through the mountains.

Right: The very last Thunderflashes of Larissa-based 348 'Eyes' Mira were due to have been grounded in March 1991, but this was not the first time such a move had been announced. The aircraft, all of early 1950s vintage, came from the Dutch, West German and United States air forces. Six remained to carry out daylight photo missions until 1991. As a reconnaissance aircraft the type was always range-limited, hence the pair of extra fuel tanks. When the RF-84s were actually serviceable and flying, they made a strange and evocative sight.

Left: One might think that the single squadron of Northrop RF-5s, operated by 349 'Kronos' Mira, provides a more modern reconnaissance asset. They are capable of carrying four KS-92 cameras in the nose to provide full panoramic photographic coverage around the aircraft. However, all the Greek air force's F-5s have been allotted a combat role, and this includes the RF-5s. None of the aircraft actually have any of their camera equipment fitted, and all are cannon-armed. With the arrival of the RF-4E Phantoms in the late 1970s, some of the initial RF-5s were converted to straight F-5A standard. Those remaining, and others received later from Jordan, fly with the 349 Mira, as part of the 110 Pterix, from Thessaloniki.

Right: The Phantom needs a lot of room to slow down and a drag chute is an absolute necessity. This RF-4E has just returned to its home base at Larissa. The 348 'Matia' Mira Tatikis Anagnoriseos (tactical reconnaissance squadron) shares Larissa with two fighter-interceptor squadrons. Six RF-4s survive from the eight delivered. The photo-Phantoms are equipped to the same standard as the F-4Es, being Sidewinder-compatible and fitted with RWRs.

Left: Greece has become a major owner of second-hand Starfighters. Having operated F-104s in its own right for years, its force of Starfighters grew rapidly during the 1980s, as the F-16 spread through the other air forces of Western Europe. Many of these aircraft are currently held as attrition reserves. Included in the total of ex-German and Dutch air force machines obtained was this F-104G, which had spent much of its former life with Germany's Marineflieger.

Tucking up its wheels as it takes off from Souda is one of 45 A-7H Corsair IIs which make up a pair of attack squadrons, the 340 'Alepou' and 345 'Lailaps' Mira. Though charged with an attack role, these aircraft have a secondary air-defence task, with Sidewinder launch rails on the fuselage sides.

Above: The main training unit of the Elliniki Aeroporia is the 120 Pterix, which incorporates three squadrons, two of which operate the Rockwell T-2 Buckeye, more normally associated with the US Navy. The 37 surviving T-2Es provide advanced flying training for the air force's pilots with 362 'Nestor' Mira, and weapons training with 363 'Danaos' Mira. Both squadrons are based at Kalamata, which they share with the T-37s of 361 Mira.

Above: Greece's single Cessna T-37 squadron is the 361 'Mystras' Mira, part of 120 Pterix, the training wing. The aircraft that it operates, both T-37Bs and T-37Cs, have origins nearly as diverse as the colour schemes they wear. This silver and faded-Dayglo T-37C retains its former USAF serial.

Below: Very obviously a former Royal Jordanian Air Force aircraft, this world-weary T-37B entered Elliniki Aeroporia service as recently as 1988, when it arrived with seven others to supplement the 361 Mira's fleet. Students come from the Cessna T-41 primary trainer to undergo a further 80 hours on the T-37s.

Above: Looking surprisingly smart by Greek standards, in shiny silver and with freshly painted Dayglo trim, it's easy to forget that this T-37B spent much of its working life over the Jordanian desert. Throughout it all it has retained a USAF serial. The T-37s are the first jet aircraft air force cadets experience.

Below: The Buckeye was designed to teach budding naval aviators the skills of carrier landings, and as such Rockwell built it tough enough to withstand even the treatment meted out by the worst aviators! No replacement is imminent. Students fly 130 hours on the type before moving to front-line units.

Below: In their day, vast numbers of Lockheed T-33 and RT-33s served with the Greek air force, and the type is still a common sight today. About 60 aircraft are still active. The faithful 'T-Bird' still serves as an IFR trainer, target tug and communications aircraft at several bases. This T-33A, with a USAF-style 'buzz-number' written large on its nose, belongs to the 366 Sminos (flight). Three other such flights operate up to 15 T-33s each. This aircraft is seen taxiing in at Tanagra.

Above: Smoke vents from the Pratt & Whitney R-2800 radial piston engine as one of the 355 'Ifaistos' Mira's glorious yellow Canadair CL-215s fires up for another water-bombing mission.

Left: Now reaching the end of their long life with the Elliniki Aeroporia, a total of 10 aged Grumman HU-16B Albatross still provide a sea surveillance service and search-and-rescue cover with the 353 'Albatros' Mira at Elefsina.

Left: The bright yellow band around the rear fuselage of this Agusta-Bell AB 205 marks it as one of the search and rescue helicopters which are attached to several bases. Fourteen of the type are operated by the 358 Mira, and these aircraft also have a secondary VIP role.

Above: The Hellenic air force operates a variety of transport types, among which are the 12 Lockheed C-130H Hercules allocated to 356 Mira at Elefsina. Five of these aircraft come under army control for airborne and support missions.

Left: The Japanese-built **NAMC YS**-11 is a rare and unusual sight wherever it is found, and few are more striking than this brightly painted example operated by the 356 Mira at Elefsina. A total of six aircraft, which had previously flown for the national airline Olympic, were delivered in 1980. All the YS-11As have a **VIP** transport role. This aircraft, however, has a primary task of calibrating the instrument landing systems installed at Greek air force bases, and of checking **VOR** navigation beacons and **DME** installations. With so much overwater flying involved in Greek air force operations, precise and accurate navigation is essential.

Above: Wearing a more military colour scheme, the standard for the type, this **NAMC YS-11-200** is one of the five surviving in service with 356 'Iraklis' Mira at Elefsina. While not a common type, the aircraft is built sturdily and is powered by a pair of super-reliable Rolls-Royce Dart turboprops. This will ensure its longevity in Greek service.

Above: Always a respected executive transport, the Gulfstream 1, known universally as the G1, has found a place with the Elliniki Aeroporia. A single example carries **VIP** passengers in some style for 356 'Iraklis' Mira.

Below: Also serving in the **VIP** transport role is this Dornier Do 28 Skyservant. Attached to 112 Pterix, the Do 28D-2s are more commonly found at individual air bases as liaison aircraft.

Above: The Greek Dornier Do 28s are all ex-Luftwaffe aircraft and were delivered in 1984 as a replacement for obsolete Noratlas transports, which were also ex-Luftwaffe. Their operating unit is 355 'Ifaistos' Mira, part of the 112 Wing of Air Material Command.

LOCKHEED HERCULES Variants

Part 3: HC-130P – HTTB

The final part of our Hercules Variants feature covers the most recent versions of this versatile machine, and also includes the significant numbers of English-built and civilian C-130s. Several of the versions covered have yet to enter service, and two of these had not even flown by the late summer of 1991. On the other side of the coin, two variants (the EC-130Q and the RC-130S) have been withdrawn from service, demonstrating the slowed-down pace of Hercules development. Lockheed's one-off High Technology Test Bed is also included; in many ways, this aircraft demonstrates the future of the type.

HC-130P

Twenty HC-130Ps (65-0988, 65-0991/65-0994 and 66-0211/66-0225) combined features of the Air Force HC-130Hs, including enlarged radome and ARD-17 tracker, with the refuelling capability of the HC-130Ns. Two were destroyed on the ground in Vietnam, one was lost in a training accident, and 12 remain in service with AFSOC, MAC and ANG squadrons.

Below: HC-130Ps have served in varying colour schemes, including overall gloss grey and three-tone 'European One' camouflage. They have a Fulton-type nose, Cook tracker, T56-A-15 engines and permanent underwing fuel tanks.

HC-130P

Observation window (both sides)

T56-A-15 engines

Fulton STAR recovery system

AN/ARD-17 Cook aerial tracker antenna

Reshaped Fulton nose radome

Inflight refuelling pods underwing

Above: Intended specifically to refuel helicopters, the HC-130P distinguished itself in Vietnam, supporting rescue missions.

EC-130Q

In service with VQ-3 at NAS Agana, Guam, and VQ-4 at NAS Patuxent River, the EC-130Gs were supplemented and eventually replaced with 18 EC-130Qs (BuNos 156170/156177, 159348, 159469, 160608, 161223, 161494/161496, 161431 and 162312/162313) which had C-130H

Right: The EC-130Q has been largely replaced by the Boeing E-6 in its task of communicating with US Navy ballistic missile submarines in time of war.

frames and were powered by 4,910-
hp T56-A-16s. They were fitted with
ngtip pods housing additional
ectronic equipment and with dual
iling antennas. Extended from the tail
ne and through the aft ramp, the
tennas were fitted with stabilising
nes and were respectively 26,000 ft
.9 km) long and 5,000 ft (1.5 km) long.
rmally, the long antenna was streamed
,000 to 20,000 ft (4.9 to 6.1 km) with
e aircraft flying in tight orbits to keep
th antennas nearly vertical. In the late
80s, their TACAMO equipment, which
d been improved several times for
ore effective EMP (Electro Magnetic
ulse) hardening, was removed and was
stalled in the Boeing E-6As which
placed them, first with VQ-3 from
ugust 1989 after that squadron was
located to NAS Barbers Point.
llowing removal of TACAMO
quipment, the aircraft are being
perated as TC-130Q trainers and utility
ansports.

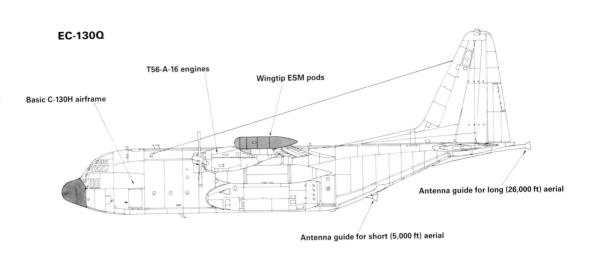

EC-130Q

Basic C-130H airframe · T56-A-16 engines · Wingtip ESM pods · Antenna guide for long (26,000 ft) aerial · Antenna guide for short (5,000 ft) aerial

KC-130R

he 14 KC-130Rs (BuNos 160013/160021,
60240 and 160625/160628) have C-130H
irframes and 4,910-eshp T56-A-16
ngines. Total fuel capacity, including two
uselage tanks, has been increased from
0,560 US gal (39973 litres) for the
KC-130Fs to 13,280 US gal (50269 litres).

*Right: A Marine KC-130R refuels a
YAV-8B development aircraft. The
US Marine Corps first evaluated
the Hercules in the inflight-
refuelling role during 1957. Unlike
earlier tanker versions like the
KC-130F however, the Corps' 14
KC-130Rs are not readily
convertible to transport
configuration. These aircraft, which
permanently retain their underwing
refuelling pods, serve with two of
the Marines tanking squadrons.*

LC-130R

Six ski-equipped aircraft with C-130H
airframes and 4,910-eshp T56-A-16
engines were delivered to the US Navy
(BuNos 155917, 159129/159131 and
160740/160741) to supplement the
LC-130Fs of VX-6 and support National
Science Foundation operations in the
Antarctic.

*Right: The small number of
LC-130R Hercules procured by the
Navy spend their lives flying
between their home base at Point
Mugu and American scientific
bases at the South Pole and in
Antarctica. They can be fitted with
special equipment for measuring
temperatures, and more recently,
pollution.*

Lockheed Hercules variants

RC-130S

One of the recommendations made in March 1966 as part of Operation Shed Light, a high-priority research and development programme initiated by the Air Force to attain a night-strike capability, called for the development of a Battlefield Illumination Airborne System (BIAS) to perform real-time reconnaissance for Army field units and to serve as hunter-illuminator for strike aircraft flying close air support sorties at night. To that end, two JC-130As (56-0493 and 56-0497) were fitted in late 1967 with a large fairing mounted on each side of the forward fuselage, each housing 56 searchlights with a combined illumination of 6.14 million candles. The two 'Bias Hunter' RC-130Ss were also fitted with various sensors, including infra-red devices, to locate the enemy.

Tests proved the 'Bias Hunter' concept technically sound but operationally unrealistic as, having to fly in tight orbits and at low altitude to illuminate their targets, brightly lit RC-130Ss would themselves have become easy targets for enemy gunners. Accordingly, the programme was quickly terminated and searchlights and other specialised equipment were removed from the two test aircraft. Redesignated C-130As, they were flown by AFRES and ANG units until 1988, when 56-0497 was placed in storage at AMARC while 56-0493 ended its career as a logistic support aircraft with the 162nd TFG, Arizona ANG, at the Tucson IAP.

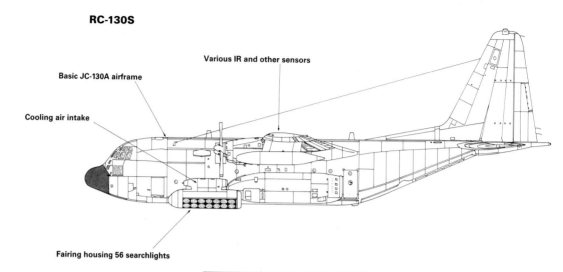

RC-130S

Various IR and other sensors

Basic JC-130A airframe

Cooling air intake

Fairing housing 56 searchlights

Right: A pair of C-130As was radically modified to serve briefly as RC-130S 'Bias Hunter' testbeds. The basic concept was flawed, since it required the aircraft to fly low and slowly while illuminating itself, as well as its target, with an enormous battery of searchlights.

KC-130T

Like the KC-130Rs that preceded them into service with the Marine Corps, the 20 KC-130Ts (BuNos 162308/162311, 162785/162786, 163022/163023, 163310/163311, 163591/163592, 164105/164106, 164180/164181, 164194/164195 and 164441/164442) are tanker/transports with C-130H airframes but are powered by 4,910-eshp T56-A-423 engines. They differ from the earlier Marine Corps tankers primarily in being fitted with modernised avionics including a new autopilot, an AN/APS-133 solid-state search radar, INS, Omega and TACAN.

Above: A KC-130T of VMGR-234, stationed at Glenview Naval Air Station. A sizeable fleet of Hercules tankers is operated by six USMC squadrons.

Above: The tanker Hercules has not escaped the adoption of low-visibility grey colour schemes throughout the US Navy.

KC-130T-30H

Due for delivery to the US Marines' 48th Reserve Group at NAS Glenview near Chicago in October and November 1991 were two examples of a brand new C-130 tanker variant. This is a stretched derivative of the KC-130T, using the 15-ft fuselage stretch of the C-130H-30 and L-100-30. The stretched tankers will be able to accommodate larger internal fuel tanks, taking advantage of the Hercules' increased maximum take-off weight capability.

AC-130U

A $155-million contract for the development of a new C-130 gunship was placed with the North American Aircraft Operations division of the Rockwell International Corporation in 1987. The choice of Rockwell was a natural one, in view of the company's unrivalled experience of sophisticated avionics applied to large military aircraft gained during the B-1B Lancer programme, and during the 'Pacer Strike' upgrade of F-111Ds and F-111Fs. The prototype AC-130U (87-0128) was funded in the FY 1986 budget, and was completed (virtually as an unarmed C-130H) at Lockheed's Marietta plant in 1988. It was flown to Rockwell's

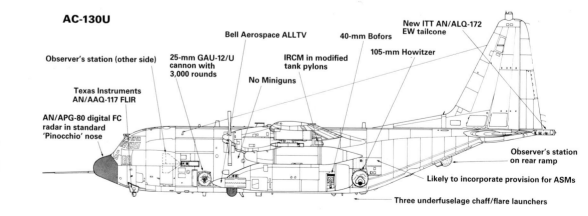

AC-130U

New ITT AN/ALQ-172 EW tailcone

Bell Aerospace ALLTV

40-mm Bofors

105-mm Howitzer

Observer's station (other side)

25-mm GAU-12/U cannon with 3,000 rounds

IRCM in modified tank pylons

No Miniguns

Texas Instruments AN/AAQ-117 FLIR

AN/APG-80 digital FC radar in standard 'Pinocchio' nose

Observer's station on rear ramp

Likely to incorporate provision for ASMs

Three underfuselage chaff/flare launchers

Right: Latest Hercules gunship is the AC-130U. Carrying only three guns, including the usual 40-mm Bofors and 105-mm howitzer, it also features a modern fire-control system and state-of-the-art detection and self-defence systems.

Palmdale facility for fitting out on 28 July 1988 and was rolled out as an AC-130U on 20 December 1990. It made its first flight in the new configuration on 20 December 1990 and will conduct trials at neighbouring Edwards AFB until 1992-93. The prototype is being followed by five aircraft funded in FY 1989 and six in FY 1990.

The 12 aircraft are to be delivered to the 16th SOS at Hurlburt Field, where they will replace the AC-130H. These will then be passed on to the AFRes, allowing the retirement of the ageing AC-130As. The new gunship has dramatically improved survivability, with improved Spectra ceramic armour, explosion-suppressing fuel tanks, state-of-the-art avionics and countermeasures equipment and with automatic gun training allowing the aircraft to fly a less predictable flight path, making significant deviations during the normal banked turn. Armament is reduced to three cannon, with a 25-mm General Electric GAU-12/U forward (with 3,000 rounds) and with a 40-mm Bofors and a 105-mm howitzer aft. The crew of 13 consists of pilot, co-pilot, flight engineer and navigator on the flight deck, with up to seven seated in the Battle Management Centre at monitoring consoles and four IBM IP-102 computers, and observers on the rear ramp (prone) and behind the cockpit on the starboard side.

The weapons can all be slaved to the fire control radar, a digital Hughes AN/APG-80 derived from the AN/APG-70

fitted to the F-15E. This is backed up by a Texas Instruments AN/AAQ-117 FLIR (mounted under the port side of the nose) and a Bell Aerospace ALLTV (All Active Low Light Level TV) set, turret-mounted in the port main undercarriage sponson. The cockpit is fitted with a new HUD, and the aircraft has combined INS and GPS/Navstar for navigation. Three under-fuselage chaff/flare launchers can dispense 300 chaff bundles and either 90 MJU7 or 180 M206 IR decoy flares. An ITT Avionics AN/ALQ-172 jammer is installed in the tailcone. Other avionics systems and defensive aids are similar to those fitted to the MC-130H. Externally, the AC-130U can be distinguished by the lack of the distinctive 'Black Crow' truck ignition sensor radome and associated blast compensator, and by the recontoured forward part of the undercarriage fairing. The aircraft also has no separate beacon tracking radar, leaving a space between the 40-mm and 105-mm guns.

Above: The AC-130U has an observation bubble on the rear ramp and an extended tailcone housing AN/ALQ-142 ECM equipment.

Forestry air tankers

Developed by FMC Corporation of San Jose, California, the Modular Airborne Fire Fighting System (MAFFS) was first tested at Edwards AFB in July 1971, the test aircraft being a C-130A (56-0498) of the California ANG. MAFFS was adopted by the Air Force in 1973 – when eight systems were purchased for initial installation in the cargo compartment of Hercules of the 1550th CCTW at Kirtland AFB, New Mexico, and later installation in C-130Bs of the North Carolina and Wyoming ANGs and C-130Es of the California ANG – and has also been fitted to Greek, Italian and Portuguese C-130Hs.

MAFFS consists of seven airborne modules and one ground compressor and is used to fight forest and brush fires by spraying Monsanto Phos-Check retardant to inhibit the combustion potential of trees and shrubs and, by acting as a fertiliser, to promote the rapid regrowth of fire-denuded terrain and to prevent erosion. The airborne modules – five tanks and two clusters of compressed air canisters – are mounted on special pallets which can be loaded in 90 to 120 minutes. The rear pallet also incorporates a flow and mixture control panel and an aft-facing seat for the loadmaster. Each system, which weighs 10,550 lb (4785 kg) (empty) and has a 3,000-US gal (11356-litre) capacity, can be filled with retardant and compressed air in 15-20 minutes. The entire mix of water and retardant is discharged through two downward nozzles protruding from the aft loading ramp either in a single pass covering an

area 150 ft (46 m) wide and 2,000 ft (610 m) long or in up to five passes over smaller areas.

A more permanent conversion has been developed by Hemet Valley Flying Service of Hemet, California, for surplus C-130As acquired by the US Forestry Service. It consists of an eight-compartment tank, each with its hydraulically operated doors, and holding a total of 4,000 US gal (15141 litres) of Phos-Check fire retardant. First used in the western US during the summer of 1990, dedicated C-130 air tankers are now offered to foreign customers, with France's Sécurité Civile being the first potential customer to evaluate the fire-fighting C-130.

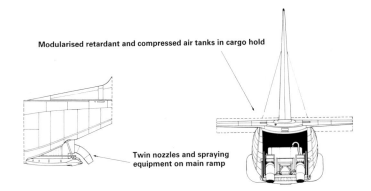

Modularised retardant and compressed air tanks in cargo hold

Twin nozzles and spraying equipment on main ramp

Below: MAFFS-equipped C-130s have been operated by a number of AFRes squadrons for several years and provide valuable fire-fighting coverage.

L-100

Developed for the civil market and receiving FAA certification on 16 February 1985, the L-100 was the equivalent of the C-130Es but did not carry pylon tanks and had all military equipment removed. Including the demonstrator (c/n 3946, N1130E) – which, by flying on two engines for all but 36 minutes, remained airborne 25 hours 1 minute when first flown on 20-21 April 1964 – 22 L-100s were built for commercial operators. Nine L-100s were later modified to the L-100-20 stretched configuration with a 5-ft (1.52-m) fuselage plug forward of the wing and a 3.3-ft (1.02-m) plug aft, and 26 new L-100-20s were produced for civil customers and the air forces of Gabon (one aircraft), Peru (five) and the Philippines (three).

Two L-100s and nine L-100-20s were modified to the L-100-30 configuration (with fuselage stretched an additional 8.3 ft/2.54 m) and over 70 have been built to this standard, including aircraft for the air forces of Dubai (one aircraft), Ecuador (one), Gabon (two), Indonesia (one), Kuwait (four) and Pakistan (one). The type remains in production for US and foreign civil customers and foreign government agencies.

Below: Like any Hercules, the L-100 can carry outsize loads, but is also compatible with standard commercial cargo pallets. Its rough field capability is appreciated by many military operators, including Pakistan.

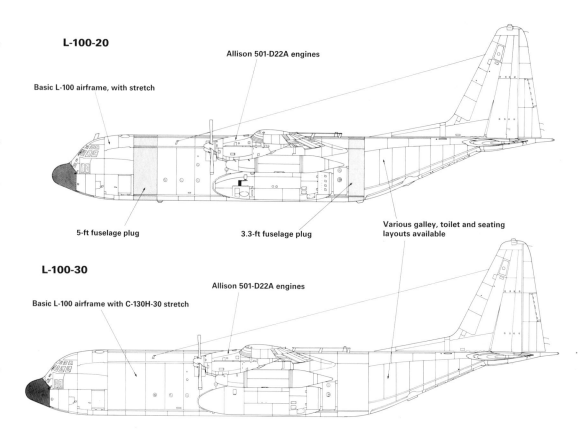

L-100-20

Allison 501-D22A engines

Basic L-100 airframe, with stretch

5-ft fuselage plug

3.3-ft fuselage plug

Various galley, toilet and seating layouts available

L-100-30

Allison 501-D22A engines

Basic L-100 airframe with C-130H-30 stretch

Above: Southern Air Transport's fleet of L-100-20s and -30s frequently operates in support of the US military.

UK Variants

Hercules C.Mk 1

Built by Lockheed, with some components made by Scottish Aviation, the 66 C-130Ks (which had received USAF serials 65-13021/65-13044, 66-8550/66-8573, and 66-13533/66-13550 for contractual purposes but were delivered as XV176/XV223 and XV290/XV307) were essentially C-130Hs powered by 4,508-eshp T56-A-15s and fitted by Marshall of Cambridge (Engineering) Ltd with British electronics, instrumentation and other equipment. The C-130K first flew at Marietta, Georgia, on 19 October 1966 and, as the Hercules C.Mk 1, entered service with No. 242 OCU at Thorney Island, Hants, in April 1967. Four Hercules C.Mk 1s (XV180, 194, 198 and 216) have been written off, and the 62 others have been modified into versions described separately.

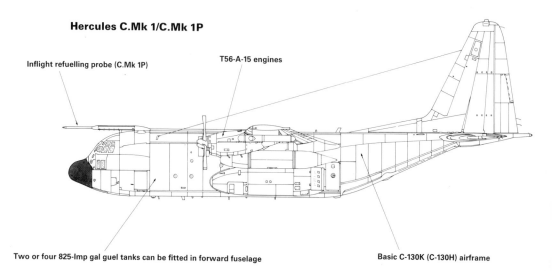

Hercules C.Mk 1/C.Mk 1P

Inflight refuelling probe (C.Mk 1P)

T56-A-15 engines

Two or four 825-Imp gal guel tanks can be fitted in forward fuselage

Basic C-130K (C-130H) airframe

Hercules C.Mk 1K

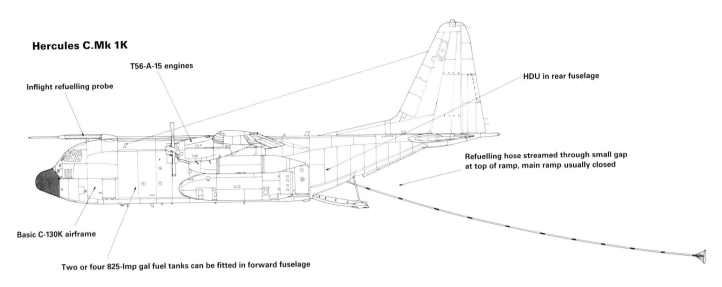

Inflight refuelling probe

T56-A-15 engines

HDU in rear fuselage

Refuelling hose streamed through small gap at top of ramp, main ramp usually closed

Basic C-130K airframe

Two or four 825-Imp gal fuel tanks can be fitted in forward fuselage

During Operation Corporate, the British re-taking of the Falkland Islands in 1982, the Engineering Wing at Lyneham fitted two or four 825-Imp gal (3750-litre) tanks in the forward fuselage of Hercules C.Mk 1s to extend their range and enable them to support the Task Force from Wideawake airfield on Ascension Island. Aircraft with two tanks became known as LR2s and those with four as LR4s. A further increase in range was obtained by having Marshall of Cambridge fit an air-refuelling probe to 25 aircraft which became Hercules C.Mk 1Ps (XV178/179, 181/182, 185/187, 191, 195/196, 200, 205/206, 210/211, 215, 218, 291/293, 295, 297/298, 300 and 306) while six others were fitted with both the air refuelling probe and a hose drum unit in the fuselage to serve as Hercules C.Mk 1K tankers (XV192, 201, 203/204, 213 and 296). Beginning in 1987, C.Mk 1Ps and C.Mk 1Ks began receiving AN/ALQ 157 IR jamming equipment and chaff/flare dispensers, while more recently five C.Mk 1Ps have been fitted with Racal 'Orange Blossom' ESM pods beneath their wingtips to provide a measure of surveillance capability, a useful feature for aircraft assigned to No. 1312 Flight at Mount Pleasant in the Falklands.

Above: RAF Hercules C.Mk 1s were delivered in this desert-type camouflage scheme, with black undersides for night operations.

Below: The black and white checkerboard ramp was applied to allow photos of A & AEE trial air-drops to be calibrated.

Above: During the operation to retake the Falkland Islands in 1982, several C.Mk 1s were converted to provide extra refuelling assets on the long flights to the South Atlantic.

Below: This Hercules C.Mk 1P was specially painted to celebrate one million hours of RAF Hercules flying. The Gulf war radically increased this already impressive total.

Left: Based with No. 1312 Flight at Mount Pleasant in the Falklands, this C.Mk 1P carries Racal 'Orange Blossom' ESM pods for maritime surveillance.

Lockheed Hercules variants

Hercules W.Mk 2

To replace a Vickers Varsity operated by the RAF Meteorological Research Flight from Farnborough, Hants, Marshall of Cambridge modified a Hercules C.Mk 1 (XV208) into the Hercules W.Mk 2. First flown on 21 March 1973, this research aircraft has an 18-ft (5.49-m) long instrumentation boom on the nose – forcing the relocation of the radar scanner on a pod above the flight deck, scientific instruments in the fuselage, and instrumentation pods beneath the wing.

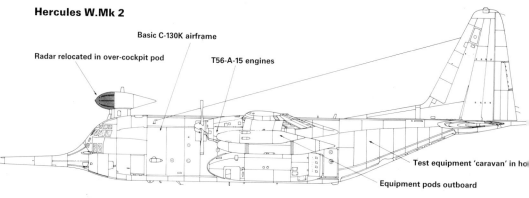

Hercules W.Mk 2

Basic C-130K airframe

Radar relocated in over-cockpit pod

T56-A-15 engines

Instrumentation boom

Test equipment 'caravan' in hold

Equipment pods outboard

Left: Perhaps the most radically modified of all Hercules is the single Hercules W.Mk 2 operated by the RAE for meteorological research.

Right: The prominent nose boom which replaces the standard weather radar on the W.Mk 2 provides sensing information for the array of instruments in the aircraft's hold.

Hercules C.Mk 3

Following the modification by Lockheed of XV223 as the prototype of the Hercules C.Mk 3 with fuselage stretched by 15 ft (4.57 m) to increase capacity from 92 to 128 infantrymen or from 64 to 92 paratroopers, 29 other Hercules C.Mk 1s were brought up to C.Mk 3 standard by Marshall of Cambridge. The Lockheed-

Above and below: Almost half of the Hercules operated by the four squadrons of the Lyneham Transport Wing have been converted to C.Mk 3 standard. This entails a radical improvement in the carrying capacity of the aircraft, ensuring they rarely 'bulk out' before reaching their weight limits.

Lockheed Hercules C.Mk 3

1 Radome
2 Weather radar scanner
3 Scanner tracking mechanism
4 Pitot head, port and starboard
5 Radome hinge
6 Radar mounting framework
7 Front pressure bulkhead
8 Downward vision windows
9 Instrument panel
10 Instrument panel shroud
11 Windscreen panels
12 Overhead switch panel
13 Co-pilot's seat
14 Cockpit eyebrow windows
15 Pilot's seat
16 Control column
17 Rudder pedals
18 Cockpit floor level
19 Nose landing gear wheel bay
20 Ground intercom socket
21 Twin nosewheels
22 Nosewheel leg door
23 Battery compartment
24 Radio and electronics racks
25 Portable oxygen bottle
26 Pilot's side console
27 Electrical system panel
28 Systems engineer's seat
29 Navigator's station
30 VHF aerial
31 Navigator's instrument panel
32 UHF aerial
33 Crew rest bunks
34 Cockpit emergency escape hatch
35 Control cable runs behind bulkhead
36 Galley unit
37 Fire extinguisher
38 Crew closet
39 Flight deck access ladder
40 Crew entry door
41 Integral airstairs
42 Cockpit section production joint double frame
43 Cargo-handling system roller conveyors
44 Main cabin bulkhead
45 Stretcher installation, maximum load 96 stretchers

46 Stretcher/troop seating mounting beam
47 Overhead equipment stowage rack
48 Cabin roof frames
49 Forward fuselage 'plug' section, 2.54 m (100 in) long
50 Aerial lead-in
51 Fuselage skin plating
52 Cabin wall trim panels
53 Forward fuselage plug section attachment double frame
54 Troop seats (stowed), maximum 92 fully equipped paratroops
55 Floor beam construction
56 Cabin window panels

nodified aircraft flew on 3 December 979 and Marshall completed the nodification programme in November 985. Commencing during the following ear, C.Mk 3s (XV176/177, 183/184, 188/ 0, 193, 197, 199, 202, 207, 209, 212, 4, 217, 219/223, 290, 294, 299, 301/305 nd 307) were fitted with the air efuelling probe as Hercules C.Mk 3Ps.

Below: The decision to buy the Hercules for the Royal Air Force ame with the cancellation of the indigenous transport design, the HS681 in 1965. Sixty-six aircraft, known as C-130Ks to the manufacturer, were delivered as adly needed replacements for geing Hastings and Beverleys. No eplacement for the long-serving Hercules is in sight.

Hercules C.Mk 3/C.Mk 3P

Inflight refuelling probe (by retrofit) on 29 aircraft

T56-A-15 engines

Basic C-130K airframe with stretch

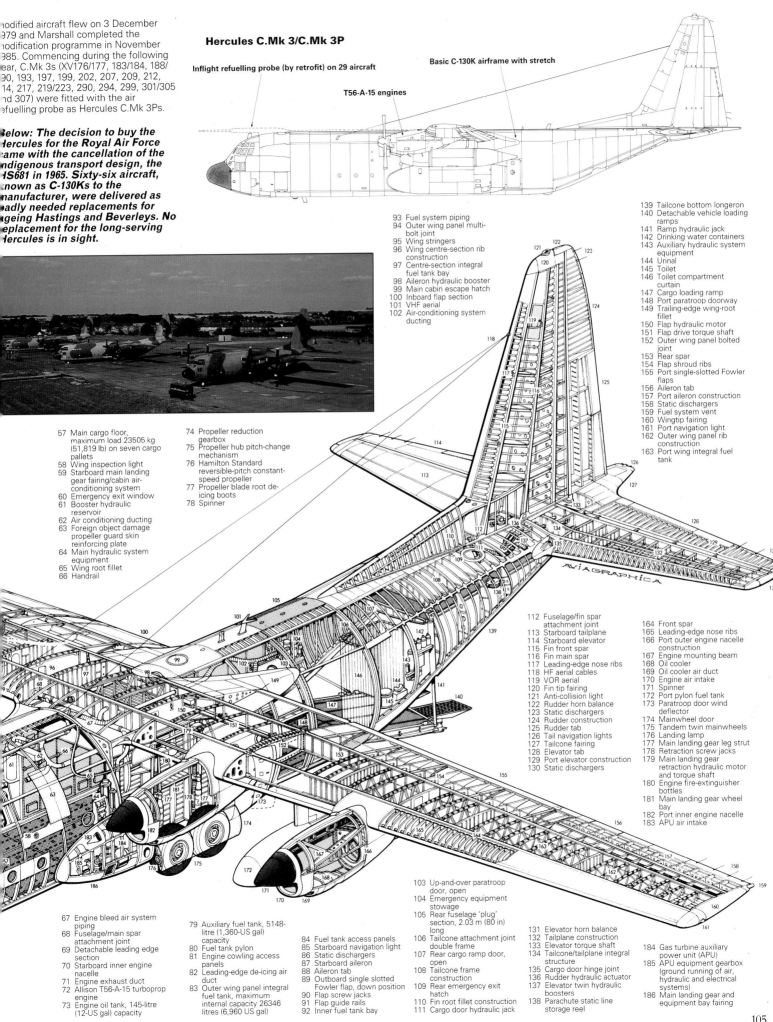

57 Main cargo floor, maximum load 23505 kg (51,819 lb) on seven cargo pallets
58 Wing inspection light
59 Starboard main landing gear fairing/cabin air-conditioning system
60 Emergency exit window
61 Booster hydraulic reservoir
62 Air conditioning ducting
63 Foreign object damage propeller guard skin reinforcing plate
64 Main hydraulic system equipment
65 Wing root fillet
66 Handrail

67 Engine bleed air system piping
68 Fuselage/main spar attachment joint
69 Detachable leading edge section
70 Starboard inner engine nacelle
71 Engine exhaust duct
72 Allison T56-A-15 turboprop engine
73 Engine oil tank, 145-litre (12-US gal) capacity

74 Propeller reduction gearbox
75 Propeller hub pitch-change mechanism
76 Hamilton Standard reversible-pitch constant-speed propeller
77 Propeller blade root de-icing boots
78 Spinner

79 Auxiliary fuel tank, 5148-litre (1,360-US gal) capacity
80 Fuel tank pylon
81 Engine cowling access panels
82 Leading-edge de-icing air duct
83 Outer wing panel integral fuel tank, maximum internal capacity 26346 litres (6,960 US gal)

84 Fuel tank access panels
85 Starboard navigation light
86 Static dischargers
87 Starboard aileron
88 Aileron tab
89 Outboard single slotted Fowler flap, down position
90 Flap screw jacks
91 Flap guide rails
92 Inner fuel tank bay

93 Fuel system piping
94 Outer wing panel multi-bolt joint
95 Wing stringers
96 Wing centre-section rib construction
97 Centre-section integral fuel tank bay
98 Aileron hydraulic booster
99 Main cabin escape hatch
100 Inboard flap section
101 VHF aerial
102 Air-conditioning system ducting

103 Up-and-over paratroop door, open
104 Emergency equipment stowage
105 Rear fuselage 'plug' section, 2.03 m (80 in) long
106 Tailcone attachment joint double frame
107 Rear cargo ramp door, open
108 Tailcone frame construction
109 Rear emergency exit hatch
110 Fin root fillet construction
111 Cargo door hydraulic jack

112 Fuselage/fin spar attachment joint
113 Starboard tailplane
114 Starboard elevator
115 Fin front spar
116 Fin main spar
117 Leading-edge nose ribs
118 HF aerial cables
119 VOR aerial
120 Fin tip fairing
121 Anti-collision light
122 Rudder horn balance
123 Static dischargers
124 Rudder construction
125 Rudder tab
126 Tail navigation lights
127 Tailcone fairing
128 Elevator tab
129 Port elevator construction
130 Static dischargers

131 Elevator horn balance
132 Tailplane construction
133 Elevator torque shaft
134 Tailcone/tailplane integral structure
135 Cargo door hinge joint
136 Rudder hydraulic actuator
137 Elevator twin hydraulic boosters
138 Parachute static line storage reel

139 Tailcone bottom longeron
140 Detachable vehicle loading ramps
141 Ramp hydraulic jack
142 Drinking water containers
143 Auxiliary hydraulic system equipment
144 Urinal
145 Toilet
146 Toilet compartment curtain
147 Cargo loading ramp
148 Port paratroop doorway
149 Trailing-edge wing-root fillet
150 Flap hydraulic motor
151 Flap drive torque shaft
152 Outer wing panel bolted joint
153 Rear spar
154 Flap shroud ribs
155 Port single-slotted Fowler flaps
156 Aileron tab
157 Port aileron construction
158 Static dischargers
159 Fuel system vent
160 Wingtip fairing
161 Port navigation light
162 Outer wing panel rib construction
163 Port wing integral fuel tank

164 Front spar
165 Leading-edge nose ribs
166 Port outer engine nacelle construction
167 Engine mounting beam
168 Oil cooler
169 Oil cooler air duct
170 Engine air intake
171 Spinner
172 Port pylon fuel tank
173 Paratroop door wind deflector
174 Mainwheel door
175 Tandem twin mainwheels
176 Landing lamp
177 Main landing gear leg strut
178 Retraction screw jacks
179 Main landing gear retraction hydraulic motor and torque shaft
180 Engine fire-extinguisher bottles
181 Main landing gear wheel bay
182 Port inner engine nacelle
183 APU air intake
184 Gas turbine auxiliary power unit (APU)
185 APU equipment gearbox (ground running of air, hydraulic and electrical systems)
186 Main landing gear and equipment bay fairing

HTTB

As part of a multi-phase development programme to obtain STOL data for use in designing future tactical transports, Lockheed has modified an ex-Kuwaiti L-100-20 into its High Technology Test Bed (HTTB). Modifications progressively introduced over the years include (**1**) test instrumentation; (**2**) dorsal fin extension and lateral strakes (horsals) ahead of the stabilisers; (**3**) double-slotted fast-acting flaps; (**4**) drooped wing leading edges; (**5**) wing spoilers; (**6**) extended chord ailerons and rudder; (**7**) high-sink-rate undercarriage; (**8**) steerable FLIR turret; (**9**) laser ranger; (**10**) 5,250-shp Allison 501D Series IV turboprops with digital controls and 13.75-ft (4.19-m) propellers; and (**11**) digital flight control system. Registered N130X, the HTTB first flew on 19 June 1984 after receiving the first two modifications. Some of these modifications may be incorporated in the proposed C-130J.

The HTTB remained in use with Lockheed, and was used for testing and evaluating various new items of equipment and new operational techniques. During development, the HTTB set two 'time-to-climb' world records, then lifted the largest load carried by a STOL aircraft to a height of 2000 metres. In July 1990, the aircraft conducted various STOL tests. On 13 July the HTTB landed with an air distance of 600 ft berween a 50-ft obstacle and touchdown, and a stopping distance of 900 ft. This was achieved with a gross weight of 130,000 lb and followed an 80-kt approach with a glideslope of 6°.

In July 1991 the HTTB completed initial tests of a new integrated Inertial Navigation and Global Positioning System, consisting of two Litton LTN-92 Inertial platforms and a Collins GPS. This recorded position errors of less than 100 ft throughout a typical flight.

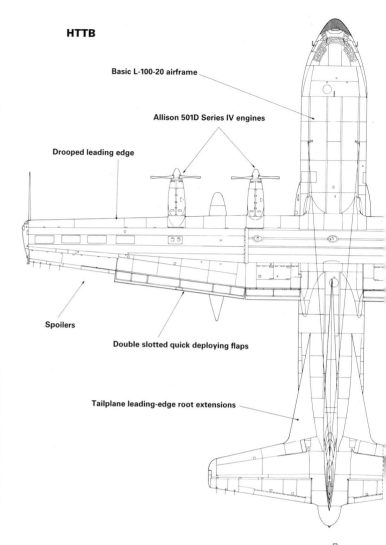

HTTB

Basic L-100-20 airframe

Allison 501D Series IV engines

Drooped leading edge

Spoilers

Double slotted quick deploying flaps

Tailplane leading-edge root extensions

Below: In the HTTB programme Lockheed succeded in producing a fully STOL-capable Hercules. At gross weights of 130,000 lb a full-stop landing could be achieved within 1,200 ft.

Below: The startling performance of the HTTB, a converted L-100-20, was due to its sophisticated computer-controlled flight control system and many aerodynamic refinements. These include double-slotted flaps, direct lift control spoilers and powered, extended-chord control surfaces.

Reshaped nose

Digital flight control system

Underwing equipment pod

Dorsal fin extension

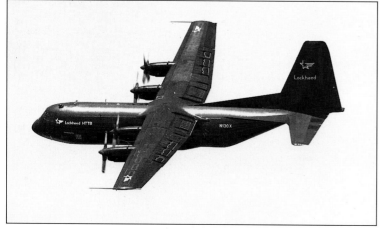

Above: HTTB, flying for seven years with various equipment fits, has been made available to both universities and industry for research.

EC-130V

EC-130V

Basic HC-130H airframe

AN/APS-145 radar in rotodome above fuselage

T56-A-15 engines

Above: The EC-130V carries an E-2C type AN/APS-145 radar antenna in the rotating radome above its fuselage.

The growing drugs problem in US cities has led to a major intensification in the interdiction campaign against the drug runners, and the State Department, Customs Service and (since the Anti-Drug Abuse Act of 1986) the Coast Guard have been more generously funded, allowing the wholesale acquisition of new and more effective equipment. Most drugs consignments are smuggled in either by air (in low-flying light aircraft) or by fast boat. In order to intercept these the US Coast Guard relies on good intelligence and airborne radar systems (which are used to alert Customs or Coast Guard vessels) and 'interceptor' aircraft like the Sikorsky Black Hawks. Since January 1987 the Coast Guard has used up to eight Grumman E-2C Hawkeyes transferred from the US Navy, the surviving seven of these aircraft now flying with CGAW-1 (Coast Guard Airborne Warning Squadron One) from St Augustine, Florida. These aircraft quickly showed their worth, but also demonstrated the need for a longer-endurance, longer-range AEW aircraft, and it was decided to produce an AEW C-130 Hercules, using the HC-130H airframe and the E-2C radar for maximum commonality. Conversion of the Coast Guard's final HC-130H (1721, commissioned in May 1968) to EC-130V standard was undertaken by General Dynamics Fort Worth, and the aircraft made its first flight in its new configuration on 31 July 1991. The three radar operators sit at positions which are pallet-mounted, allowing the aircraft to be quickly re-configured if necessary. Design and modifications were completed within 18 months, under a contract which also included training and spares. Trials at the Carrier Airborne Early Warning Department of the Naval Test Directorate at Patuxent River were completed by October 1991.

Communications antennas

Observation window (both sides)

Unidentified antenna fairings (both sides)

Various cooling air intakes

Below: After initial flight trials at General Dynamics' Fort Worth facility, the EC-130V was sent to Patuxent River for acceptance trials.

Below: The EC-130V combines the capability of the E-2C Hawkeye (used in small numbers by the Coast Guard) with the endurance of the C-130.

Best in the Business

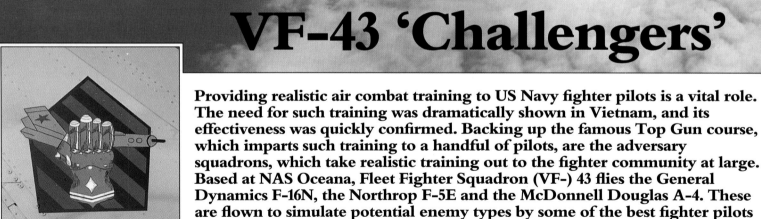

VF-43 'Challengers'

Providing realistic air combat training to US Navy fighter pilots is a vital role. The need for such training was dramatically shown in Vietnam, and its effectiveness was quickly confirmed. Backing up the famous Top Gun course, which imparts such training to a handful of pilots, are the adversary squadrons, which take realistic training out to the fighter community at large. Based at NAS Oceana, Fleet Fighter Squadron (VF-) 43 flies the General Dynamics F-16N, the Northrop F-5E and the McDonnell Douglas A-4. These are flown to simulate potential enemy types by some of the best fighter pilots in the US Navy. Some of these pilots describe VF-43's vital role.

Main picture above: The three major types used by VF-43 are seen flying in formation. Inset above: The insignia of VF-43 consists of a MiG-21 being crushed in an armoured gauntlet.

Far right: A VF-43 pilot in the cockpit of his F-16N. The introduction of the F-16N gave the adversary units a more realistic MiG-29 simulator.

On any given day off the Virginia coast, dogfights take place involving as few as two aircraft, and as many as . . . well, whatever it takes. F-14s, F/A-18s and a few veteran Marine F-4s wheel and dodge through the sky, trying to catch elusive bogeys. The little gray bandits are hard to see and, once spotted, are even tougher to catch. What makes the situation worse is that the bogeys are flown by some of the best fighter pilots in the business. They are the adversary pilots of VF-43.

VF-43 is based at the Navy's Master Jet Base at NAS Oceana, Virginia Beach, Virginia, near Norfolk. The squadron is one of a dozen fleet and reserve adversary squadrons that the Navy uses to give Navy and Marine squadrons training in aerial combat.

Squadrons have always indulged in internal training, with impromptu, as well as scheduled, 'hassles' a part of squadron routine. However, it was the relatively poor showing by *all* US fighter squadrons in Vietnam, where the ratio between

American kills and losses to those of North Vietnamese MiGs varied between 1:2 and 1:1.5, the lowest ever recorded since World War I, that prompted a review of the situation. (The Navy ratio was little better at 3.5:1.)

The Air Force and Navy addressed the problem separately, and eventually arrived at the same solution, which was to use specialized training syllabuses and dedicated squadrons of highly trained and motivated pilots. These experienced aviators' skills could

hopefully be transferred to newer aviators about to go into combat. The Air Force called these squadrons 'aggressors', while the Navy referred to them as 'adversaries'.

The wide-ranging Air Force aggressor program has fallen on hard budgetary times, with their units disbanding and giving some of their aircraft, notably the F-5s, to the Navy, which struggles to hold on to its ambitious program.

Fightertown

The most famous adversary unit is the Navy Fighter Weapons School, Top Gun, at NAS Miramar, near San Diego, California. From its meager beginnings in 1969 with a few war-weary A-4Es painted in various 'enemy' camouflage schemes, Top Gun soon proved its worth.

In 1972, as the Vietnam air war, dormant since the swirling battles of 1966-68, exploded into free-for-all fighting over North Vietnam, US Navy fighter crews waded into the MiGs and established a 12.5:1 kill-loss ratio. They shot down 25 North Vietnamese fighters, nearly half of the total number destroyed by Navy and Marine crews during the entire war.

Credit for this greatly improved showing went largely to the training the F-4 crews received at Top Gun. Indeed, the Navy's only pilot ace,

The Northrop T-38 Talon was one of the early aircraft types used by VF-43, and proved a popular adversary type with its high performance, agility and small size.

then-Lieutenant Randy Cunningham of VF-96, marvelled at how much the dogfights with Communist MiGs resembled the 'pretend' hassles at Miramar.

After Vietnam, the gospel of adversary training grew.

At first, most adversary units used the ubiquitous A-4. There were plenty of the ageing Vietnam veterans around, especially since most fleet squadrons were transitioning or disestablishing. The only regular Navy user of the A-4 was the Training Command, with two-seat TA-4Js. The Marines still had a few single-seat A-4E and A-4M VMAs, and the H&MSs – headquarters and maintenance squadrons – flew TA-4Fs and -Js. A few two-seat -Fs had been transformed into OA-4Ms with specialized radio equipment for forward air control duties.

A 'super-hotrod'

Top Gun operated a stripped-down version of the A-4 called the 'Mongoose'. It was little more than a flying engine with a seat, fuel tanks and rudimentary avionics. But, boy, could it turn! The Mongoose A-4E set the pattern for A-4 adversaries. Eventually, several squadrons flew A-4Fs with uprated engines, but without the -F's characteristic dorsal avionics hump.

Dubbed the 'Super Fox', the adversary A-4 offered a nearly 1:1 thrust-to-weight ratio, and a roll rate of almost 720° per second. Until the advent of the F-16N, the Navy's best all-round adversary aircraft was the Super Fox. Today, it still is the

At one time, the Top Gun hangar at Miramar was decorated with MiG silhouettes representing enemy aircraft shot down by graduates from the school.

centerpiece of both Naval Air Reserve squadrons, VFC-12 and VFC-13, and also flies with several fleet adversary units, including VF-43.

By the early 1980s, it was evident that, while the A-4 and F-5 were fine imitators of subsonic threat aircraft and third-generation Soviet types like the popular MiG-21, the new group of Soviet fighters, including late-model MiG-23s, and especially the MiG-29 and Su-27, required a new adversary aircraft. There was really only one choice as

far as the Navy was concerned: the General Dynamics F-16 Fighting Falcon.

The US Air Force had already ordered the F-16 in large numbers, but, even though the F-16 had tremendous advantages, the Navy had to convince Congress that the new fighter was vital to its mission. VF-43 helped analyze the F-16 as the next-generation adversary in 1982.

VF-43's lion cubs

To give the Navy breathing space to consider its choice, and to allow a different type to offer its services to the adversary program, Secretary of the Navy John Lehman announced in 1984 that the Navy would accept an Israeli offer of a free-lease agreement of 12 early-model Kfirs, which were designated F-21s in Navy service. VF-43 pilots received initial training overseas and, during ceremonies in April 1985, with Secretary Lehman providing the keynote address, VF-43 accepted the first of the delta-winged Kfirs.

The F-21s flew with VF-43 for three years, by which time the Navy had decided to make a limited purchase of F-16s, equipping VF-126 and Top Gun on the West Coast, and VF-45, and later VF-43, on the East Coast. VF-45 at NAS Key West, Florida, received the F-16s first, while VF-43 flew the F-21s.

The F-21 was fast and very strong, but, although the American pilots liked the new visitor, its performance and limited endurance did not exactly give everything that the adversary program hoped for. Until the F-16s arrived, the

Challengers needed their A-4s. The F-5s had been sent to NAS Miramar, and were recalled when the Kfirs left in April 1988. The Israeli aircraft, which were maintained by a dedicated group of Israeli technicians, had flown more than 9,700 hours in 9,800 sorties, an impressive record.

On to the Fighting Falcon

As the F-21s left, a cadre of pilots was already undergoing training in the F-16 at Luke AFB, Arizona. Borrowing a few F-16s from VF-45, when the Key West squadron could spare the valuable jets, VF-43 began Falcon operations in June 1988. Eventually, the squadron's own aircraft arrived in mid-1989. Thus, with its varied duties and responsibilities, VF-43 became a unique squadron flying four

Below: VF-43 operated 12 leased early-model Kfirs for some three years, but the type's short endurance proved a major weakness. While the Kfir was in service, VF-43's F-5Es were transferred to Miramar.

distinctly different types of aircraft, including several different sub-types.

Supporting various fleet squadrons, maintaining and flying all these different aircraft, as well as all the regular squadron activities, makes VF-43 a busy squadron. Commander R. E. 'Smoke' Davis is the Commanding Officer of the 'Challengers'. A native of Forsyth,

Georgia, he graduated from Georgia Tech in 1971. He received his gold wings in 1973, and flew F-4s with VF-74 in USS *Forrestal* and *Nimitz*. He served as an ACM instructor with VF-171.

Transitioning to the F-14, Commander Davis served with VF-84 in *Nimitz*. He reported to VF-43 in September 1988 as the Executive Officer (XO), and 'fleeted up' to CO.

"The Navy screening process looks at your entire record, and for all aviation squadrons, it's a fleet-up process. You're screened for command, then assigned to a squadron as XO. Then you fleet up to CO. About your 14th or 15th year, you have a command screen board, secret, where everyone's record is inspected. The board is made up of aviator captains, with one admiral, from different communities. The needs of the service play a part in determining who gets screened. For instance, if there is a need for more fighter COs,

Above: The US Navy and the USAF are not the only operators of dedicated adversary training squadrons. The F-5E serves with the US Marines VMFT-401 at Yuma, and in 'Marines' titles with the NFWS at Miramar (illustrated).

Above: Secretary of the Navy John Lehman formally handing over the first IAI Kfir (F-21A in USN service) for service with VF-43.

they will get more. Then consideration is given to who can fit where.

"I was selected, I believe, because of my ACM (air combat maneuvering) instructor time, in Key West. I had the experience and a good reputation, although to get this plum was due to a little luck, with whatever 'secret' handshakes went on in the back rooms.

The rewards of the job

"I don't think I have had a particular 'high' point, as such, although my change of command, when I took over, was certainly a high point. It's such a great job. The thing that gives me the most satisfaction is managing an outfit with this many people and different types of airplanes, and this many complex, dangerous missions. I can't take credit for everything that goes on, because I've got so many good people working for me. They take care of flying the airplanes, different quals, ACM, spin training, contract

This F-21A wears the distinctive fin badge of VF-43. Experience with the Kfir reinforced the Navy's desire to procure an adversary version of the F-16.

maintenance, Navy maintenance. It's not always fun, but when I look back it makes me feel good, thinking of all our accomplishments.

"For me, the high point in flying is obviously flying the F-16. I've flown F-4s and F-14s, and a fam hop in an F/A-18, but the F-16's the most fun airplane I've ever flown. The F-5 and A-4 are fun, too, but they're a different generation. The F-16's the most user-friendly plane I've ever flown. You can pick your arena, and each of our aircraft has its little niche, or edge, where they can outperform the other, but the F-16 is fun. It'll keep a 40-year-old man in shape trying to keep up with these 26-year-old lieutenants. And the mission is fun, too. Lots of ACM.

A good team

"There are the little 'nit-noid' management problems which you'd find anywhere, in any squadron. I have 200 troops working for me. Most of them are great, but, as always, there are a few who cause problems, and that's true anywhere. Typical squadron. My adversary instructors are the pick of the litter. I'm not too concerned about talent. And since we fly every day, our proficiency is at a high level. We could go out and win all the time. So, what I look for is standardization; are we doing the same thing, in the way we're supposed to? We try hard to take the ego out of it.

"The fighters don't want to lose, and since we're both the 'bad' guys and the judges, we have to take our ego out of it and get used to getting shot.

"From the other side, I have to keep the guys from getting involved, and get those who do back on the straight-and-narrow. I'm grading the same thing that the fighters are. We basically judge them on how they did. Once we get through how and what they did, the real meat of the debriefing is *why*. Why did you do good, or why did you do bad?

"How did you use your missiles and tactics, planning and deployment? Did you miss the shot because you had your switches set up wrong? Did you go off in two different directions because of improper radio discipline?

Left: Unusually, this VF-43 F-5E carries an enormous centreline fuel tank. This would severely limit the little fighter's performance and manoeuvrability. At one time, adversary aircraft wore a variety of schemes, but a standard grey camouflage is now virtually de rigueur.

Above: At one time, even VF-43's spin training T-2 Buckeyes wore an aggressor-style grey colour scheme. This was later abandoned for flight safety reasons.

Below: Today, VF-43's Rockwell T-2s wear standard training colours and are used for giving F-14 pilots the spinning and 'Out of Control Flight' (OOCF) indoctrination impossible in their own aircraft.

Above: The VF-43 instructor does his walk-around while the F-14 pilot 'pupil' straps in.

Above: An F-5E and an F-5F of VF-43, the 'Challengers'. The F-5F in the background was obtained from another unit, and was soon painted in a more useful grey colour scheme.

"When you go into the debrief, the people can go back to figure what they did right, and keep doing it. And find out what areas need improvement, refinement. Not every one of the bogeys will attend the debrief, but the bogey mission commander conducts the debrief for the fighters.

"We don't play the bogeys' radio transmission. Most of that is concerned with safety of flight. As the adversaries, we have a special responsibility to maintain the safety aspect, not get emotionally involved, or try to push the fight past the edge of the envelope.

Fighting safely

"We have training rules that we brief before the flight; they're pretty standard, regarding separation, mid-airs, out-of-control flight,

simultaneous runs on a bogey or fighter. The fighters are also supposed to discuss the training rules in their own brief, after we leave, as well as their 'secret' gameplans to beat us. We also brief weather, airspeeds, hard decks. As the senior, or more experienced, folks out there, we're supposed to be the ones to call a knock-it-off, or know when enough's enough.

"One-v-one maneuvering's a very perishable skill. I don't care how good you are. If you haven't done it for a while, it'll take a while to get back in. Now, a new guy will find ACM is like riding a bicycle: you might keep falling off, but once you've learned how to ride, you won't fall off, but you might not be ready to ride the Tour de France without a little warm-up.

"Now, generally speaking,

experience doesn't necessarily translate into talent. You get a fleet-experienced lieutenant who is certainly capable of beating a lot of lieutenant commanders or commanders who have less talent but more experience. And vice versa."

Commander Davis is fortunate in having a lot of capable people working for him. Although wanting to come to VF-43 is desirable, for most of the pilots their selection is part of the natural process of qualification, timing and needs of the service.

One of the crew

Lieutenant David 'Sly' Fox, from Kansas City, Missouri, graduated from the US Naval Academy, Class of 1983. He flew F-14s with VF-41, and is VF-43's Quality Assurance

(QA) Officer. Although relatively new at the squadron, he already has definite ideas about his responsibilities.

"I joined the squadron in May 1990, and I like it a lot. It's the best job in the Navy for a fighter pilot. New pilots usually get checked out in either the A-4 or F-5, and then, after they've flown one airplane for two or three months, they qualify in the second airplane. I qualified in the A-4 first, then the F-5. I fly them both now. I'm slated to go to F-16 school next month, probably at MacDill AFB in Tampa, Florida. That's where their F-16 'RAG' is, the 56th Tactical Training Wing.

"Hopefully by the eight- or nine-month mark, a pilot is current in all three adversary airplanes. Generally, we don't *fight* all three airplanes, but we're NATOPS-qualled in them.

We can fly them around, on cross-countries, but we generally limit ourselves to fighting just two different planes in one period.

"Most of the guys in the squadron have been through Top Gun, in one way or another. Maybe they flew F-14s in the Power Projection Course, or maybe they went through the Adversary Course as a pilot from this squadron. Although both courses run simultaneously, they're two different classes. I went through the Power Projection Course in an F-14. That's the five-week course for fighter pilots.

"All the crews that went through Top Gun obviously love to fly the airplane and they're good enough to be selected by their COs to go to Top Gun; they're probably pretty

good at what they do already. Then they go out to Miramar and train hard, getting into the nuts and bolts of flying, as well as becoming an effective teacher regarding air combat and how to win.

Pure fighter pilots

"It's a natural progression for us to come to this squadron after Top Gun. Perfect. Even though we're adversaries – the bad guys – we go up and fight twice a day, maybe more, on the average, especially during the big exercises. Usually each flight is about an hour. Pilots average 30–35 hours a month in the squadron.

"We only fly in good weather; you can't fight in bad weather. We don't fight at night, so we don't fly

at night, except to maintain our basic qualifications, 12 hours a year. So, we're talking VFR, daytime, good weather, and fighting the airplane. For a fighter pilot, it doesn't get any better.

"Sometimes we'll go on dets, take detachments to Key West, or Fallon, maybe Cecil in Jacksonville, to help support other fleet units.

"The airplanes we fly, of course, are different, each with its good and bad points, depending on the mission. The F-16 is obviously the

Below: The VF-43 flight line on a typically busy day. VF-43's main 'trade' comes from the F-14 squadrons co-located at Oceana, but also from Navy and Marine F/A-18 units on the East Coast.

Left: The conversion of the USAF's aggressor squadrons to the F-16 gave the US Navy's adversary units a much-needed influx of F-5E airframes. Here two VF-43 F-5Es fly over Virginia.

queen. It's a superb airplane, a fourth-generation adversary. We'll give the fighters anything they want unless it's a FFARP mission – Fleet Fighter Air combat maneuvering Readiness Program. FFARP is a once-a-year, or at least, once-a-turn-around affair for every aircrew in a squadron, involving 12 sorties. If it's not a FFARP mission where the scenario is set out for us, we'll let the fighters decide what they want.

"We'll fight the best we can,

given the parameters of the particular aircraft we're supposed to be, i.e., a MiG-21, -23 or -29. Based on the aircraft we're flying, we can simulate the threat very well, depending on what weapons we're *supposed* to be carrying.

"Another point about this job is that we get awfully good at fighting. ACM isn't like riding a bike; you can't get right back on it after going away for two months and be as good as you were in only a few minutes. It's a dynamic environment and every fight is just a little different. It's important to just maintain situational awareness, your ability to analyze the energy states of the bogey, to recognize angles and manage your own energy, and as

Above: VF-43 pilots debrief in the crewroom after a satisfying DACM hassle with some Oceana-based F-14 Tomcats.

Inset: The new VF-43 flying suit patch features a MiG-29 in place of the original MiG-21. Main picture: Pre-flighting a VF-43 F-16N.

well remembering the switchology for your weapons systems requires constant practice, or you get 'cold'.

"If a fighter beats us, he's good. He shouldn't beat us because we're so proficient; after all, it's our job. There's no pressure on us. The new guys normally don't do very well. Of course, you occasionally run into a 'natural' who does really well. But on the whole, we shouldn't lose. And we don't. But we don't give away anything, either. We fight hard. We fly the airplane the best we can because if we give the fighter crews a false sense of security, if we go easy, let them win, that isn't doing anybody any good.

Below: An F-16N of the Fighter Weapons School holds as an F-14 overshoots. All US Navy F-16Ns wear the same basic colour scheme, and all are maintained by General Dynamics.

"Now, with the more inexperienced crews, or those who haven't fought in a while, you kill them pretty quick. It's not pretty. But you don't want to go out in the first fight and let them end up thinking they're better than they really are. But, in the next engagement, you go a little easier. You don't want to beat them into the ground.

The skills to succeed

"You've got a responsibility to build up the people in the squadrons so that when they deploy, they're confident that they can win, and they can. As I said, they've proved it to us because we didn't give them anything.

"When we return, we debrief the mission, what the fighters could have done a little better, good points, and *teach* them how to beat us. That's the name of our game.

"In a fighter squadron, FFARP events carry a lot of pressure; some of it is self-induced. Let's face it, fighter pilots have pretty big egos. Nobody wants to lose. It's hard to admit that you lost.

"Again, there's no pressure for us adversary pilots. We do it so much, every day, that we're very effective instructors. We see a lot of mistakes over and over, we see them coming, and we try to brief the fighters on things we've seen. But there's nothing like doing it, getting your feet wet, making a few mistakes and learning.

"As far as which pilots go to VF-43, well, they probably finished first in their first fleet squadron, whether it's F-14s, or . . . we have a few folks from F/A-18 squadrons. They're good pilots. The selection process is fairly normal, however,

including annual fitness reports which go to Washington. Those people who 'break out' of the pack, so to speak, are probably going to get what they want for their next assignment.

"Some people would rather go to a VX test and development squadron, or to the RAG, for their own reasons. But orders to VF-43 are the 'cream orders' for an East Coast fighter pilot – *I* think.

"My CO in VF-41 had some friends at Top Gun. After I completed the course there, they told him that they wanted me to come to Top Gun as an instructor during my next tour. I thought long and hard about that. But, although I was an appealing prospect, I didn't go. I wanted to stay on the East Coast. With a new family, additional living expenses and so on, moving to the West Coast would have been a problem. I can do the same thing right here.

Beyond Top Gun

"Top Gun is a great organization, but it's more of a training officer's class. They take the cream of the squadrons, put them through the five-week program and send them back to their squadron so they can train the rest of their unit crews. But, the three Navy adversary squadrons – VF-43, VF-45 and VF-126 – take *entire* squadrons through a training program. We just rewrote our syllabus, made it more

Below: The F-16Ns of Key West-based VF-45 wear yellow-outlined red buzz codes, and have a red star on the tailfin. VF-43 borrowed F-16Ns from VF-45 until their own aircraft arrived.

intense, and we take every crew through it.

"How well each squadron does is important, besides the operational aspect. Efficiency awards, bragging rights around the base – you know what I mean. I think our mission is just as important, maybe more so, than Top Gun, because we take a whole squadron. Top Gun is for the select few who get to go to the school, whereas we train guys right now who go on cruise in a couple of months, maybe to the Red Sea, or off the coast of Israel. This is the last training many of them get before they go do it for real. Their confidence has to be real.

Merits of the mounts

"The single-seat A-4s – we also have a few two-seaters – are great airplanes for one-v-one fights. We make the fighters work real hard to beat us. The A-4E and F have a lot of power, very good handling at slow speed, and are very good simulators of the MiG-21 below 300 kt. *Above* 300 kt, the F-5 better simulates the MiG-21, as well as the

MiG-23. It doesn't turn as well as the -21, and bleeds a lot more energy a lot faster than the A-4.

"You have to know what you want to do. With the amount of *g* you put on the airplane and the speed you maintain, you know what you can simulate. When there's five or six planes out there, the F-5 is great because it's so small and hard

Right: 'Challengers'' 'Skipper', Commander 'Smoke' Davis, climbs aboard his F-16N before an ACM sortie.

Below: The entry ladder is removed. The civilian ground crew at VF-43 are employed by General Dynamics. The F-16N contract included full maintenance support.

A pair of VF-43 F-16Ns take off, while an F-14 launches from the parallel runway.

to see. You can make a big vertical move and no-one will see you.

"Even the other bogeys don't see you. We're constantly talking to each other on our own frequency. Although the F-14 is a good killing machine, it's big, and people don't lose sight of it. But the F-5 is different.

"Safety is paramount. We're talking as to where the fighters are, 'Sly's rolling in on the eastern fighter,' or 'there's another one up there that I didn't see.' There's a lot of talk among the bogeys.

"My goal is to join the Blue Angels. I've been talking with them and next spring, I hope to get selected for the team. The flying will never get better than what I'm doing now, but I've always had a dream to be one of the Blues. I'm going to try. It'll be tough, but maybe I'll get lucky. My timing is good, flight time, my career path. Who knows?"

Lieutenant Commander Dan 'Vegas' Cannan from Rochester, New York, balances the junior officer's viewpoint. Also a graduate of the Naval Academy (Class of 1978), Lieutenant Commander Cannan was originally a Radar Intercept Officer (RIO) with VF-41, deploying in *Nimitz* (CVN-68) in 1981. He later took pilot training and became an F-14 driver with VF-31 in *Forrestal*. All this experience qualifies Lieutenant Commander Cannan to head the squadron's operations department.

Operations Officer

"I really wanted to come to VF-43 and talked with the detailer. Of course, knowing the skipper helped a lot. A little of the 'good 'ol boy' network. My squadron skipper wanted me to go to VX-4, but I wanted to stay at Oceana. There was a spot at -43, too, so it all worked out. I reported in November 1988.

"The squadron had just given the Kfirs back and I was looking forward to flying F-16s. But when I got here, they hadn't gotten them yet. I was a little disappointed. It's the most technologically advanced aircraft we have. It makes flying a lot of fun.

"As Operations Officer, my main job is managing the people I have working for me, making sure all the scenarios, especially for the FFARP exercises, are good, everything's working. I keep track of how much money, how much flight time we have left. I try to let the guys do their job, providing guidance when they need it.

"I usually fly one, maybe two hops a day – if I can. Sometimes weather causes problems, especially in the winter. We get spoiled in the squadron flying in good weather. The fighters are more practiced in instrument conditions, particularly since they have better systems. The A-4 and F-5 have only one radio, one TACAN. You lose either one, and you're hard-pressed to get back to the field. Sometimes the fighters tease us, 'How come you guys didn't go flying?' Since the F-16 has two radios, we use that to do a weather recce before the day's flight schedule begins.

"The FFARP training is fairly generic. It includes world-wide threats, Third World, a mix. Some of the threats will have a fourth-generation, top-of-the-line fighter, with lesser generation missiles, such as a MiG-29 without the missiles a -29 might carry. Or, sometimes, a Third-World country will have F-5s, or even A-4s, so, of course, we can use our aircraft as those threats. Sometimes we can address specific concerns of squadrons deploying to a specific area, but you can't always know what certain countries will do. So, we generalize, and fly our airplanes more aggressively. Generally speaking, if our guys can handle anything *we* throw at them, they can handle anything on cruise.

"As adversary pilots, we're trying to give the fighters the best possible training. Sometimes we have to remember, especially when we're flying a plane like the F-16, not to take advantage of the aircraft's abilities if the threat we're simulating wouldn't have those advantages. Sometimes during an especially involved fight, you'll see someone turning really hard and you say, 'Oh, no, stop that! You're not that kind of an airplane! You can't do that!'

More than just flying

"But we critique ourselves, and that's all part of our job as professional bogeys. We're teaching the fighters how to do it right. We take real pride in providing that service. Then, occasionally, we take our thinking caps off and have at it, fighter against bogey. Sometimes we fight against each other within the squadron, one-v-one. Then it becomes individual ability instead of what type of aircraft you're supposed to be."

Besides its more glamorous ACM and adversary activities, VF-43 also runs a spin-training syllabus, more formally called the Out Of Control

Flight (OOCF) Program. Begun in 1979, the OOCF syllabus uses T-2C Buckeye trainers, long a staple in the Navy's Training Command undergraduate pilot program. Easy and forgiving to fly, the T-2 offered an ideal platform for indoctrinating F-14 crews in the pitfalls of spins, as well as showing them how to get out of them. VF-43's pilot roster includes one or two qualified IP in the OOCF program.

VF-43, while primarily a pilot's squadron, also uses two Naval Flight Officers (NFOs). The NFOs are experienced RIOs. Lieutenant David 'Genghis' Kahn, from Allentown, Pennsylvania, graduated from Syracuse University in upstate New York. He had the distinction of serving in VF-74 during that squadron's tour as the first deployed F-14A(Plus) squadron, in *Saratoga* (CV-60). He works in Lieutenant Commander Cannan's Ops Department as the Schedules Officer.

The big picture

"VF-43 *is* a pilot's squadron, but the NFOs have several functions. For instance, I write the flight schedule, and I am an RTO, Range Training Officer. We monitor the ACM engagements on the Tactical Air Combat Training Systems (TACTS) range. All the pilots are qualled and are RTOs, too, but I'm a *command* RTO. We watch the fight, and give ground control for the intercepts. We also control the fighters and bogeys during FFARP exercises.

"During a mission, as an RTO, I'm responsible for getting the aircraft joined up and on the range, getting the adversaries together, and the fighters together, making sure there's no separation, completing the weapons checks, and checking that the simulated missiles carried are good; the planes carry simulator pods. I make sure the correct simulation is loaded on the TACTS range. You can actually call up range and bearing from one aircraft to another. I give 'bogey dope', or GCI information, to control the bogeys, and orchestrate their maneuvers as they simulate whatever threat is required. The RTO is also a back-up safety observer to make sure no one goes below the hard deck, usually

Above: A VF-43 F-16N pulls hard, vortices streaming from the blended wing/fuselage junction. The F-16N's high α capability is not sufficient to simulate aircraft like the Su-27 and MiG-29.

Below: An F-16N breaks from a mixed formation of VF-43 aircraft. An F-5E leads, followed by the two F-16Ns, with an A-4 bringing up the rear.

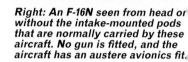

Right: An F-16N and an A-4 of VF-45 in formation. Below: The patch worn by General Dynamics maintenance personnel.

5,000 ft MSL. You evaluate the shots, whether someone gets a kill.

"The RTOs will debrief the bogey mission commander, and give him a printout of the shots during the hop. We usually don't debrief the fighters, but we can if we want to, or they ask us. But usually the bogey mission commander does the debrief.

"I've learned a lot from watching the engagements, what works and what doesn't. It will make me a better RIO. I also get some stick time in -43, which will help me better understand the pilot's responsibilities. I'll take it back with me to my next squadron."

With constantly changing world affairs, and financial considerations always taking center stage, support programs like the Navy's adversary squadrons are always looked at closely. Budget planners in Washington, looking for ways to save money, look everywhere. Commander Davis is well aware of not only the importance of his squadron's mission, but also its occasionally tenuous existence.

Support from above

"The adversary program is very important and has a lot of support throughout our chain of command. We've come a long way from the early days, and the adversary instructors certainly provide a valuable fleet training resource. I don't think there's any doubt, from the fleet lieutenant to the DCNO(Air), that the adversaries have a worthwhile mission. The problem comes down to the budget and the so-called 'Peace Dividend'. Cuts will have to be made somewhere as we go towards a 'leaner' Navy. The question is, where will the cuts be made?

"The adversary squadrons are not deployable, and a budget cutter could make a ready case that here's a squadron that could be disestablished without impacting fleet readiness. Our F-16s don't even have guns; we're just a training asset. It's up to the operators to let the budget cutters know that they can't measure training readiness like that.

"As far as dollars go, it's not a quantifiable number. I wonder how many airplanes we've *not* crashed during ACM training now that we have professional adversary squadrons. It used to be just a few planes hassling. Pilots would say, 'I'll meet you out there, 50 miles east, and we'll go at it.' The cost of one or two F-14s or F/A-18s could more than make up for the adversary program."

Below: Structural problems have now grounded most of the adversary F-16Ns, and the burden has fallen back onto the older types, which were slowly being phased out.

Right: An F-16N seen from head on without the intake-mounted pods that are normally carried by these aircraft. No gun is fitted, and the aircraft has an austere avionics fit.

Below: Two F-16Ns of VF-43 in formation with a pair of Tiger IIs from the same unit. All the aircraft carry TACTS pods and the F-16s also carry AIM-9 acquisition rounds.

The Soviet Withdrawal from Europe

Part One: HUNGARY

Above: Seventeen humpbacked MiG-29 'Fulcrum-Cs' line up on the flight line at Sarmellek on 4 October 1990, waiting to leave for their new home – a military airfield near Minsk. Each carries a pair of underwing ferry tanks.

Left: The Regiment Commander taxis out in 'his' MiG-29. Moments later he 'beat up' Sarmellek in spectacular fashion. Sarmellek was built in 1952, and taken over by the Soviets in 1962.

In the first of a series of articles documenting the Soviet withdrawal from Eastern Europe, *World Air Power Journal* details the departure of the air forces of the Southern Group of Forces (once known as the 59th Air Army) from Hungary. The Soviet air forces in non-Soviet Eastern Europe previously represented a massive 20 per cent of total Soviet tactical aircraft strength, and included the lion's share of the most modern equipment and the best-trained pilots. A modest increase in size during the early 1980s was accompanied by a revolutionary improvement in capability, as fighter regiments converted to strike or attack duties. Within a few years, warming relations with the West led to another change, with many offensive aircraft being replaced by fighters and interceptors. Then the withdrawal began.

At the height of the Cold War the Soviet Union maintained massive armed forces on the territories of its Warsaw Pact allies. Soviet forces tended to represent the highest-quality assets, while the forces of other Warsaw Pact nations (which came under Soviet control) were generally used to augment them. Thus the most front-line fighter regiments tended to be Soviet, while further back from the Iron Curtain were the East German, Czech, Polish and Hungarian fighter units (generally equipped with older and inferior aircraft types). Similarly, the Soviet Union provided the vast majority of ground-attack and strike units, denying its allies access to long-range offensive aircraft. Thus while Soviet aircraft provided 43 per cent of

Above: A mixed bunch of Soviet military personnel, dependants and Hungarian civilians watch with mixed emotions as the regiment's 'Fulcrum-Cs' taxied out for the last time.

overall Warsaw Pact combat aircraft strength, it provided 60 per cent of the fighter bombers, and 100 per cent of the bombers.

During the early 1980s, Soviet air forces in Eastern Europe underwent a series of changes. Aircraft strength increased modestly, but overall capability underwent a revolutionary change, with large numbers of fighter regiments being replaced by MiG-27, Su-17 or Su-24 attack and strike units, and with the widespread introduction of 'smart' munitions. At the same time there was a major shelter-building programme, reducing the vulnerability of aircraft on their airfields.

Deployment

Soviet air force units were deployed in most Warsaw Pact countries, although not in Bulgaria (which was regarded as being geographically irrelevant) and not in Romania (where Ceausescu maintained a show of independence). Elsewhere,

Soviet aviation units were assigned either directly to the support of the relevant Group of Forces (Western in East Germany, Northern in Poland, Central in Czechoslovakia and Southern in Hungary) or to Strategic Air Armies which reported directly to the Soviet High Command.

Strategic forces

The two Strategic Air Armies with forces deployed outside the Soviet Union were the 4th (headquartered at Vinnitsa in the Ukraine), which controlled units in East Germany and Poland, and the 24th (headquartered at Legnica, Poland), which controlled units in the USSR and in Hungary. The 46th Air Army (headquartered at Smolensk) would have also sent aircraft to FOLs in western Poland in time of war. Most Soviet air power in Eastern Europe was more tactical in nature, and most units were therefore assigned directly to the relevant Group of Forces in each country. The air army in each country originally had a separate numerical designation, though these designations were later dropped.

Below: This 'Fulcrum-C' carries an excellence award below the cockpit.

Thus the 16th Air Army became known simply as the Air Army of the Western Group of Forces, while the 37th Air Army in Poland became the Air Army of the Northern Group of Forces and the 59th Air Army became the Air Army of the Southern Group of Forces. The previous identity of the Air Army of the Central Group of Forces in Czechoslovakia is unknown at the moment.

Divisions, regiments and squadrons

Each air force typically consists of a number of divisions, in which three (or sometimes four) polki (regiments) are grouped. The division will normally be a single-role unit, with fighters and fighter-bombers on neighbouring airfields belonging to different divisions. In Germany, where the concentration of Soviet forces is greatest, the air force is split into two geographical corps, to which the various divisions reported.

The Soviet regiment is broadly equivalent to a Western wing, and will normally occupy a single air base, although some larger bases in the Soviet Union itself can house a whole division. At the other end of the scale, some specialised aircraft types may be deployed as independent expanded *eskadrils* (squadrons), with a reconnaissance *eskadril*, for example, sometimes occupying a whole base. Such independent *eskadrils* report directly to a divisional, or sometimes an air force, headquarters.

Regimental structure

The basic structure of Soviet regiments changed slightly during the early 1970s, increasing in size from an average of 37 aircraft (three 12-aircraft squadrons with a single HQ aircraft) to an average of 45 aircraft (three 15-aircraft squad-

rons, sometimes with an extra training flight). Attack regiments are usually slightly smaller. In wartime a reserve squadron would be added to each regiment.

Virtually every regiment in Frontal Aviation has at least a limited ground-attack role. Front-line tactical fighter regiments, for example, normally include at least one squadron which

Above: The typically Soviet-looking cockpit of a Su-24MR 'Fencer-E' reconnaissance aircraft. Full dual controls are provided for the navigator, who sits in the right-hand seat.

Below: The Kunmadaras 'Fencer-Es' lacked the prominent overwing fences seen on German-based recce Su-24 variants, but were otherwise identical to the aircraft used by the Welzow wing. About 12 were based at Kunmadaras.

Above: The Su-24's retractable refuelling probe is clearly visible in this head-on view, as is the slab-sided reconnaissance pod on the centreline.

rains in a secondary ground-attack role.

Squadrons normally consist of three four-aircraft *zvenos* (flights), although expanded squadrons may have their own three-aircraft training flight or have three 'spare' aircraft. Independent squadrons are often larger, with four or five flights. The basic Soviet tactical unit is the *para*, or pair.

59th Air Army

Hungary was for many years the home of the Soviet 59th Air Army, which, as noted above, latterly became known as the Air Force of the Southern Group of Forces. This had its headquarters at Tokol, a large air base near Budapest. Hungary also hosted a single nuclear strike regiment of the 4th Strategic Air Army. The Soviet forces left their seven airfields in Hungary between March 1990 and June 1991, and the withdrawal, and their post-war composition, are outlined here.

Strategic Sukhois

The single strategic unit in Hungary was a nuclear strike regiment equipped with the Su-24MK 'Fencer-D'. This was based at Debrecen, which also housed a Yak-28 EW unit, probably an independent squadron, for many years. Some of the Su-24s, perhaps equipping one of the regiment's three squadrons, may have been EW versions which replaced the Yak-28 'Brew-

ers'. By 1990, Debrecen also housed a MiG-27D 'Flogger-J' regiment, and at least one squadron of MiG-23MFs. The fighter 'Floggers' were the first to leave officially, departing in March 1990 for a base in the Murmansk area. They included MiG-23MFs 92 and 93, and MiG-23UB 21.

The MiG-27Ds wore blue codes and carried a winged horse badge. The 38 aircraft (including some MiG-23UBs) left at the end of May 1991 for Novgorod. The aircraft included MiG-23UBs

Above: Flush antennas, perhaps serving a SLAR, are clearly visible in this close-up view of the nose of an Su-24MR at Kunmadaras.

63 and 65 (flown by Regiment Commander Colonel Victor Zsavrazsnov) and MiG-27Ds 01, 02, 07, 08, 10, 11, 29, 40 and 41.

The base officially closed on 31 May 1991. The departure of the MiG-27s was marked by a major ceremony, with the base being thrown open to press and public alike. This was the first time that a Hungarian was allowed on to a Soviet airfield in Hungary for many years. A military band played, the Soviets paraded their unit standards, and the pilots lined up for inspection by a senior officer before they climbed into their cockpits. Unfortunately, the departures began at 0400, so any onlookers had to be dedicated. By contrast, the departure of the 'Fencers' was not publicised at all.

A single fighter division controlled three fighter regiments, based at Tokol, Kiskunlachaza and Sarmellek. Although many Western analysts never caught up with the change (and contrary to the Warsaw Pact air force analysis in *World Air Power Journal*, Volume 3), all of these units were equipped with the MiG-29 'Fulcrum', having re-equipped from MiG-21bis (at Tokol and Sarmellek) and MiG-23 aircraft during 1986 and 1987.

MiG-29 departures

Kiskunlachaza was the first of the fighter bases to close, on 20 May 1990, its complement of aircraft flying home for re-assignment to an unknown base. At Sarmellek, one squadron departed in late November, and the last of Sarmellek's red-coded MiG-29 'Fulcrum-Cs' followed on 4 October, with the base closing officially on 20 October 1990. They included 01, 34 and 35, and reportedly relocated to a base near Minsk. These aircraft may have been newly re-

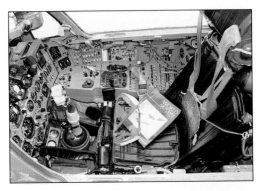

Left: A well-known aviation periodical was seen in the cockpit of one of the Kunmadaras-based 'Fitter-Ks'.

Below: One of the two-seat Sukhoi Su-17UM 'Fitter-Gs' is shown at Kunmadaras. This carries unidentified EW pods on its inboard underwing pylons, perhaps indicating an Elint or 'Wild Weasel' role. Long-range fuel tanks are carried outboard. Bottom (main picture): One of the single-seat Kunmadaras Su-17M-4 'Fitter-Ks'. The centreline reconnaissance pod is identical to those seen on 'Fitter-H' aircraft.

Left: Blue-coded Mikoyan MiG-27D 'Flogger-Js' line up in the early morning sun at Debrecen. The regimental badge was a winged horse, superimposed on a blue and white banner.

located at Sarmellek from Tokol, since they carried red codes, whereas the 'Fulcrums' from the base which visited the Kecskemet air show in August 1990 wore blue codes (01 and UB 70) and Guards badges.

The MiG-29s at Tokol may have been the last Soviet aircraft to leave Hungary, the base finally closing on 5 June 1991. Tokol, also the HQ for the fighter division, and indeed the whole Air Army, also housed a major maintenance and overhaul facility. Mil Mi-8 and Mi-17 'Hips' from many WarPac countries (and from Iraq) were overhauled here.

'Fencer' farewell

Kunmadaras, east of Budapest, housed a reconnaissance/EW regiment equipped with Su-17 'Fitters' and Su-24MR 'Fencer-Es', and almost certainly at least one MiG-27 'Flogger' squadron, and perhaps a whole regiment. These aircraft were visible in the background when the 'Fencers' and 'Fitters' departed on 21 April 1991. No formal farewell ceremony was held, and the departure was announced only a few hours in advance. Fortunately, a handful of journalists was on hand to photograph the aircraft as they left.

The Su-24s wore white codes, and included 01, 02, 03, 04, 05, 06, 07, 09, 10, 11 and 12. The Su-17s included red-coded 'Fitter-Ks' 21, 22, 23, 24, 25,

Above: One of the Debrecen-based MiG-23UBs takes off, afterburner torching brightly.

26, 27, 28, 29 and 31, and Su-17UMs 33, 34 and 35. The single-seaters carried a fuselage-mounted multi-sensor reconnaissance pod (like that normally associated with 'Fitter-H'), while the two-seaters carried small underwing EW pods, perhaps denoting a 'Wild Weasel' or Elint role. The airfield officially closed on 10 May 1991, the 'Floggers' having left quietly in the meantime.

The Soviets in Hungary were always very secretive, and even at the end staged formal withdrawal ceremonies which left aircraft in place at the various bases. At other bases, no public access

Below: The Debrecen MiG-27Ds left after a dawn ceremony in which the regimental standard was paraded.

was arranged, and aircraft left without fanfare, sometimes by night. Thus it still remains unclear as to exactly what aircraft types were based at the two remaining Soviet airfields in Hungary, Csakvar and Kalocsa. These two bases probably housed an Mi-8/Mi-24 attack helicopter wing or two, and perhaps a transport squadron or regiment. The two bases closed on 28 June 1990 and 17 July 1990, respectively.

In future volumes of *World Air Power Journal* we will examine the ongoing Soviet withdrawal from Poland and the former German Democratic Republic.

Cobra Ball and Cobra Eye

Alaskan Observers

Telint gathering is one of the most specialised disciplines in military aviation, requiring the use of aircraft to photograph missiles and re-entry vehicles in flight and to record the telemetry data being relayed to and from the missile. The best-known unit involved in this work is the USAF's 6th Strategic Reconnaissance Wing, based close to the action in Alaska.

Since 1963 the 6th Strategic Reconnaissance Wing (and its predecessors) have flown missions from Alaskan bases aimed at gathering intelligence from Soviet missile tests. Today the main operational equipment is the Boeing RC-135S Cobra platform.

Five miles above the stormy Bering Sea a strip-alert Boeing KC-135R on temporary duty with the Alaska Tanker Task Force completes a heavy fuel offload. The black-winged receiver backs out quickly, turns steeply, and disappears into the night.

Inside the mysterious airplane there is a flurry of activity. After cross-checking each other's positions, the two navigators plot the shortest route to the mission location while the pilots plan a heavyweight climb profile to reach the airplane's maximum altitude. Aft of the cockpit door the remaining crew members are readying the complex sensors which peer unblinkingly into the darkness, looking and listening.

This is the RC-135S Cobra Ball, one of two based at Eielson AFB, Alaska, and flown by crews assigned to the 24th Strategic Reconnaissance Squadron (SRS), 6th Strategic Reconnaissance Wing (SRW). Along with the newest addition to the RC-135 fleet – the RC-135X Cobra Eye – the Cobra Ball operates in conjunction with the Cobra Dane land-based radar at Shemya AFB, Alaska, and the Cobra Judy sea-based radar on board the USNS *Observation Island* as a 'national technical means' of verification and compliance with strategic arms agreements. The Cobra Ball and Cobra Eye fly peripheral reconnaissance missions in international airspace while tracking trajectories and studying ballistic missiles and their associated re-entry vehicles.

The airplanes are normally on 24-hour alert at the 6th SRW's Detachment 1 located at Shemya – popularly known as 'the Rock' – where crews spend two-week tours on alert. Shemya is one of the Near Islands located at the extreme western tip of the Aleutian archipelago at the confluence of the Pacific Ocean and the Bering Sea. This unique location subjects the island to extremely hazardous weather conditions, such as simultaneous 70-mph winds and dense fog. As a result, only the most experienced crews in Strategic Air Command (SAC) are selected to fly the Cobra Ball and the Cobra Eye.

Mission history

The first strategic airplane dedicated to direct intelligence-gathering associated with intercontinental ballistic missiles (ICBMs) was a Boeing B-29 equipped with an infra-red sensor designed to 'sniff' the missile's plume once it was launched. As far as is known, this programme was fairly limited in its scope and technical prowess and its longevity is believed to have been brief.

The first significant reconnaissance platform dedicated to gathering intelligence data on ICBMs was the Boeing EB-47E(TT). During 1958 Boeing converted three B-47E Stratojets into 'Tell Two' telemetry intelligence (Telint) platforms. The Tell Twos were assigned to the 55th SRW at Forbes AFB, Kansas, and routinely operated from Incirlik AB, Turkey, beginning in 1958, and later from other bases in North Africa such as Wheelus AB, Libya, through 1967. In late 1966 at least one Tell Two operated from Shemya. One Tell Two crashed at Incirlik in April 1965.

The EB-47E(TT) carried electronic equipment designed to monitor missile tests from launch to re-entry. Despite the successes of this programme, the Tell Two suffered from a lack of substantive optical collection capability. By late 1961, Air Force Systems Command (AFSC) had begun tests at Wright-Patterson AFB, Ohio, and at Shemya to correct this deficiency.

Nancy Rae

Using Boeing JKC-135A 59-1491 under the operational name Nancy Rae, AFSC developed an optical system to observe and record ballistic vehicle characteristics. Initial flight tests of the airplane and its sensors included flights from Shemya with AFSC and SAC crews on board.

Nancy Rae was transferred to SAC on 1 March 1963, and assigned to the 4157th Strategic Wing (SW) at Eielson. General Dynamics modified the airplane and on 7 October 1963, it was redesignated an RC-135S. It then returned to the 4157th SW and became known operationally as Wanda Belle.

In addition to the Wanda Belle RC-135S, the 4157th SW operated three KC-135A-II Office Boy reconnaissance platforms (redesignated RC-135Ds on 1 January 1965). These three airplanes may have operated in conjunction with the Wanda Belle under a programme known as 'Jig Time'. This association seems to have led aviation historians to conclude that 59-1491 was at some time designated an RC-135D. Clearly

Right: The first RC-135S was 59-1491, originally modified to this configuration under the Nancy Rae codename, which changed to Wanda Belle in its entry into service with the 4157th SW, and finally to Rivet Ball in 1967. Notable features of this first optical tracking and photographic platform were the large optical windows in the side of the fuselage, glass bubble dome in the spine (with black anti-glare paint), 'towel-rail' antennas and underfuselage radome.

This is not the case, as the Wanda Belle was designated an RC-135S over a year before the RC-135D designation was created. In January 1967 the operational name of the RC-135S was changed from Wanda Belle to Rivet Ball.

The Rivet Ball's appearance was radical in the reconnaissance world, but clearly showed its lineage from AFSC testbeds such as those used in the Radiation Monitoring Program (RAMP) and the Terminal Radiation Program/Midcourse Acquisition and Tracking System (TRAP/MATS). The original RC-135S had 10 large-diameter optically-ground windows along the starboard side of the fuselage. Special optical sensors were housed behind these windows. Atop the fuselage was a small glass observation dome. The mission tactical co-ordinator (TC) sat beneath this fairing and, using an old B-50 gunsight, would visually search for the re-entering ballistic missile (or any of its components). Once sighted, the computerised automatic system would then take over to track the objects with the optical sensors. Data was recorded and the airplane returned to Shemya (weather permitting) or Eielson where the tapes and mission reports were prepared for immediate shipment to US intelligence agencies.

Lisa Ann

Beginning on 30 September 1963, Ling-Temco-Vought (LTV) modified a former Military Air Transport Service (MATS) C-135B transport into the sole RC-135E. Delivered on 30 March 1966 to the 4157th SW, the airplane was known operationally as Lisa Ann. In January 1967 the operational name was changed to Rivet Amber.

Like the Wanda Belle, the appearance of the Lisa Ann was anything but orthodox. The

RC-135E had a 12-ft high by 20-ft long fibreglass antenna embedded in the forward fuselage. This antenna did not completely encircle the fuselage and covered only the starboard side from the nose gear well aft to the wing root. The antenna was part of a phased-array radar used for precise

Right: The 55th Strategic Reconnaissance Wing operated the Boeing EB-47E(TT) Tell Two aircraft on Telint gathering missions, notably from Turkey. These operated on an alert basis, launching to record Soviet ICBM tests.

Above: Partnering the RC-135S in the 4157th Strategic Wing's reconnaissance line-up were three KC-135A-II Office Boy aircraft, more commonly known as the RC-135D Cotton Candy.

Right and below: Two views of the sole RC-135E Lisa Ann show the large pods under the wing roots, containing a small auxiliary jet for radar power to port and a heat exchanger to starboard. The large phased-array radar for accurately tracking missiles and re-entry vehicles was located behind the starboard-side dielectric fairing, which may have been responsible for the inflight break-up that caused the Lisa Ann's loss in 1969.

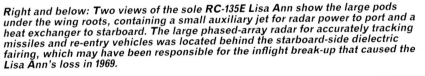

Left: With the loss of 59-1491 Rivet Ball, the 6th Strategic Wing was left without an optical platform, and so the hasty modification was authorised of a pair of C-135B transports to RC-135S Cobra Ball standard. This is the first aircraft in its original configuration.

Above: Cobra Ball I 61-2663 in its current configuration, with only one 'towel-rail' retained.

Below: A characteristic feature of the RC-135S is the teardrop-shaped fairing on the rear fuselage sides containing Sigint receivers.

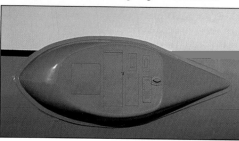

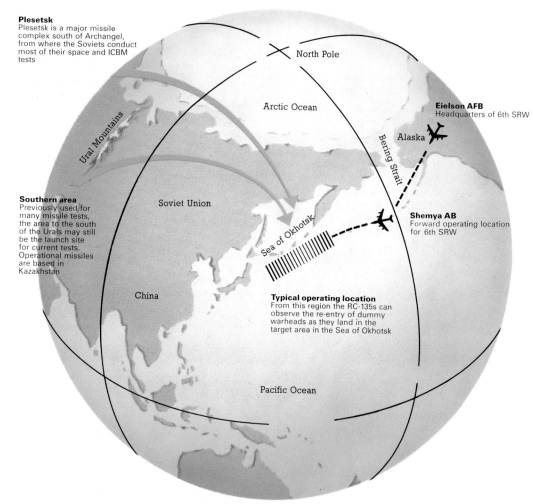

Plesetsk
Plesetsk is a major missile complex south of Archangel, from where the Soviets conduct most of their space and ICBM tests

North Pole

Arctic Ocean

Ural Mountains

Eielson AFB
Headquarters of 6th SRW

Alaska

Bering Strait

Southern area
Previously used for many missile tests, the area to the south of the Urals may still be the launch site for current tests. Operational missiles are based in Kazakhstan

Soviet Union

Sea of Okhotsk

Shemya AB
Forward operating location for 6th SRW

China

Typical operating location
From this region the RC-135s can observe the re-entry of dummy warheads as they land in the target area in the Sea of Okhotsk

Pacific Ocean

The principal operating area for the 6th SRW's fleet is off the Sea of Okhotsk, where re-entry vehicles are aimed from Soviet ICBM tests. Most of these are launched from Plesetsk, south of Archangel, although some may still launch from Kazakhstan and the area south of the Urals. The 6th SRW is headquartered at Eielson AFB in Alaska, but RC-135s forward deploy to Shemya to decrease reaction time to missile launches.

tracking of ballistic missiles. This is the only operational RC-135 variant ever equipped with any kind of side-looking aerial radar (SLAR), despite the widespread reporting of this feature in the aviation literature.

Forward and aft of the fuselage area which housed the powerful radar were thick bulkheads made of lead designed to protect the crew from the considerable radiation produced when the

radar was operating. Once the radar was on, passage from front to back was impossible, an issue of no little concern to the pilots and navigators at the front of the airplane who might need to use the latrine located at the back of the jet!

The other distinguishing feature of the Lisa Ann was the two 37-in diameter by 127-in long pods beneath each wing adjacent to the fuselage. As with so many other misconceptions about the RC-135E, these were neither 'sampling pods' nor extra engines (spawning an 'it just won't die' myth of a 'six-engined' KC-135).

The powerful phased-array radar on the Lisa Ann required a tremendous amount of electrical power, far more than the RC-135E's four engine-driven electrical generators could provide. LTV resolved this power problem by installing a Lycoming T55-L-5 turbojet engine connected to

a 350-kVA generator beneath the left wing.

The phased-array radar and other equipment on the Lisa Ann produced a considerable amount of heat, which would have been both uncomfortable for the crew and damaging to the delicate equipment. Dissipating it proved to be a major problem, solved by installing a heat-exchanger in the pod beneath the right wing.

Major changes

On 1 March 1967, the 4157th SW was inactivated and the 6th SW (formerly the 6th Bombardment Wing from Walker AFB, New Mexico) activated in its place. Prior to this organisational change the crews who flew the Wanda Belle, Lisa Ann and Office Boy airplanes were assigned directly to the 4157th SW's Reconnaissance Division. Following the activation of the 6th SW the crews were assigned to the 24th SRS, whose motto is 'We Observe the Unknown'.

The Rivet Ball and Rivet Amber continued to work together over the next two years observing and recording a burgeoning foreign ICBM development and testing programme. On 13 January 1969, this highly-specialised fleet was cut in half with the loss of the Rivet Ball.

While landing on the icy runway at Shemya, the RC-135S was unable to stop. The Rivet Ball's Pratt & Whitney J57 turbojets lacked thrust reversers, and even the emergency shutdown of the engines failed to prevent the airplane from sliding off the runway and down a steep embankment. Although there was no fire, explosion or loss of life, the fuselage was broken in half, rendering it uneconomical to repair.

Tragedy followed on 5 June 1969, when the RC-135E disappeared utterly into the Bering Sea while returning from Shemya to Eielson. No trace of the airplane or the 19 crew members board has ever been found. Speculation over the disappearance has ranged from structural failure to a Soviet submarine that shot down the airplane with a surface-to-air missile, collected the debris, and then returned to the Soviet Union. Given the extensive nature of the fuselage modifications coupled with two brief transmissions received from the airplane during its last moments, the Rivet Amber likely broke up in flight due to aerodynamic stresses to the highly-altered fuselage. That no trace of the wreckage was found can be attributed to the airplane's inflight break-up, the consequences of impact with the water, and the violent waters of the Bering Sea swallowing the debris.

Replacements

Soon after the loss of the Rivet Ball, two AFSC C-135B testbeds were selected as replacements. This redundancy provided both greater mission coverage and a measure of programme security in the event of the loss of yet another RC-135S. E-Systems modified C-135Bs 61-2663 and 61-2664 into an entirely new RC-135S configuration under the Big Safari programme. The first of these two airplanes – 61-2663 – was designated an RC-135S on 24 October 1969, and was delivered to the 6th SW on 11 January 1970, with the operational name of Cobra Ball I. Cobra Ball II – 61-2664 – arrived at Eielson soon thereafter. No serious plans were made to replace the Rivet Amber.

The Cobra Ball has appeared in a variety of external configurations as its mission evolved and its associated equipment upgraded. The position

The Cobra Ball I nudges towards a KC-135 tanker over Alaska. A distinctive feature of the 6th SRW's aircraft is the black starboard wing and engine nacelles. This negates any glare from these large surfaces which would affect the sensitive side-facing cameras.

Left: The 6th SRW has applied some high-quality nose art to its aircraft, including this maiden of the north. The fist clenching a lightning flash and olive branch is the badge of Strategic Air Command.

Below: A sizeable crew is carried by the Cobra Ball aircraft. The flight crew consists of the standard pilot and co-pilot, behind whom sit two navigators. Doubling up at this station helps to ensure that the aircraft does not stray into prohibited airspace. Back in the cabin are five electronic warfare officers and two equipment technicians.

and number of windows, the shape and location of antennas, and other details vary significantly from the Rivet Ball and from Cobra Ball to Cobra Ball. The Cobra Ball is equipped with TF33-P-5 turbofan engines with thrust reversers, a significant addition after the lesson learned with the loss of the Rivet Ball.

In December 1979 RC-135T 55-3121 was transferred from the 305th Air Refueling Wing (AREFW) at Grissom AFB, Indiana, to the 6th SW. This former reconnaissance platform was equipped with an air refuelling receiver (ARR) receptacle and entered use at Eielson as a flight crew proficiency trainer. Despite its RC-135T

appellation, the airplane had no reconnaissance mission or capability.

On 15 March 1981, RC-135S 61-2664 crashed while attempting to land at Shemya in extremely bad weather, killing six crewmen. Plans to convert sister ship C-135B 61-2662 into a replacement Cobra Ball were undertaken within two weeks, even to the degree that the high-priority acquisition and modification of the airplane received the approval of President Ronald W. Reagan, who then lay in a Washington, DC, hospital after the 30 March 1981 assassination attempt. This immediate approval underscored the importance of the Cobra Ball mission to

Above: Cobra Ball II shivers in the freezing conditions of the Shemya night. The aircraft displays one of many window/antenna arrangements applied to the Cobra Ball fleet, with only three optical windows and no slab fairing on the forward fuselage.

Above: The Cobra Ball II and six crew were lost in 1981. The aircraft was attempting a landing in appalling weather at Shemya, where a memorial was erected with the aircraft's serial plate.

existing and future arms agreements and the monitoring of compliance with them.

After the AFSC satellite communications (Satcom) test equipment was removed, E-Systems converted the airplane into the Cobra Ball III. Redesignated an RC-135S on 2 November 1983, it was delivered to the 6th SW 11 days later.

Other airplanes and missions

From mid-January through to the end of February 1982, the RC-135T had its J57 turbojet engines replaced with former airline Boeing 707 JT3D turbofan engines with thrust reversers. In its absence, the 6th SW used NKC-135E 55-3129 as a trainer.

The Cobra Ball has been used for missions other than reconnaissance, most notably search and rescue. When a US Navy Lockheed P-3 Orion ditched in the bitterly cold northern Pacific Ocean, a Cobra Ball directed the rescue efforts of the nearest surface vessel – a *Soviet* fishing trawler – to successfully recover most of the

crew. This marked the first use of satellite communications in rescue operations. Since the Cobra Ball was unable to communicate directly with the trawler, its satellite messages were sent to a SAC command post which then telephoned the messages to a port city in the eastern Soviet Union which in turn transmitted them to the trawler.

On 30 July 1982, an RC-135S assisted in the rescue of the crew of a US Coast Guard Lockheed C-130 Hercules which had crashed on Attu Island near Shemya. The Cobra Ball has also been used in the medical evacuation of critically ill personnel from Shemya to the hospital at Elmendorf AFB at Anchorage, Alaska.

On 25 February 1985, the RC-135T crashed into a mountain near Valdez, Alaska, following a missed approach in poor weather. All three crewmen on board perished. Despite intensive search efforts (including search flights by Lockheed SR-71As) the wreckage was not located until 2 August 1985.

Prior to the crash of the RC-135T, plans were underway to transfer it to the 55th SRW (now at Offutt AFB, Nebraska) in July 1985 for use as a reconnaissance trainer by RC-135U/V/W flight crews assigned to the 38th SRS. The RC-135T would be replaced by newly-converted TC-135S 62-4133, which was delivered to the 6th SW on 22 July 1985.

By outward appearances the TC-135S replaced the RC-135T because it crashed, but the TC-135S had been intended to replace the RC-135T any-

The fated Cobra Ball II seen at Offutt AFB, Nebraska, the SAC headquarters. This base houses the RC-135U/V/W fleet of the 55th Strategic Reconnaissance Wing, which often uses Alaskan bases to fly standard signals intelligence gathering missions.

way. The 55th SRW was thus forced to continue using KC-135E 59-1514 as a trainer until funds could be made available for the conversion of TC-135W 62-4129.

The next generation

On 1 April 1988, the 6th SW was redesignated the 6th SRW to emphasise its primary reconnaissance role (the wing also hosts the Alaska Tanker Task Force – ATTF – and Eielson is home to the KC-135Es and KC-135Ds of the 168th Air Refueling Squadron (AREFS) of the Alaska Air National Guard).

After nearly six years of modification and technological delays, the 6th SRW received its newest airplane on 16 July 1989. RC-135X 62-4128 – known operationally as the Cobra Eye – is jointly sponsored by the US Army and Air Force and collects data on strategic weapons systems and targets of interest to the US Army's Strategic Defense Command and the US Strategic Defense Initiative Organization (SDIO).

The first RC-135X operational reconnaissance mission took place on 15 August 1989. In recognition of their efforts to make this extremely complicated reconnaissance platform fully operational, the crew received the 1989 General Jerome F. O'Malley Award for the Best Reconnaissance Crew in the Air Force.

Cobra crews

Crews from the 24th SRS deploy to Shemya for two weeks and return again after periods of from one to four weeks. Every effort is made to keep assigned crews together for each trip, although illness, temporary duty to other bases, training programmes and 'baby watch' all mean that substitutions are common. At least one pilot and one navigator from a given crew must fly together on operational missions. This improves safety and crew co-ordination, reduces the potential for accidents and enhances mission effectiveness.

Crew selection is critical to the Cobra Ball and Cobra Eye programmes. Since two airplanes have been lost in landing accidents at Shemya, there is considerable emphasis on safety and training, particularly approaches and landings. Not every pilot selected for training has completed this rigorous check-out programme.

The aircraft commander (AC) must be an instructor pilot and have a minimum of 2,500 total flying hours just to be eligible for selection to the

programme. Once selected, aircraft commanders must become qualified in receiver air refuelling (if not already), fly a minimum number of operational sorties as an observer with a fully-qualified crew, and complete a demanding Shemya check-out programme. This requires the prospective AC to fly a number of each type of instrument approaches to each runway at Shemya under both day and night conditions and make at least three Shemya landings with direct crosswinds between 20 and 25 kt.

Following this training programme the AC must pass a comprehensive inflight evaluation. After successfully completing this check ride he must then certify his mastery of operational and mission knowledge in an oral examination before the 6th SRW wing commander. At this point he is then assigned to a mission-ready crew.

No co-pilots are assigned to the Cobra Ball and Cobra Eye directly from pilot training. All average a minimum of approximately 500 total flying hours. Although the co-pilot check-out programme is not as rigorous as it is for ACs, it is still very demanding.

Given the combination of routinely flying under extreme weather conditions (Cobra Ball and Cobra Eye crews *train* in weather conditions that other SAC crews might see only once or

Hangarage for the RC-135s is provided at both Shemya and Eielson, although all but the most routine maintenance is carried out at Eielson. This aircraft is the Cobra Ball III, which arrived in service in November 1983. The aircraft is still current, in this external configuration.

Swiftly approved and converted, 61-2662 was the replacement for the crashed Cobra Ball. Refuelling for the 6th SRW's fleet is provided by KC-135s of the Alaskan Tanker Task Force, based at Eielson and including the based aircraft of the Alaska Air National Guard's 168th Air Refueling Squadron. Shown here is a CONUS-based KC-135A on TDY to the ATTF.

twice during a three-year assignment) on missions of national priority, all under the aegis of highly experienced instructor pilots, Cobra Ball and Cobra Eye co-pilots rank among the best-trained future ACs in SAC.

RC-135S and RC-135X crews fly with two navigators. Like the co-pilot, the second navigator – known as the 'Nav 2' – must have previous experience prior to assignment to the 24th SRS. The Nav 2 duties include manual reckoning as an independent means of confirming the aircraft's position as determined by the airplane's inertial navigation system.

After some 200 hours of flying Cobra Ball or Cobra Eye missions, Nav 2s can upgrade to first navigator – 'Nav 1'. The Nav 1 is responsible for all of the navigation and mission timing (with tolerances measured in feet and seconds rather than the more traditional miles and minutes). As with the pilots, both navigators must pass a comprehensive inflight examination and certify their mission readiness before being assigned to operational crews.

The backenders

Fliers in the Air Force are often thought of only as pilots and occasionally as navigators or

Cobra Ball and Cobra Eye: Alaskan Observers

Above: Another refuelling view of a Cobra Ball shows off to good effect the black wing and engine nacelles, which have their original grey finish on the outside. With the exception of the rear fuselage teardrop Sigint receivers, virtually all of the aircraft's sensors are ranged to starboard, requiring the aircraft to be facing the right way during the critical portion of the Telint mission.

Below: After having used RC-135T 55-3121 for some time as a crew trainer, the 6th Strategic Wing had the specially-converted TC-135S 62-4133 delivered. For a while it wore a smart fin-stripe and wing badge on the 'Milky Way' SAC sash on the fuselage.

weapons systems officers. Seldom does anyone remember the many mission specialists (the 'backenders') who operate the complicated equipment aboard some of the Air Force's most sophisticated airplanes. Often denigrated as 'SLEBs' – self-loading excess baggage – these mission specialists are the very reason that the more visible and recognised flight crew 'drives the bus'.

The mission crew on the Cobra Ball includes five electronic warfare officers (popularly known as 'ravens'), one of whom is the TC, a photo technician (PT), and an inflight maintenance technician (IMT). The ravens operate the reconnaissance equipment and co-ordinate with the flight crew to place the airplane in the best position to observe the re-entry. The PT ensures that the optical equipment on board is working properly and can repair it in flight if necessary. The IMT monitors the onboard systems and can repair them during flight should they fail. A Cobra Eye backend crew includes only a sensor operator, a sensor technician and a TC.

Flying missions in the Cobra Ball and Cobra Eye is undeniably a team effort, and effective crew co-ordination means safe flying and a successful collection.

A trip to 'the Rock'

Mission planning for a deployment to Shemya begins two days prior to departure. The flight crew plans the route from Eielson to Shemya, reviews and schedules necessary training and files the appropriate paperwork. The mission crew reviews its training requirements and anticipated mission requirements for the deployment.

The day prior to departure the crews meet for a morning pre-deployment briefing which includes current intelligence, threat analysis and mission requirements. Nothing is scheduled for the afternoon so that crew members can arrange their personal affairs prior to departure.

The most common activity during the afternoon is grocery shopping. Crews are housed in dormitory-like facilities within the airplane hangars at Shemya to ensure a quick response to an impending launch. There is a large kitchen on each floor and some crews plan common meals – especially at holidays, although the most common food is anything frozen and anything that can be cooked in the kitchen's several microwave ovens. (Both the RC-135S and RC-135X have microwave ovens on board, and crews provide their own inflight meals.)

The trip to 'the Rock' often includes a practice air refuelling from one of the ATTF KC-135s. The flight is usually made in the squadron's TC-135S unless it is undergoing maintenance. In the absence of the TC-135S, Cobra Ball and Cobra Eye flight crews are also qualified to fly the KC-135As and KC-135Qs at the ATTF, and some crews are also qualified in the ATTF's KC-135Rs.

With an air refuelling *en route* to 'the Rock', the flying time is in the order of 4½ to 5 hours. Halfway there the crew crosses Bethel, Alaska, and joins the Amber 590 Pacific Oceanic jet route. Airliners flying between the United States and the Orient often fly on this jet route, and Cobra Ball crews share this airspace with airliners of a variety of nations. This is purely coincidental, despite several conspiracy-minded lunatics who claim that this is a secret rendezvous procedure to mask the reconnaissance plane by flying it in concert with a civil airliner on a scheduled route.

Crews will not begin their descent into Shemya if the weather is below required minima. Instead, the crews orbit above the island until they have just enough fuel to return to Eielson. If at that point the weather is suitable, they land at Shemya; otherwise they return home and try again the next day.

After landing the airplane is refuelled (if needed) and maintenance personnel correct any discrepancies. The most eager people meeting the relay are the crew members going home. Long lines form as suitcases and ice chests filled with food are passed down to waiting pick-up trucks while dirty laundry bags and empty coolers are passed up into the airplane's waiting cargo bins.

The arriving crew members attend a short briefing to review mission changes, weather forecasts (aptly described in unprintable terms) and items of administrative interest. By this time the 'go-home' crew is airborne *en route* to Eielson, with flight times home typically around three hours.

Fantasy island

Shemya Island is some two miles wide by four miles long. It has few creature comforts, and both crews and permanent party personnel assigned to Shemya are both resourceful and innovative in avoiding boredom. By far one of the most popular things to do at Shemya is an 'Island Tour', where a crew piles into its four-door pick-up truck and drives around the island.

Shemya was first used in 1943 as a base for Convair B-24 and Lockheed P-38 operations against Japanese targets, including adjacent Attu Island. Among the landmarks which remain from this period are the bunkers and fortifications prepared to repel a Japanese invasion. Two graves on the island are the final resting place of two Russians, probably fur trappers, who were buried on the island in 1926 and 1930. A large open-pit quarry fills the centre of the island and is known as the 'Grand Canyon'.

No island tour would be complete without seeing the 'drive-in movie theatre', the nickname for the immense Cobra Dane over-the-horizon

Above: In addition to its training role, the TC-135S is used as a support vehicle for the wing's deployment to Shemya, shuttling replacement crews and supplies to 'the Rock'. The aircraft has no reconnaissance equipment, and so has a capacious cabin for freight carriage.

Above: The TC-135S seen shortly after its conversion from EC-135B standard and its delivery to the 6th Strategic Wing. The primary role of the aircraft is to provide continuation training (including inflight refuelling) for the Cobra Ball/Eye crews, for which reason the aircraft features the black wings and 'thimble' radome of the operational machines. Consideration was given to sending Cobra Ball aircraft to the Gulf to help in the 'Scud' war, but in the event only the TC-135S was used in Desert Storm, being employed on transport and crew shuttle duties in support of the 55th SRW's RC-135U/V/W war detachment.

Left: Exceptional 6th SRW nose-art quality is maintained by the TC-135S, which features this Pegasus design. The aircraft itself is named North Star.

phased array radar located on the northwest corner of the island. Final stop for any island tour is Building 600, home of Shemya pizza and ice cream (deliveries permitting), and a small exchange and commissary facility popularly known as 'Macy's'.

Several days each week (weather permitting), military supply planes and commercial airliners visit Shemya with perishables and mail. The arrival of fresh milk or a two-day-old newspaper at Macy's is likely to cause a rumble as everyone rushes to buy what they need before the stock is depleted.

A 'gronk'

Each airplane at Shemya is housed inside its own large hangar to protect it from the severe weather. The airplane is 'cocked on', ready for an immediate engine start, much like the tankers, airborne command posts and bombers which sit alert at SAC bases around the world. A tug is hooked to the Cobra Ball, ready to push it out-

The sole RC-135X is seen on test during its development. Notable is the large 'farm' of wool tufts on the sensor fairing on the forward starboard fuselage, these being photographed to test the airflow around the bulge. The aircraft was modified from a C-135B.

side at a moment's notice. Since missions are often flown without notice, ground crews and flight crews pride themselves on the speed and efficiency of their 'back-out'.

The klaxon that launches an operational reconnaissance mission can sound at any time, and usually does. Known as a 'gronk' or a 'horn', this klaxon notification begins a series of events involving flight crews, mission crews, maintenance and staff personnel, the base fire department, and airfield controllers who work together to launch the airplane in a matter of minutes.

With everyone onboard the jet, the crew chief removes the boarding stand and closes the entry hatches, and the tug begins to push the airplane outside the hangar. The co-pilot updates the weather, computes the take-off data and completes the scramble checklist. Both navigators ensure that the airplane's sophisticated inertial navigation system is warming up properly and that all mission materials are on board.

Once outside the hangar the tug stops, and the RC-135's engines are started quickly and the airplane is stabilised on internal power. Now disconnected from all ground equipment, the Cobra Ball taxies to the runway and gets a 'last-chance' inspection by the detachment commander to ensure that all hatches and panels are

Cobra Eye introduces a very sophisticated optical tracking system for missiles and re-entry vehicles, a far cry from the early days of Nancy Rae when the targets were acquired visually. The Cobra Eye data has significant SDI application.

shut, the flaps and trim are properly set and there are no abnormalities with the airplane.

At the end of the runway, the Cobra Ball turns around to align itself with the runway and sits in silence as the crew completes last-minute cockpit checks. When ready to launch, the co-pilot flashes the landing light and the tower clears the airplane for an immediate departure. In a matter of minutes, the Cobra Ball is airborne with an absolute minimum of radio traffic to avoid compromising the mission.

The mission

As the Cobra Ball begins to climb towards its cruising altitude everyone on board is working at a fever pitch. The aircraft commander flies the airplane while the two navigators provide headings and wind drift information. The co-pilot begins the huge stack of mission paperwork, which includes flight time records, an engine analysis sheet, a structural performance data sheet and training records. The co-pilot also

completes the complicated message and call sign charts used to communicate with other agencies throughout the mission.

Soon after launch the crew learns if a tanker has been launched to refuel the Cobra Ball in flight, extending its duration and loiter time on station, a fairly regular occurrence. Because of the bad weather at Shemya, the Cobra Ball must return there with sufficient fuel to try a few approaches and then divert back home to Eielson. Even on a short training mission a tanker is commonplace to ensure that the Cobra Ball has sufficient fuel after leaving its orbit area to return to Shemya, orbit as long as needed and then either land or divert to Eielson.

The raven crew is busy readying its equipment. The system runs self-tests which determine the degree to which the equipment is operating properly. Any discrepancies are corrected immediately by restarting the system or having the PT or IMT repair or replace the defective part.

By the time the airplane is levelled off at its cruising altitude most of this activity has abated and the crew begins the most tedious portion of the mission – the wait. Sometimes the wait is short, a blessing for everyone on board. Sometimes the wait is long, agony for everyone on board. Word of a second tanker usually means a very long mission – perhaps 12 hours or so. Rare are the 'megadeath' sorties, those with a third or fourth tanker, which can last up to 24 hours or more. Experienced flyers remember to bring their lunch boxes and drinks, mindful that an 18-hour sortie without at least a snack can become a nightmare. New crew members make that mistake only once.

Bringing home the bacon

Since the Cobra Ball and Cobra Eye react in anticipation of a ballistic missile launch, there is no guarantee that any will take place. On these fruitless missions the crews jokingly refer to their

collection as 'tuna' in honour of the fish that ply the icy waters beneath the orbiting airplane. These uneventful missions are nicknamed 'tuna patrols'.

Should there be a missile launch, the crew works together to ensure that the airplane is at the correct altitude and on the correct heading to provide the best possible look-angle to view and record the event. Duration of the re-entry event can range from nonexistent – should the objects of interest break up during flight or re-entry – to perhaps a minute or two, depending on the number of objects which re-enter the atmosphere.

The equipment on board the Cobra Ball observes and records each object as it re-enters the atmosphere. According to published sources, the RC-135S's technical capabilities are believed to be similar to those of the Boeing EC-135E and Boeing EC-18B Advanced Range Instrumentation Aircraft (ARIA), which have both been used

Above: On the port side of the RC-135X's nose is this splendid artwork representing the Cobra Eye codename. The aircraft is probably the most advanced aerial photographic platform.

Above: Cobra Eye became operational in August 1989, and flies missions from Shemya alongside the regular Cobra Ball missions. When the onboard camera system is not in use, it is covered by a sliding door, in front of which is an airflow baffle.

Below: the RC-135X Cobra Eye aircraft is considerably cleaner aerodynamically than any of the Cobra Ball configurations. However, within the airframe is a highly sophisticated reconnaissance system, with superb missile tracking and photographic systems.

to monitor American missile tests. The Cobra Ball combines the electronic means of the ARIA with an optical capability more advanced than the RAMP/TRAP/MATS systems.

Equipment reportedly installed in the Cobra Ball includes a ballistic framing camera system (BFCS) and a medium resolution camera system (MRCS). According to one source, "the BFCS images all the objects of interest in the re-entry phase, while the [MRCS] photographs individual re-entry vehicles, . . . determin[ing] the re-entry vehicle size. Size estimates are used in turn to produce estimates of the explosive yield of the warheads."

The information the Cobra Ball collects is used to verify foreign compliance with international arms agreements and helps to determine the degree of development of foreign ballistic missile technology.

After a successful collection (or upon mission termination as directed by the Cobra Ball's command authorities), the airplane begins the trip back to Shemya. The raven crew stays busy completing its mission paperwork and logs. The co-pilot gets a weather update and computes the appropriate approach and landing data.

Shemya landings

Landing at 'the Rock' ranges from the most boring of routine landings to those guaranteed to turn even the most seasoned flier into a white-knuckled pilot. Shemya's unique weather patterns mean that not just one or perhaps two landing hazards or illusions exist simultaneously, but virtually all exist at the same time.

A night approach through multilayered cloud decks, across a black reference-less ocean with an upsloping approach end on the runway, coupled with 25 kt of direct crosswind gusting and changing directions at a moment's notice, wind shear, ground fog, limited forward visibility and a case of the 'leans' (spatial disorientation) all combine to make each approach a unique experience.

The pilots and navs work together to land the airplane. Using sophisticated computers onboard the airplane, the navs report the airplane's actual ground speed and wind drift to the pilots, critical information in the avoidance of and safe passage through any wind shears. The navs also handle communication with the safety observers on the ground who monitor each approach and landing and who can, in the event of trouble, direct a go-around. The tower observer provides constant wind reports throughout the approach.

The pilot flying the airplane must use precise instrument techniques to fly the instrument approach to decision height where he will determine if it is safe to continue the approach to land. The natural tendency at this point is to peek out of the window and to fly the airplane towards the runway using only visual cues, but strong and gusty crosswinds will usually blow the airplane off course too far for a safe landing before the pilot can visually recognise the drift. Since the runway at Shemya is fairly short and often wet or icy, it is critical that the airplane be on speed and altitude as it begins its transition to land. Even five kt of excess airspeed can be enough to make the airplane land too long, leaving inadequate stopping distance in the remaining runway.

The other pilot completes the pre-landing checklist, gets landing clearance and provides the

At rest the Cobra Ball is an impressive sight. It is one part of a combined US effort aimed at gaining Telint from ICBM test launches, working in close concert with a fixed phased-array radar (Cobra Dane) on Shemya island and a similar but smaller shipboard radar (Cobra Judy).

pilot flying the approach with updates on airspeed, altitude and course deviations. He also looks out of the windows to identify visual cues associated with the runway environment that will help the pilot safely land the jet.

Shemya landings, especially those in severe or gusty crosswinds, are quite unlike the ideal airliner landing. A firm, solid landing at 'the Rock' helps overcome potential problems with crosswinds and hydroplaning on wet runways and kills excess energy, allowing the airplane to slow more effectively. The Cobra Ball and Cobra Eye use thrust reversers to slow down; these add an increased measure of safety to each landing.

After the mission comes maintenance and post-mission crew debriefs, and the necessary evil of completing the mission paperwork. A cold beer or other liquid refreshment helps relieve the accumulated hours of tension acquired during the flight. Not surprisingly, crews soon find themselves asleep after what is usually a long and tiring mission. After a minimum of crew rest, they are ready to respond again to the next klaxon.

Global implications

There is an undefined mystique about black airplanes. The Lockheed U-2 and SR-71 represent quintessential strategic aerial reconnaissance platforms. The Lockheed F-117 epitomises the future development of discreet operational platforms.

The black-winged Cobra Ball and Cobra Eye extend this mystique. The remote operating locations haunted by the RC-135S and RC-135X add to their nebulous reputations.

The world today is less at risk from a nuclear exchange between the superpowers because of the efforts of the men and women who have flown the dangerous and demanding no-notice operational reconnaissance missions aboard these black-winged jets. When world leaders sign international accords agreeing to limit the number and capabilities of their nuclear-tipped missiles, they do so with the understanding that national technical means like the Cobra Ball will verify their good faith in complying with these agreements. This verification reinforces the trust necessary to ensure that a nuclear exchange must never happen.

A Cobra Ball launches from Shemya on a 'gronk' alert mission. These are carried out swiftly to maximise the chance of getting in position before the missile re-entry vehicles arrive in the target area, and are as radio-silent as possible for security reasons.

Airplane Roster

MDS	Operational Name	Delivered	Status
55-3121 RC-135T		Dec 79	crashed 5 Feb 85
59-1491 JKC-135A	Nancy Rae	1961	redesignated 28 Feb 63
RC-135S	Wanda Belle	1 Mar 63	redesignated 31 Dec 66
RC-135S	Rivet Ball	1 Jan 67	crashed 13 Jan 69
61-2662 RC-135S	Cobra Ball III	2 Nov 83	current
61-2663 RC-135S	Cobra Ball I	24 Oct 69	current
61-2664 RC-135S	Cobra Ball II	Jan 70	crashed 15 Mar 81
62-4128 RC-135X	Cobra Eye	16 Jul 89	current
62-4133 TC-135S		22 Jul 85	current
62-4137 RC-135E	Lisa Ann	30 Mar 66	redesignated 31 Dec 66
RC-135E	Rivet Amber	1 Jan 67	crashed 5 Jun 69

Unit Service Chronology

4157th SW		
1961	28 Feb 67	
6th SW		
1 Mar 67	31 Mar 88	
6th SRW		
1 Apr 88	current	

Above: Refuelling is often necessary on Telint missions, as the RC-135 may have to wait some time for the missile launch due to technical delays. In addition to optical equipment the Cobra Ball carries receivers to record telemetry data being downlinked from the missile.

Above: Shemya is singularly bleak and uninviting, and the short and often icy runway makes landing in bad weather very difficult. All of the 6th SRW's aircraft are now powered by the TF33 turbofan, which has thrust reversers and sufficient power for safe go-rounds.

Below: Just another day at the 'office' for 6th SRW crewmen. Shemya is blighted with some of the worst weather to be encountered by airmen anywhere in the world, so the hand-picked 6th SRW crews are among the most experienced at bad-weather flying.

Far East Air Arms: Southern Region

The southern Far East region, encompassing South East Asia and the island states, represents a fascinating mix of nations with widely contrasting economic backgrounds and political ideologies. Some of the nations are extremely rich (Brunei, Singapore) while others (Laos, Kampuchea) are among the lowest in economic standing in the world. Although superpower influences are not as great as in the northern Far East region, the continuing battle between Communist and capitalist causes wide rifts not only between several nations in the area, but also within many of the countries themselves. The effects of the 'domino' theory in South East Asia (where Thailand faces Communist pressure from Laos, Kampuchea and Vietnam) requires that Thai forces be on constant alert. Air power in the region is on the whole relatively capable, with F-5s and A-4s the dominant types. More importantly, and as a counter to Vietnam's MiG force, Thailand, Indonesia and Singapore have all introduced the F-16 in recent years.

Brunei's (at present) small Air Wing has only helicopters its front-line equipment. The BO 105CB is in use with No. Sqn at Brunei Airport.

Training for the Air Wing's helicopter fleet is accomplishe using the Bell 206 JetRanger, which serves with No. 3 Squadron.

The principal equipment for No. 1 Sqn at Berakas Camp is the twin-engined Bell 212, used for oil rig support and arm transport.

Most of the Bell 212s wear a camouflage scheme, but this machine has a smarter civil-style scheme for staff transpo. The larger 214ST is used for rescue duties.

BRUNEI

Royal Brunei Armed Forces – Air Wing

Enjoying the world's highest per capita income thanks to massive oil resources, Brunei has plenty of money to spend on defence, should it wish. In fact, although Brunei's air arm has been operating helicopters since 1965, expansion has only gathered pace since the country assumed full responsibility (from the UK) for external as well as internal affairs, in 1984.

In late 1989, an intention to order 16 BAe Hawk 100/200s was announced, as part of an expansion plan which also includes developing a fixed-wing maritime patrol capability, possibly with CN-235s from the IPTN production line in Indonesia.

Having previously operated Bell 205A Iroquois, the air wing later standardised on twin-engined Bell 212s, and now flies 12 on oil rig patrol and army support duties. Six MBB BO 105CB armed helicopters were acquired in 1981. A single Bell 214ST is used for SAR, while two Bell 206B JetRangers are trainers.

Fixed-wing training is conducted on four SIAI-Marchetti SF.260W Warriors.

Order of Battle

UNIT	EQUIPMENT	BASE
1 Sqn	Bell 212, 214ST	Berakas Camp
2 Sqn	BO 105	Brunei Airport
3 Sqn	SF.260, Bell 206	Brunei Airport

BURMA (MYANMAR)

Myanmar Air Force

Ever since independence in 1948, the government in Rangoon has struggled to exert control over the far-flung forested uplands to the north and east. For almost all of that time, military or military-controlled regimes have fought periodic campaigns against entrenched Communist and ethnic guerrillas. These include the Karen and Shan, which seek independence, and in the meantime finance their insurgency by cultivating and selling opium.

Burma was renamed Myanmar in 1989, and continues to profess strict non-alignment. It has therefore received little military aid from the major power blocks, and the repressive nature of the current government makes the provision

[map showing Brunei Airport, Berakas Camp, BRUNEI, MALAYSIA (SABAH), MALAYSIA (SARAWAK), INDONESIA (BORNEO)]

rrently the only fixed-wing type in the Brunei Air Wing is the *SIAI-Marchetti SF.260W Warrior*, used for training pilots destined for the helicopter force. e role of these aircraft will expand as the nation acquires its first fixed-wing equipment in the shape of the Hawk light attack fighter, 16 of which are on er to provide a considerable increase in available air power for the small, oil-rich state.

licopters have proved very useful to *Burma (Myanmar)* during the fighting against ethnic d Communist guerrillas operating in the country. Bell *UH-1s* were supplied in the d-1970s, and several are still in service.

an attempt to upgrade its forces in the face of stiffening guerrilla resistance, the yanmar air force has recently acquired *SOKO G-4 Super Galebs* from Yugoslavia, the first xport success for this light attack platform/advanced trainer.

The *Myanmar* air force bases its aircraft at Mingalodon and Meiktila, but other air bases in the nation are available, those in the north being close to the areas of fighting.

of such aid even more unlikely. The country is unable to finance major weapons purchases on its own account.

The Tamdaw Lay therefore flies a mix of propeller-driven transports and trainers on army support duties. The only jets to see recent service are six survivors of about 15 Lockheed T-33A armed trainers supplied by the US in the late 1960s, but these are now grounded. In 1975-76, a dozen SIAI-Marchetti SF.260 piston-engined trainers were acquired, followed by 15 Pilatus PC-7 turbo-trainers in 1979-80 and four of the more powerful PC-9 version in 1986. These have been equipped at various times with air-to-ground rockets and (at least the PC-9s) with podded light machine-guns.

A few of these aircraft have been lost to anti-aircraft fire, believed to be from small-arms, but the greatest threat to continuing offensive operations by the Tamdaw Lay is probably shortages of spare parts and avgas, which forced the sale of the SF.260s. In 1990, Myanmar attempted to acquire a jet trainer/ground-attack aircraft in the form of 20 G-4 Super Galebs from Yugoslavia. These, however, are powered by Rolls-Royce engines, and may be embargoed because of Burma's poor human-rights record. Accordingly, China is offering to supply F-6 (MiG-19) fighter-bombers instead, along with F-7 (MiG-21) interceptors.

The familiar 'Huey' has been the major helicopter type, although the fleet has dwindled through accidents and shoot-downs since 18 were supplied by the US in 1975. They have been supplanted by some Mil Mi-2s from Polish licence-production, and 20-30 PZL W-3 Sokol medium-lift helicopters have been ordered. Some of the 14 Aérospatiale Alouettes received may still be flying, but 10 avgas-reliant

Kawasaki-Bell 47Gs were sold.

Transport aircraft play an important part in shuttling troops and equipment to remote areas. Five Fairchild-Hiller FH-227 (licence-built Fokker F27) turboprops were acquired second-hand in 1978. They were militarised by the addition of a side-cargo door, and replaced the TL's remaining C-47s. Another F27 was used as a staff transport, but two FH-227/F27s have been written off, and the military also uses the F27s of Myanmar Airways. For light STOL transport, Pilatus supplied at least four PC-6A Porters and five PC-6B Turbo-Porters. Some Cessna 180s are also in use.

The main TL base is at Mingaladon, which is also Rangoon's civil airport. The second base is at Meiktila, closer to the counter-insurgency areas. The country's other main airfields are at Lashio, Mandalay and Moulmein.

Order of Battle

EQUIPMENT	QUANTITY
Armed trainers	
SOKO G-4 Super Galeb	6
Pilatus PC-7	c.15
Pilatus PC-9	4
Transports	
Fairchild/Hiller FH-227	4
Pilatus PC-6A Porter	4
Pilatus PC-6B Turbo Porter	5
Cessna 180	
Helicopters	
Bell UH-1	survivors of 18
PZL/Mil Mi-2	
PZL W-3 Sokol	

INDONESIA

Indonesian Air Force (TNI-AU)

Indonesia is the world's fifth most-populous nation, spread across 13,000 islands in a 3,000-mile-long chain. Despite this, the Indonesian air force is one of the region's smallest, with only three combat jet squadrons. It was not always thus, since the air force was the recipient of over 170 Soviet fighters and transports during the period following independence, when President Sukarno ruled. But Soviet influence was eradicated when he was removed in 1965 following an abortive Communist coup, and the army under President Suharto has ruled the country ever since, in practice.

Although the Suharto regime has retained a large number of men under arms – the air force alone has 27,000 – it has not invested heavily in modern weapons. It has, however, sponsored a number of high-profile development projects, one of these being a state aircraft industry. A fair proportion of the CASA C.212 Aviocar transports, AS 330 Puma and MBB BO 105 helicopters produced under licence by IPTN from the mid-1970s has been delivered to the Indonesian armed forces, although an equal

proportion has gone to the country's airlines and oil industry support organisations. The latest production programmes at IPTN are similarly designed for both civil and military consumption – the CN-235 regional transport, plus the AS 332 Super Puma and the Bell 412 medium helicopters.

The rather top-heavy structure of the Indonesian air force was slimmed down in 1985 when two operational commands were formed. These control air activity in the western (Koopsau 1, HQ Jakarta) and eastern (Koopsau 2, HQ Ujung Pandang) halves of the archipelago.

Before the recent arrival of 12 General Dynamics F-16 multi-role fighters (eight single-seat F-16As and four two-seat F-16Bs), the sole air-defence squadron was the one based at Madiun and operating the 12 Northrop F-5Es and four F-5Fs received in 1980.

Madiun is also the home base for the first batch of 14 A-4E Skyhawk attack aircraft and two TA-4H trainers, also received in 1980. These were reconditioned former Israeli aircraft, although the religious sensitivity of this Muslim country meant that the sale was negotiated via the US. A second batch of similar size followed in 1985, to equip a second squadron.

The Skyhawks are equipped for aerial refuelling, enabling them to be rapidly deployed with the aid of two KC-130B Hercules transports. The Indonesian air force was an early customer for the Herc, taking 10 C-130Bs in the late 1950s

Indonesia received the British Aerospace Hawk in the mid-1980s for its advanced training requirement. These serve with 103 Skwadron at Madiun.

Indonesia's small attack force comprises two squadrons McDonnell Douglas A-4E Skyhawks, one at Madiun and at Pekanbaru.

For most of the 1980s the F-5Es of 14 Skwadron Udara represented Indonesia's air defence, but these have since been augmented by F-16s.

Used principally for counter-insurgency operations, the Rockwell OV-10F Bronco can carry rocket pods and has internal machine-guns.

The large expanse of area covered by the islands of the Indonesian nation requires a large transport force. Fokker F27s help equip Jakarta-based 2 Skwadron Udara.

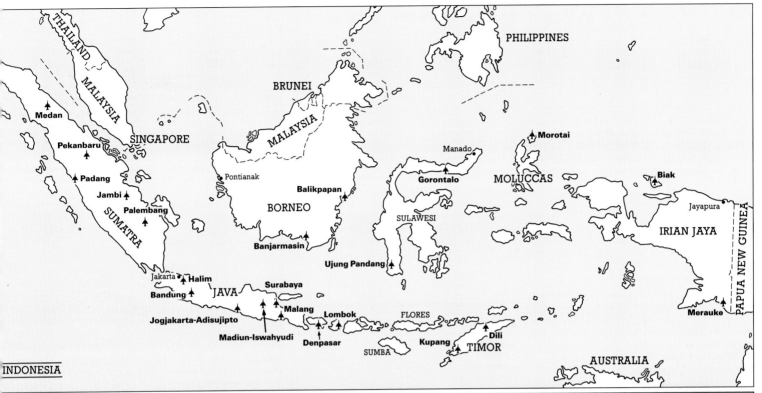

INDONESIA

...kwadron is a transport
...t with F27s, C-47s and
...212s.

Long-range VIP transport was the domain of this Boeing
707. Other Boeings on strength are 737 Surveillers, although
these are currently undergoing a refit.

An unusual type in TNI-AU service is the FFA AS.202 Bravo,
which equips the primary training unit (101 Skwadron) at
the Air Force Academy.

...kwadron has a fleet of
...t aircraft for transport
...ies.

Prime transport of the TNI-AU is the Lockheed Hercules,
which equips two squadrons. One of the squadrons
contains several of the stretched C-130H-30 model.

Used widely on a variety of duties, the Polish-designed
PZL-104 Wilga was built under licence in Indonesia for the
army, which knows it as the Gelatik.

...Skwadron is one of the
...o A-4E units, based at
...diun.

14 Skwadron is one two
TNI-AU air defence units,
equipped with F-5Es.

A division badge is worn on
the fins of A-4 Skyhawks and
F-5E Tiger IIs.

After a primary course on the Bravo, students move to the
Beech T-34C Turbo-Mentor for the basic course,
accomplished with 102 Skwadron of the Academy.

(and another three from surplus USAF stocks in 1975). A second Hercules squadron was formed when, from 1978, the service took delivery of 12 later-model Hercules, comprising seven stretched C-130H-30s and an L-100-30, three C-130Hs, and another C-130H equipped for maritime patrol. This last was a strange choice, given that the service also decided to buy three maritime patrol versions of the Boeing 737-200, equipped with Motorola side-looking radar. These Boeings were under-used, but are currently undergoing an upgrade.

Eight Fokker F27 Friendships delivered in 1978 provide the main capability in a third transport squadron, backed up by 10 NC.212 Aviocars, which have replaced most of the C-47s. A light transport squadron also operates some NC.212 Aviocars, plus a miscellany of Cessnas (six 180s, five 207s, four 401s and two 402s). After protracted delay, the first CN-235s are now being delivered.

The 16 Rockwell OV-10 Bronco light attack aircraft delivered from 1976 have seen combat action, for this massive country is by no means peaceful. The Broncos have been used during army campaigns to suppress independence-seeking guerrillas in East Timor and elsewhere. Helicopters are also important for this purpose, but the army and the air force appear to be rivals in supplying the equipment. The air force contribution comprises two squadrons equipped with Pumas, Super Pumas and 12 Sikorsky S-58Ts (turbine conversions of the UH-34D). Eight SA 330s were supplied from France before IPTN delivered a further seven, and the more recent (but low-rate) AS 332 production has been split between the navy and air force.

A squadron based at Semarang and specialising in SAR flies 10 AB 204 Iroquois, five Alouette IIIs and four fixed-wing Grumman HU-16 Albatross amphibians.

Flying training is conducted by the Air Force Academy at Jogjakarta, where two equal batches of 20 Swiss AS.202A Bravo piston monoplanes were delivered in 1981 and 1984. Students progress to the Beech T-34C (16 delivered in 1978 and nine more in 1984). Those selected for combat jets continue their course on the 15 survivors of 20 BAe Hawk T.Mk 53s delivered 1980-84. Multi-engined training for transport selectees is conducted with two Beech King Airs and C-47s, and a pair of Dakotas are also used to train navigators.

Indonesia's first SAMs are BAe Rapiers, operated by the TNI-AU for air base defence.

Order of Battle

UNIT	EQUIPMENT	BASE
? Sqn	F-16	Madiun-Iswahyudi
2 Sqn	F27, NC.212, C-47	Jakarta-Halim
3 Sqn	OV-10	Bacau
4 Sqn	NC.212, Cessna 180/207/ 401/402	Malang
6 Sqn	Puma	Jakarta-Halim
11 Sqn	A-4E	Madiun-Iswahyudi
12 Sqn	A-4E	Pekanbaru
14 Sqn	F-5E	Madiun-Iswahyudi
17 Sqn	Puma, S-58T	?
31 Sqn	C-130	Jakarta-Halim
32 Sqn	C-130	Malang
101 Sqn	AS.202	Jogjakarta-Adisutjipto
102 Sqn	T-34C	Jogjakarta-Adisutjipto
103 Sqn	Hawk	Madiun-Iswahyudi

Indonesian Army Air Arm (TNI-AD)

Although large, the army operated few helicopters until the mid-1970s, but has since more vigorously embraced the air-mobile doctrine. It is now in the process of receiving 28 IPTN-produced Bell 412 medium-lift machines, adding to the 13 Bell 205A-1 Iroquois supplied from the US in the late 1970s. Sixteen NBO 105s from IPTN were received in an initial batch, and can carry gun or rocket pods, with more delivered recently. Training is conducted on some 20 Schweizer-Hughes 300C two-seat helicopters.

Fixed-wing assets include four NC.212 Aviocars and a large number of PZL-104s, the Polish high-wing STOL light plane which was the first aircraft to be licence-produced in Indonesia, as the Gelatik.

Order of Battle

EQUIPMENT	QUANTITY
Helicopters	
Bell 205A-1	13
IPTN/Bell 412	28
IPTN/MBB NBO105	16
Schweizer-Hughes 300C	c.20
Fixed-wing liaison/transport aircraft	
LIPNUR/PZL-104 Gelatik	2
IPTN/CASA NC.212 Aviocar	4

Indonesian Navy (TNI-AL)

The naval air arm received 12 GAF Nomad Searchmaster B and six Searchmaster L twin-turboprops from 1975-79 to form a maritime patrol squadron, and plans to augment them with the longer-range CN.235, equipped with a bigger search radar. Based at the naval headquarters, Surabaya, the Nomads are also detached to Tanjung Pinang and Manado.

For ASW/ASV operations, 10 Westland Wasp HAS.Mk 1 helicopters were acquired from the Netherlands and refurbished by Westland. They fly from three former Royal Navy 'Tribal'-class frigates. Following receipt of four NAS 332B Super Puma transport helicopters from IPTN, the naval air arm embarked on an ambitious programme to acquire 22 radar- and Exocet missile-equipped NAS 332Fs from the same source. The French machines are capable of flying from the navy's four LSTs.

A transport squadron flies four NC.212s, six C-47s, some Bell 212s and four Rockwell Lark Commander light planes. Surprisingly for such a small air arm, the navy conducts its own basic flying training, with a half-dozen Piper PA-38 Tomahawks and some PA-34 Seneca twins.

Order of Battle

UNIT	EQUIPMENT	BASE
400 Sqn	NAS332, Wasp, NBO 105	Surabaya
600 Sqn	NC.212, C-47	Surabaya
800 Sqn	Nomad	Surabaya

Police Air Wing (Polisi)

Received at least seven NBO 105s from IPTN, supplementing Bell 206 JetRangers. Also flies a few assorted Cessnas and Aero Commanders.

The main weapon of the TNI-AD is the NBO 105, which outrigger pylons for weapons carriage. Here rocket pod are carried.

TNI-AL assets include the locally-built NAS 332F Super Puma, which features search radar and Exocet missiles the anti-shipping role.

The navy's patrol force employs the GAF Nomad Searchmaster, these augmenting TNI-AU assets which include a C-130H-MP.

400 Skwadron is the TNI-AL's rotary-wing unit at Surabaya.

The Searchmaster-equip 800 Skwadron is expectin CN.235s.

Long out of service with its prime user (the Royal Navy), the Westland Wasp soldiers on with the TNI-AL. This example is carrying an ASW torpedo.

KAMPUCHEA

Military air activity in Cambodia virtually ceased after the Khmer Rouge ousted the US-supported government in 1975. Prior to this, the Cambodian air force received substantial US military aid, including T-28Ds, AC-47s and AU-24s for attack roles; C-47s, C-123s, UH-1s and O-1s for transport; and T-37s and T-41s for training. Almost 100 of these were flown to Thailand as the Pol Pot regime took control. The remainder fell into disrepair.

The Khmer Rouge's ally China supplied a few J-6 (MiG-19) fighter-bombers, but they offered little resistance to the invasion by Vietnam in late 1978. This was conducted with the help of Vietnam's captured US aircraft, including F-5s, A-37s and UH-1s.

No attempt to re-organise the Kampuchean air force took place until 1984, however, when the government sent some pilots to the USSR for training. Since then, activity has been largely confined to helicopters. At least six Mil Mi-8s and two Mi-24 'Hind' gunships have been used in army campaigns against the banished, but not vanquished, Khmer Rouge, and against the two other guerrilla factions opposing the Phnom Penh government.

In 1989, 'Unit 701' was declared operational on the MiG-21, coinciding with the start of withdrawal of Vietnamese forces. The MiGs are at Pochentong, the main air base near the capital.

Order of Battle

EQUIPMENT	QUANTITY
Fighter/ground attack	
MiG-21 'Fishbed'	one squadron
Shenyang J-6 (MiG-19)	
Helicopters	
Mi-8 'Hip'	at least 6
Mi-24 'Hind'	at least 2

LAOS

Air Force of the Laos People's Army

When the Communists finally took full control of the government in 1975, an exodus of aircraft to Thailand with escaping pro-Western Laotians took place, similar to that from Cambodia. Thailand later allowed Laos to reclaim most of these aircraft – T-28s, C-47s, U-17s and T-41s that had been supplied from 1961 by the US – but they apparently were not returned to regular flying duties, probably due to lack of spares.

Instead, the USSR began supplying transport aircraft in 1976, and MiG-21 fighters the following year. Some 40 'Fishbeds' have been received for two squadrons at the main base, the Vientiane airport at Wattay. The original eight MiG-21Fs and two MiG-21U two-seaters were supplemented in the 1980s by MiG-21PFMs.

The Indonesian Police Air Wing is primarily a rotary-wing force, with Bell 206s (illustrated) and NBO 105s.

Among the types previously operated by the Kampuchean air force is the MiG-17. Today this secretive air arm has a squadron of MiG-21s for air defence.

A handful of fixed-wing types serve with the Indonesian Polisi, including this Aero Commander.

US-supplied aircraft from the 1960s such as this T-28 Trojan are no longer in service with the AFLPA.

Land-locked Laos is wedged firmly between Thailand and Vietnam, with close ties to Moscow. The small air force is largely centred around the capital, Vientiane.

The AFLPA transport force doubles as the national airline, and comprises seven Antonov An-24s, two Yak-40s, three Fairchild C-123Ks and a Viscount. Helicopters include two Sikorsky S-58s and 10 Mil Mi-8 'Hips'.

Order of Battle

EQUIPMENT	QUANTITY
Air defence/interceptors	
MiG-21PFM 'Fishbed'	c.30
MiG-21F 'Fishbed'	8
MiG-21U 'Mongol'	2
Transports	
An-24 'Coke'	7
Yak-40 'Codling'	2
Fairchild C-123K	3
Vickers Viscount	1
Helicopters	
Mi-8 'Hip'	10
Sikorsky S-58	2

The RMAF's primary air defence mission is handled by a squadron of F-5Es, but these could be augmented by RAAF Hornets and RAF Tornado F.Mk 3s if required.

MALAYSIA

Royal Malaysian Air Force (RMAF)

Like neighbouring Indonesia, Malaysia has not invested much money in air power, relative to the size of the country. In fact, defence spending was halved in the 1980s, but in 1988 the UK agreed to supply a $1.7-billion arms package on attractive loan and barter terms. Despite the RMAF's lack of enthusiasm, the government originally intended that 12 Panavia Tornado combat aircraft should form a major part of this package. Late last year, however, Malaysia decided instead to purchase 18 BAe Hawk 100s and 10 Hawk 200s, for delivery in early 1994.

Pending arrival of the Hawk, the RMAF's front-line fighter force consists of a single squadron of 14 Northrop F-5E Tiger IIs, armed with AIM-9J Sidewinder missiles. Four F-5F two-seaters and two RF-5E reconnaissance versions are flown by a second squadron, and both are located at Butterworth. This base used to house three squadrons of Royal Australian Air Force Mirage III fighters, but the Australian presence has been wound down and now comprises only a periodic detachment of six F/A-18 Hornet fighters and P-3 Orion maritime patrollers.

The RMAF's other combat jets are based at Kuantan, where two squadrons received 34 single-seat and six two-seat A-4 Skyhawks in 1986-87. In 1979, the RMAF bought 88 former-US Navy A-4C/Ls in storage, planning to overhaul and conduct an ambitious upgrade for 70 of them. This was later abandoned on cost grounds, and Grumman refurbished them to produce the 40 A-4PTM (Peculiar To Malaysia) models. These aircraft can potentially carry AGM-65 Mavericks for air-to-ground missions, and AIM-9s for air-to-air combat. Thirty-four are left, but will probably be withdrawn when the Hawks arrive.

Together with a squadron of three Lockheed C-130H-MP maritime patrol versions of the Hercules, the four fast jet squadrons report to Air Defence Command. This is also responsible for ground radar and anti-aircraft units. Malaysia has not previously operated any type of surface-to-air missile, but BAe Rapiers and Shorts Javelins form part of the British arms package.

In addition, the southern part of Malaysian airspace is defended by Singapore's Bloodhound SAMs, since these are declared to the In-

tegrated Air Defence System (IADS), which also comprises RSAF F-5s, RAAF F-18s and (theoretically) RAF Tornado F.3 fighters, which would deploy from the UK if requested.

Air Support Command controls the eight transport and helicopter squadrons, and the three flying training units. Six C-130Hs were received in 1976, and are often augmented by the three C-130H-MPs received in 1980. But otherwise, fixed-wing tactical transport is performed by 15 elderly DHC Caribou STOL aircraft, which survive from 24 received in the 1960s. A staff and VIP transport squadron flies a Dassault Falcon 900, an AS 332 Super Puma, two BAe 125-400Bs, and 11 Cessna 402Bs. Two refurbished Grumman HU-16B amphibians were acquired for flights to remote offshore islands.

About 40 Sikorsky S-61A-4 helicopters were received from 1968-78, with most still in service, flying alongside 25 smaller Aérospatiale Alouette IIIs in four squadrons. Like the two Caribou squadrons, these are split between bases in Peninsular and East Malaysia. The army has no helicopters, and apparently aspires to none.

The RMAF's two main training aircraft could theoretically be pressed into service as ground-attack types. They are the Pilatus PC-7 (44 received 1983-84) and the Aermacchi M.B.339A (12 received, also 1983-84). They replaced BAe Bulldogs (still used for reserve pilot refresher training) and Canadair CL-41G light jet trainers (six still kept in flyable storage). Prospective helicopter pilots start on the Bell 47G (seven received).

Order of Battle

UNIT	EQUIPMENT	BASE
1 Sqn	DHC-4	Kuala Lumpur (Simpang)
2 Sqn	various (see above)	Kuala Lumpur (Subang/Simpang)
3 Sqn	S-61, Alouette III	Butterworth
4 Sqn	C-130H-MP	Kuala Lumpur (Subang)
5 Sqn	S-61	Labuan
6 Sqn	A-4	Kuantan
7 Sqn	S-61, Alouette III	Kuching
8 Sqn	DHC-4	Labuan
9 Sqn	A-4	Kuantan
10 Sqn	S-61, Alouette III	Kuala Lumpur (Subang)
11 Sqn	F-5F, RF-5E	Butterworth
12 Sqn	F-5E	Butterworth
14 Sqn	C-130H	Kuala Lumpur (Subang)
1 FTC	PC-7	Alor Setar
2 FTC	Bell 47, S-61, Al III	Keluang

No. 11 Squadron has the RF-5E TigerEye as its principal equipment.

Also at Butterworth is No. Sqn, the F-5E air defence u

Two Kuantan-based squadrons fly the A-4PTM Skyhawk, including several TA-4PTMs. Although attack is the main role, secondary air defence can be undertaken.

Malaysia's transport force contains a squadron of elderly DHC-4 Caribou. These tough aircraft are of great use supplying rough strips in the jungle areas.

A pair of Northrop RF-5Es carries out the tactical reconnaissance mission for the RMAF. Both serve with No. 11 Squadron at the F-5 base at Butterworth.

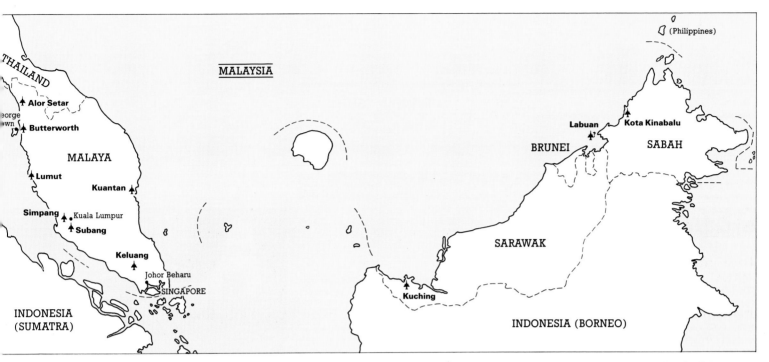

e Malaysian Federation embraces the states of Malaya, Sabah and Sarawak, creating a nation with widely dispersed territory. Virtually all of the
craft are based on the Malayan peninsula, where the main centres of population are located, but a few aircraft and bases are maintained on Borneo.
fence agreements with other South East Asian states, Australia and the UK would ensure the nation's sovereignty.

TC at Keluang is the rotary-wing training unit. Initial
ining is accomplished using the Bell 47G, a handful of
ich was acquired from Indonesia.

No. 2 Squadron is the main VIP and staff transport unit, based at Kuala Lumpur for the
transport of high-ranking officers and government personnel. One of the types that the unit
flies is this Fokker F28 Fellowship 1000.

though out of regular training service, the RMAF's
lldog 102 fleet is used by the Voluntary Pilot Training
it at Simpang.

No. 9 Sqn is one of two units
flying the A-4PTM at
Kuantan.

The Sikorsky S-61A Nuri is the main helicopter in RMAF
use, equipping four squadrons, including one on Borneo.
This aircraft serves with 2 FTC, the training unit.

TC is the advanced training unit, flying a few Pilatus
:-7s and the Aermacchi M.B.339A. As proven here, the
B.339 can carry light weapons.

The Cessna 402B is the main RMAF liaison
and staff transport type, serving with No. 2
Squadron at Simpang.

Among the varied No. 2 Squadron types is a
pair of Canadair CL-600 Challengers for
government work.

3 FTC	PC-7, M.B.339	Kuantan
VPT	Bulldog	Kuala Lumpur (Simpang)

Royal Malaysian Navy (RMN)

The RMN received six former Royal Navy Westland Wasp HAS.Mk 1 helicopters in 1989, and formed its first flying unit, No. 499 Squadron, at Lumut.

Order of Battle

UNIT	EQUIPMENT	BASE
499 Sqn	Wasp HAS.Mk 1	Lumut

PAPUA NEW GUINEA

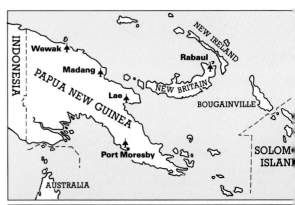

PNG Defence Force

This remote and undeveloped country has suffered recent internal rebellions and the government's writ does not always run outside the two big towns of Port Moresby and Lae. The PNGDF uses three GAF Searchmaster Bs for coastal surveillance, with a similar Nomad and a few C-47s providing transport. Three IAI Aravas and four former RAAF UH-1Hs are grounded.

Order of Battle

EQUIPMENT	QUANTITY
GAF Searchmaster B	3
GAF Nomad	1
Douglas C-47	?
IAI Arava	3 (grounded)
Bell UH-1H	4 (grounded)

Papua New Guinea's small transport force employs a GA Nomad. Similar aircraft completed to Searchmaster standard are used for coastal patrol duties.

PHILIPPINES

Philippine Air Force (PHILAF)

For air defence, Philippine reliance on the PACAF fighter wing stationed at Clark AB has grown, rather than diminished, in recent years. But the US is likely to withdraw all its forces from Clark, rather than pay the heavy 'rent' now demanded by the government in Manila. The country's airspace will then be defended by a token force of Northrop F-5A fighters. The PHILAF received 19 F-5As and three F-5Bs as long ago as 1965, and only 10 remain.

To augment the fighter force, the PHILAF bought 35 retired US Navy F-8H Crusaders in the mid-1970s, and LTV refurbished 25 of them. But corrosion, unserviceability and lack of investment in spare parts forced their retirement in 1986.

Not surprisingly, the PHILAF's main role in the 1980s was army support, rather than air defence, as the country struggled to contain Communist and Muslim guerrillas throughout the country. This effort was hampered, first by the corrupt mismanagement of the Marcos regime, and then by chronic instability following his enforced departure in early 1986.

Helicopters have been the only growth area for the PHILAF, with well over 100 Bell UH-1H Iroquois received from the US since the mid-1970s. About half of them remain, many being armed with machine-guns, and a few others allocated for SAR. Outside the US FMS procurement channel, the Marcos regime arranged for licence-assembly of the MBB BO 105, 15 of these reaching the PHILAF.

By 1983, Sikorsky was in favour, when 12 armed H-76s, five S-76s (three for SAR and two for VIP transport) and two S-70Cs were acquired. More recently, the US agreed to supply 20 MDH 500MD armed light helicopters under FMS terms in 1989, and delivery of 22 improved Model 520 Defenders began in mid-1990.

The PHILAF received over 60 armed AT-28D Trojans from the US up to the mid-1970s, and although frequently unserviceable, they participated in occasional ground-attack missions (including some in connection with coup attempts in 1987 and 1989, with several destroyed in the latter attempt). Nineteen SF.260WP Warrior lightplanes were allocated to an 'attack squadron', but some were later sold, and the rest allocated for training.

The fixed-wing transport force relies heavily on three Lockheed C-130H Hercules (delivered 1976-77) and two former civilian L-100s. Seven Fokker F27 Friendships remain from 10 originally received. Three maritime patrol versions of the F27 were received in 1981. Douglas C-47s soldier on in one transport squadron, while another squadron still flies 10 of the 12 GAF Nomad turboprops supplied from 1976, plus four received last year. A light transport squadron flies Philippine-assembled BN-2 Islanders (22 received, 1978-82) and Cessna U-17s. A so-called 'special missions wing' flies VIP transports acquired by the Marcos regime: an F27, an F28, a Boeing 707, a BAe One-Eleven and an assortment of helicopters, including an SA 330 Puma and some BO 105s.

Pilot training begins on Cessna T-41Ds (20 received) and continues on SIAI-Marchetti SF.260MPs (27 received). A few Beech T-34 Mentors are also still in use. The fighter wing trains prospective F-5 pilots on Lockheed T-33s first. A dozen are still in service, following the receipt of seven former PACAF T-33s from Clark AB in 1987.

The first eight of 18 SIAI S.211 jet trainers ordered in 1988 for local assembly have gone to the training wing. If a second batch of 18 is approved, they will be armed and will replace the T-28s.

The Philippines' major combat unit is the 6th Tactical Fighter Squadron, which provides a token air defence wi Northrop F-5As.

It is believed that three F-5Bs remain in service to provid conversion and continuation training. This aircraft wears TFS markings.

The venerable Lockheed T-33 figures prominently in the Philippine Air Force, serving with the 105th Combat Crew Training Squadron. This aircraft is an RT-33A.

...eved to be currently grounded, the *PNG Defence Forces*
...*Aravas* were used for transport. Three were delivered to
...small air arm.

...*15th Strike Wing* at *Sangley Point* has *North American*
...*8* and *AT-28 Trojans* for the light attack and counter-
...rgency roles.

...y three *C-130H Hercules* are on *PhilAF* strength, but they
...heavily utilised. They serve with the *222nd Heavy Airlift*
...adron at *Mactan*.

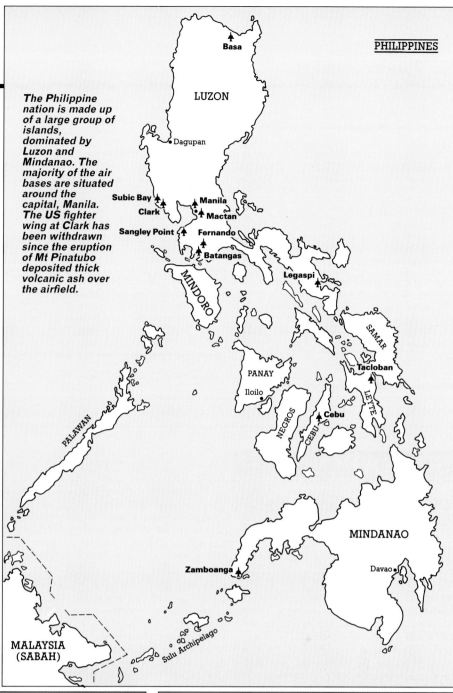

*The Philippine
nation is made up
of a large group of
islands,
dominated by
Luzon and
Mindanao. The
majority of the air
bases are situated
around the
capital, Manila.
The US fighter
wing at Clark has
been withdrawn
since the eruption
of Mt Pinatubo
deposited thick
volcanic ash over
the airfield.*

...udly carried on the tail of
... is the badge of the *6th*
...S.

The *Britten-Norman BN-2A Islanders* of the *601st Liaison
Squadron* were built under licence in the Philippines. The
unit's base is at *Sangley Point*.

Another elderly trainer used by the Philippine Air Force is
the *Beech T-34 Mentor*, a handful of which serve with the
105th CCTS, most wearing camouflage.

105th CCTS operates
...s, *T-33s* and *T-34s* on
...anced training duties.

The *Lockheed T-33* soldiers on in *PhilAF* service, the fleet
recently augmented by ex-*USAF* examples. Training is the
main role, supplying aircrew for the *F-5* squadron.

Based alongside the *C-130s* at *Mactan* are *GAF Nomad* light
transports, organised under the *223rd TAS*. These are
useful for work involving primitive airstrips.

149

Order of Battle

UNIT	EQUIPMENT
5th Fighter Wing, Basa	
6 TFS	F-5A
105 CCTS	T-33A, RT-33A, T-34A, F-5B
15th Strike Wing, Sangley Point	
16 AS	AT-28
17 AS	UH-1H
18 AS	AT-28
205th Airlift Wing, Manila	
204 ATS	C-47
208 ATS	F27
210 HS	UH-1, H-76
211 HS	UH-1, H-76
505 ARS	UH-1, BO 105, S-76
901 WS	Cessna 210
220th Heavy Airlift Wing, Mactan	
222 HAS	C-130H
223 TAS	Nomad
240th Composite Wing, Sangley Point	
27 MPS	F27MPA
601 LS	U-17, BN-2

700th Special Missions Wing, Manila	
702 PAS	various, see above
100th Training Wing, Fernando	
101 PTS	T-41, SF.260
102 PTS	S.211

Philippines Navy

Based at Sangley Point, a naval aviation unit flies four locally-assembled BN-2A Islanders and four MBB BO 105C helicopters.

Order of Battle

EQUIPMENT	QUANTITY
Britten-Norman BN-2A Islander	4
MBB BO 105C	4

In keeping with the obsolete flavour of the PhilAF, the service still uses the Douglas C-47, which serves with th 204th Air Transport Squadron.

Sizeable numbers of Bell UH-1s are in use, flying with f units. Most are for assault or armed attack, but a few w this scheme for rescue duties.

Patrol of the seas around the Philippine islands is entru to the 27th Maritime Patrol Squadron, which operates t dedicated Fokker F27MPA.

Despite the arrival in RSAF service of the F-16, one squadron of Hawker Hunters is retained, this being No. at Paya Lebar.

The four Shorts Skyvans of No. 121 Squadron at Chang perform a variety of tasks, including search and rescue paradropping and maritime surveillance.

SINGAPORE

Republic of Singapore Air Force

Singapore has built the best-equipped defence force in South East Asia, although most doubt whether an island so small could ever be defended. A well-organised reservist system is modelled on Israeli and Swiss examples, although the RSAF is primarily manned by full-timers.

The recent acquisition of F-16 fighters and E-2C Hawkeye AEW/maritime surveillance aircraft has set the seal on 20 years of remarkable expansion for the RSAF, which only sent its first pilots for jet training in 1970. The four E-2Cs received in 1987, and operational late in 1988, were the first such aircraft in the region. The four F-16As and four F-16Bs arrived in Singapore in late 1989 after an extensive crew work-up in the US. The RSAF is likely to buy a squadron of F-16C/Ds as soon as they become available for sale to the region.

The F-16s carry AIM-9P Sidewinder air-to-air missiles, as do the Northrop F-5E/Fs operated by two squadrons. Singapore received 39 F-5Es and 10 F-5Fs, and these are also used for air-to-ground roles, carrying AGM-65 Maverick TV-guided missiles or various ordnance, including laser-guided bombs. They will undergo a major upgrade, including radar replacement, and six are being converted for reconnaissance with FLIR and IRLS.

The A-4 Skyhawk has played an important part in the RSAF's development, since the work associated with refurbishing and upgrading these former US Navy attack jets has enabled a local aircraft industry to develop. Lockheed rebuilt the first eight A-4Bs to A-4S standard in the US in 1974, but all subsequent work has been done in Singapore. Forty A-4S and seven unique TA-4S two-cockpit trainers formed the initial batch for delivery to two RSAF squadrons in 1975-78. Singapore sub-

sequently bought a further 86 A-4B/Cs, and about half of these were remanufactured as A-4S1 variants for a third squadron, and as attrition replacements for the earlier Skyhawks.

A third phase of the Skyhawk programme began in 1986 when the prototype of an A-4S re-engined with a General Electric F404 turbofan was flown. Eighty production conversions are now following (designated A-4SU), while, in a separate programme, the Skyhawks are undergoing a major avionics update. A further 20 surplus US A-4s were bought in 1990, bringing the grand total acquired to 160.

Despite all the advances, the RSAF still rates the Hunter worth keeping, with one squadron continuing to fly about 15 survivors of 42 F.74/ FR.74 and T.75 aircraft. These were its first combat aircraft when delivered in 1971-72, and were subsequently upgraded to carry the AIM-9P and extra bombs/rockets.

All the RSAF combat aircraft are kept at two bases, Tengah and Paya Lebar (the former Singapore airport), where major extension and hardening have taken place. But with airspace at a premium, Singapore sends eight or more aircraft at a time to near-permanent training detachments at Williamtown, Australia, and Clark AB, Philippines.

A strong air-defence radar and missile network is also in place. The RSAF took over a Bloodhound missile squadron (which has just been withdrawn) when the RAF left in 1972. It later added Improved Hawks, BAe Rapiers, and Bofors RBS-70 SAMs.

The RSAF fleet of six C-130H and four C-130B Hercules transports is used to support the overseas training detachments (including those made by the army to Brunei and Taiwan). The C-130Bs double as tankers for extending the range of the A-4s and F-5s. Four Shorts Skyvans are used for SAR, paradropping and maritime surveillance, but the RSAF will acquire six dedicated MR aircraft, probably Fokker 50s.

The helicopter force started with eight Alouette IIIs (later sold to Malaysia), but expanded when 17 new Bell UH-1H and 30

...4 Squadron is one of the ...e Tengah-based A-4SU ...drons.

...31 Squadron at Paya ...r flies S.211s for ...nced training.

Although Singapore already had probably the best-equipped and most highly-trained air arm in the region, its capabilities were greatly enhanced by the arrival of the F-16. Here the first Singaporean F-16B touches down, still wearing traces of its 'LF' tailcode denoting its crew training period at Luke AFB, Arizona.

...e the arrival of the F-16s, the RSAF's F-5E fleet is being upgraded, including six ...aft to RF-5E standard. This F-5E is on the strength of No. 144 Squadron.

Air defence is the primary role for Singapore's F-16A/Bs, armed with up to six AIM-9P Sidewinders each. Ground attack remains a secondary role.

Seen on exercise at RAAF Williamtown, this No. 144 Sqn F-5E wears an experimental camouflage and carries a rocket pod. F-5s will assume ever-greater attack responsibilities.

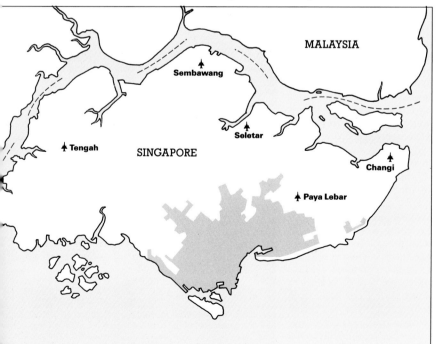

...ted at the tip of the Malayan peninsula, the independent and affluent island of ...apore is defended by a large and well-trained air force with two combat and three ...ort bases. E-2 Hawkeyes provide airborne early warning.

Bolstering the single-seat F-5 fleet are 10 F-5F two-seaters split between the two squadrons. These undertake combat duties in addition to training.

second-hand UH-1B Iroquois were received from the US in 1978-80. Eleven more Bell 205s were subsequently acquired, and 18 Bell 205/UH-1Hs are still in service, some armed with guns. Three Bell 212s were used for SAR until replaced by Aérospatiale AS 332 Super Pumas. These were the first of 22 received 1985-88, the remainder serving as tactical transports. Ten more were recently ordered.

Flying training starts with grading and basic on the SIAI-Marchetti SF.260MS and WS. Twelve of each variant are in service, and the Warriors can double as FAC aircraft. The Italian influence continues into advanced training, where 30 SIAI S.211s are used. Like the Super Puma helicopters, these were assembled locally, 1985-88, to replace BAe Strikemasters and Lockheed T-33s. Helicopter pilots start on the Aérospatiale AS 350 Ecureuil and progress to the UH-1B. Six AS 350s were bought originally, and a further 20 have recently been

ordered, 10 of them AS 350L anti-armour machines equipped with HOT missiles.

Order of Battle

UNIT	EQUIPMENT	BASE
111 Sqn	E-2C	Tengah
120 Sqn	UH-1H/B205	Sembawang
121 Sqn	Skyvan	Changi
122 Sqn	C-130B/H	Paya Lebar
123 Sqn	UH-1B, AS 350B	Sembawang
125 Sqn	Super Puma	Sembawang
130 Sqn	S.211	Paya Lebar
131 Sqn	S.211	Paya Lebar
140 Sqn	F-16A/B	Tengah
141 Sqn	Hunter	Paya Lebar
142 Sqn	A-4SU	Tengah
143 Sqn	A-4SU	Tengah
144 Sqn	F-5E	Paya Lebar
145 Sqn	A-4SU	Tengah
149 Sqn	F-5E	Tengah
150 Sqn	SF.260	Seletar

Continued updating has kept Singapore's Skyhawk for as a potent weapon in the region. These A-4SUs equip 143 Squadron at Tengah.

In addition to attack duties, the A-4S and its derivatives also occasionally used for air defence. A single AIM-9P carried under each wing.

Unique to Singapore is the TA-4S conversion trainer version of the Skyhawk, which features separate cockp as opposed to the two-place cockpit of other TA-4s.

THAILAND

Royal Thai Air Force (RTAF)

Border tension with neighbouring Laos and Kampuchea means that the RTAF remains very much poised for operational duty. Two F-5s, three A-37s, an OV-10 and a number of observation aircraft (U-17s and O-1s) were shot down during clashes with guerrillas during the 1980s. When the military threat to Thailand from Vietnam (through Kampuchea) was at its height, the US agreed to stockpile arms in-country, and generally increased its support to Thailand's defence forces.

The Thai armed forces are generally well-organised, but suffer from duplication of missions between the army, air force and paramilitary border police. The generals also play politics, but within a uniquely Thai code of ethics, which also features unswerving loyalty to the monarchy.

The RTAF became the first air force in South East Asia to receive the General Dynamics F-16 when 10 F-16As and two F-16Bs were delivered to a refurbished and hardened Korat AB in 1988-89. Four more F-16As and two F-16Bs are due to arrive this year. Pending the release by the US of radar-guided missiles and modifications to the aircraft themselves, the F-16s are confined to AIM-9J Sidewinder missiles for air combat.

In 1989, the RTAF seriously considered the purchase of much cheaper Chinese F-7M (MiG-21) fighters, to provide a 'high-low' mix with the F-16s, but never proceeded. Instead, despite fond talk of the Tornado or AMX, it apparently intends to continue operating two squadrons of Northrop F-5E/Fs, and buy some more F-16s when funds allow. The RTAF was the first F-5 operator to conduct a major avionics upgrade for the type. Now that the F-16s have arrived, the F-5s will concentrate on the air-to-ground role. The RTAF ordered the General Electric GPU-5/A 30-mm cannon pod for the F-5s, and has also been shopping for air-to-surface missiles.

The first deliveries of F-5s to Thailand were

in 1967-73, when 18 F-5As, two F-5Bs and four RF-5As were received. Only a few of these remain in use, although two extra F-5Bs were acquired from Malaysia in 1981. Two batches, each of 17 F-5Es and three F-5Fs, were delivered in 1977 and 1981, respectively. Ten more F-5Es were acquired second-hand from the US at nominal cost when the PACAF aggressor squadron at Clark AB was disbanded in 1988.

The only other combat jets are a dozen Cessna A-37B Dragonflies surviving from 16 received by default in 1975 when their South Vietnamese pilots escaped to Thailand in them.

In addition to these, the RTAF is heavily dependent on turboprops to fly light ground-attack missions. Thirty-two Rockwell OV-10C Broncos were received 1971-74, and 24 remain with two squadrons. Also in the early 1970s, the RTAF received virtually all of the 33 Pilatus Turbo-Porters which were licence-built and militarised by Fairchild as the AU-23A Peacemaker. Twenty remain in use.

Twenty GAF N22B Nomad STOL transports were acquired in 1982-83, and some were immediately pressed into service as gunships to replace six ageing AC-47s. Another veteran retired from the ground-attack role at about the same time was the T-28D Trojan, which still equipped two squadrons. FAC and target marking are performed for the attack aircraft by two squadrons of about 40 O-1s, also used for liaison flights.

Although the Army has its own large helicopter force, the RTAF maintains two squadrons of sometimes-armed choppers. One flies the 18 S-58T turbine-engined conversions of former CH-34s, and the other has about 30 UH-1H Iroquois. Three Boeing CH-47Ds were delivered recently.

Heavy transport is provided by six Lockheed C-130H Hercules (three are stretched -30 versions), backing up what seems likely to become the world's last squadron of Fairchild C-123K Providers (about 10 still airworthy). Fifteen C-47 Dakotas soldier on, including one camera-equipped RC-47. The RTAF received four BAe 748 and three DC-8-62AF transports from Thai Airways, but later sold the DC-8s, and ordered an A310 Airbus for delivery this year. Three Lear Jet 35As were acquired in 1988

No. 150 Squadron is the only unit based at Seletar, fron where it flies over 20 SIAI-Marchetti SF.260 trainers. Ha are Warriors, which double as FAC platforms.

Singapore's sizeable air arm is supplied with well-train pilots by two squadrons flying the SIAI-Marchetti (nov Agusta) S.211 advanced trainers.

helicopter training unit is **No. 123 Squadron**, which ~ides initial rotary-wing instruction on the Aérospatiale ~350B Ecureuil.

~rch and rescue is the primary role of the Aérospatiale ~332 Super Pumas of **No. 125 Squadron**, although their ~sport talents are called upon regularly.

~ rotary-wing force is concentrated at **Sembawang**, ~ere the most numerous type is the **Bell UH-1**. Most fly the ~ault transport mission, but some are used for training.

~gmenting earlier single-engined versions of the Huey are ~l 212s. Until the **Super Pumas** were acquired, Bell 212s ~formed the **SAR** mission.

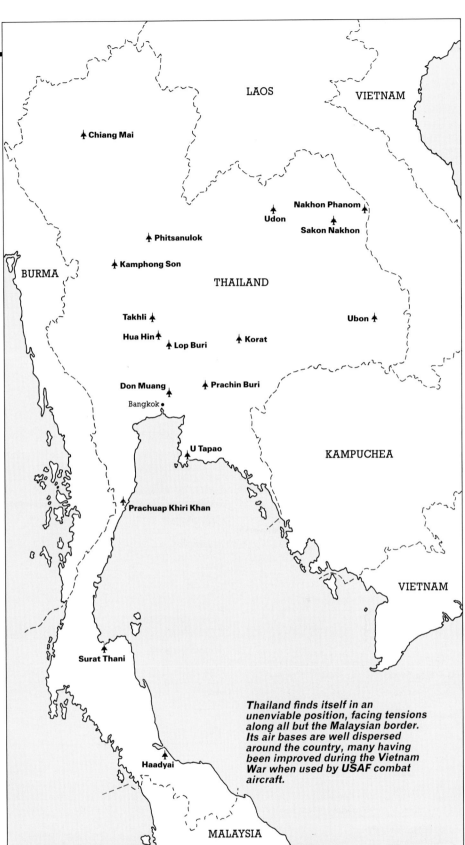

LAOS

VIETNAM

Chiang Mai

Nakhon Phanom

Udon

Sakon Nakhon

Phitsanulok

BURMA

Kamphong Son

THAILAND

Takhli

Ubon

Hua Hin

Lop Buri

Korat

Don Muang

Prachin Buri

Bangkok

U Tapao

KAMPUCHEA

Prachuap Khiri Khan

VIETNAM

Surat Thani

Thailand finds itself in an unenviable position, facing tensions along all but the Malaysian border. Its air bases are well dispersed around the country, many having been improved during the Vietnam War when used by USAF combat aircraft.

Haadyai

MALAYSIA

*Left: One of **No. 122 Sqn's C-130H** Hercules transports turns finals at **Nellis** during a **Red Flag** exercise.*

*Above: The survivors of the Hunter fleet include some two-seat **T.Mk 75s**, all now concentrated in **No. 141 Squadron**.*

for photo, ECM and target-towing missions, joining three camera-equipped Swearingen Merlin IVAs received in 1979.

Elint and communications relay are probably the main roles for three IAI Arava transports acquired in 1981, while another little-publicised RTAF squadron is that operating Lear-Siegler SkyEye RPVs for reconnaissance.

The Flying Training School used to start prospective RTAF pilots on 24 CT-4A Air-trainers, and then 18 SIAI-Marchetti SF.260MT. The fast jet selectees continued on 20 Cessna T-37s. However, in 1982 the RTAF became the only significant customer for the German RFB Fantrainer, in a co-production deal which was intended to sow the seeds of an indigenous aircraft industry. The order comprised 31 Srs 400 and 16 more-powerful Srs 600 aircraft, with the latter apparently earmarked for armed training, or even operational ground-attack work. Although knock-down kits for all 47 aircraft were supplied by late 1987, the programme has progressed only slowly.

In the meantime, a large fleet of Lockheed T-33s is retained for advanced flying training; over 50 have been received, but a number have been cannibalised for spares.

The RTAF is responsible for the Royal Flight, which consists of a Boeing 737-300, two BAe 748s and two Bell 412s.

Order of Battle

UNIT	EQUIPMENT
No. 1 Wing, Korat	
101 Sqn	RT/T-33A
102 Sqn	F-5E
103 Sqn	F-16
No. 2 Wing, Lopburi	
201 Sqn	S-58T
202 Sqn	AU-23
203 Sqn	UH-1H
No. 4 Wing, Takhli	
403 Sqn	F-5E/F
404 Sqn	Arava
No. 6 Wing, Bangkok (Don Muang)	
601 Sqn	C-130, DC-8
602 Sqn	C-123K, BAe 748
603 Sqn	C-47, Merlin
604 Sqn	O-1, T-41
605 Sqn	Lear Jet, Merlin, Nomad, King Air
No. 21 Wing, Ubon	
211 Sqn	A-37B
213 Sqn	AU-23
No. 41 Wing, Chiang Mai	
411 Sqn	OV-10
No. 46 Wing, Phitsanulok	
461 Sqn	Nomad
No. 53 Wing, Prachua Khiri Khan	
531 Sqn	O-1
No. 56 Wing, Haadyai	
561 Sqn	T-33A
No. 71 Wing, Surat Thani	
711 Sqn	OV-10, O-1
712 Sqn	AU-23
Flying Training School, Kamphong Son	
	CT-4, SF.260, T-37, Fantrainer
Royal Flight, Bangkok (Don Muang)	
	Boeing 737, BAe 748, Bell 212

Royal Thai Army

Over 100 Bell UH-1A/B/H Iroquois were received in various consignments from the US, and the service apparently intends to refurbish the 75 or so that remain. However, four twin-engined Bell 412s were received in 1986, and deliveries of 25 more 212s began in 1990.

Having previously relied upon Miniguns aboard the UH-1s, the army received its first dedicated attack helicopters in 1988 – four TOW-equipped Bell AH-1S Cobras. Four more arrived in 1990. Ten previously-acquired Bell 206A/Bs can presumably scout for the Cobras. A large fleet of 60 O-1s performs liaison flights, and spotting for artillery.

Two Shorts 330 transports were received in 1984 to augment four C-47s, while VIP/staff transport is provided by a Beech 99, a Beech King Air 200 and two Bell 214ST helicopters.

Pilot training is conducted at the army aviation headquarters, Lopburi, where 48 new-build Schweizer-Hughes TH-300Cs have augmented 23 similar, but former US Army, TH-55s.

The first land-based surface-to-air missiles to be deployed by Thailand are Selenia Aspides, ordered by the army in 1987 for the defence of the Bangkok area.

Order of Battle

EQUIPMENT	QUANTITY
Helicopters	
Bell AH-1S	8
Bell 412	4
Bell 212	25
Bell UH-1A/B/H	75
Bell 206A/B	10
Bell 214ST	2
Schweizer-Hughes TH-300C	48
Hughes TH-55	23
Fixed-wing aircraft	
Shorts 330UTT	2
Douglas C-47	4
Cessna O-1 Bird Dog	60
Beech 99	1
Beech King Air 200	1

Thai Border Police

Essentially a small army in its own right, the Border Police operates a substantial fleet of aircraft from Bangkok and Hua Hin airports. This comprises three DHC-4 Caribou, one Shorts 330, three Dornier Do 28D Skyservants, five PC-6B Turbo-Porters, 13 Bell 212s, 18 Bell 205s and 15 Bell 206s. Some of the helicopters are armed.

Order of Battle

EQUIPMENT	QUANTITY
Helicopters	
Bell 212	13
Bell 205	18
Bell 206	15
Fixed-wing aircraft	
DHC-4 Caribou	3
Shorts 330	1
Dornier Do 28D	3
Pilatus PC-6B Turbo-Porter	5

Thailand introduced the first F-16s to South East Asia, equipping 103 Squadron at Korat. Further orders have b. announced to strengthen the fleet.

An important type for the RTAF is the Rockwell OV-10C Bronco, which is used for counter-insurgency and FAC duties. It has proved its worth in border conflicts.

Thailand's A-37Bs were originally on the strength of the South Vietnamese air force until the Communist takeov. in 1975. They are used for COIN duties.

GAF Nomads serve with 461 Squadron at Phitsanulok, fr where they perform light transport missions. Some have more warlike function, having been converted to gunshi.

Douglas C-47s remain in Thai service as transports, with one aircraft equipped as an RC-47 with cameras. The AC gunships are thought to be retired.

For many years Thailand's **Northrop F-5Es** undertook the air defence of the nation, but the arrival of the F-16 and future orders for the **GD** product will see the Tiger II relegated to air-to-ground duties. Looking further into the future, the F-5 may be replaced altogether when Thailand receives the **AMX** light strike fighters ordered in September 1991.

Wearing an air defence grey camouflage, this F-5E serves with 403 Squadron, part of No. 4 Wing at Takhli. Thailand's F-5s are to be upgraded for attack work with the GPU-5/A Pave Claw cannon as carried by the F-16As of the New York Air National Guard.

The **RTAF** is a fascinating mix of old and new. Firmly entrenched in the former category, but still providing useful service, is the Lockheed T-33.

The majority of the transport force is based at Bangkok's Don Muang Airport, from where 602 Squadron flies this British Aerospace 748.

Squadron at Don Muang has a mixed fleet for special duties, including Fairchild Swearingen Merlins used for photo-survey work.

Amazingly, a large share of the RTAF's transport taskings fall on the old but broad shoulders of the Fairchild C-123K Provider, Vietnam War-era veterans which serve with 602 Squadron. The C-123K has auxiliary jets underwing.

Royal Thai Navy

The former B-52 base at U-Tapao is head-quarters for the navy's aviation element. Three Fokker F27MPAs provide longest-range maritime patrol, and are equipped with MDC Harpoon anti-ship missiles. So too, presumably, will be three former US Navy Lockheed P-3B Orions ordered in 1990. At the same time, the RTN also ordered three Do 228 maritime patrollers from Dornier. The new aircraft will replace the survivors of 10 S-2A Trackers.

Five radar- and sonobuoy-equipped GAF Searchmaster Ls are also in use, with a primary task of policing the pirate-infested coastal waters of the Gulf of Siam. Also participating in this effort (and firing machine-guns or rockets if necessary) are six Cessna 337s beefed up by Summit Aviation as T-337SPs.

Eight Bell 212s are torpedo-equipped for ASW, while four UH-1H and five Bell 214STs are general transports. Two more F27-400Ms serve as fixed-wing transports and for SAR. Amphibious aircraft comprise two Lake LA-4s and two Canadair CL-215s.

Three vessels can carry SAMs (one frigate with Shorts Seacats, and two corvettes with Selenia Aspides), while Exocet and Gabriel anti-ship missiles are on six fast attack boats.

Order of Battle

UNIT	EQUIPMENT
1 Sqn	F27MPA, S-2
2 Sqn	Searchmaster, CL-215, F27
3 Sqn	Cessna 337
4 Sqn	Bell 212/UH-1H/214ST

The Flying Training School at Kamphong Son has a mixed bag of types to cater for the various stages of pilot training. Cessna T-37Bs handle the basic jet phase.

Resplendent in black camouflage, this Cessna T-41 is one of those which supports the Cessna O-1s of 604 Squadron at Don Muang.

VIETNAM

Vietnamese People's Air Force (VPAF)

Over 1,000 US-supplied aircraft fell into Communist hands when South Vietnam collapsed in 1975, and many of them were pressed into service with the VPAF. C-7s, C-47s, C-130s, F-5s, A-37s, CH-47s, UH-1s and U-17s were kept flying, and some participated in the invasion of Kampuchea, but by the mid-1980s the inevitable lack of spares led to their grounding, despite cannibalisation.

Today's VPAF is distinctly Soviet in flavour, following the deterioration of relations with China that led eventually to a border war in the north in 1979. The USSR has only recently scaled back the massive military and economic support it has been providing. Returning the favour, Vietnam allows the basing of 16 Soviet Tu-16s and Tu-95s, protected by MiG-23 interceptors, at Cam Ranh Bay.

Some time after their arrival in 1985, Vietnamese pilots began training on the MiG-23 themselves. However, the VPAF has actually received MiG-23BM attack-optimised 'Floggers', some 50 having augmented a similar number of Su-22 'Fitters' received earlier for the strike role. There are three fighter-bomber regiments, and the third type used is the MiG-21MF – about 40 supplied.

Four air-defence regiments are all equipped with MiG-21s. About 150 interceptor versions of the 'Fishbed' are thought to be in service, including early-model MiG-21F/PFs and the more modern MiG-21bis. The formidable air-defence missile organisation that shot down so many US aircraft remains in place, using the SA-2 and SA-3.

Dating from the Vietnam War and the years of Chinese support, about 50 F-5 (MiG-17) and F-6 (MiG-19) fighters remain, but are thought to all be in storage.

At least 30 Mil Mi-24 'Hind' attack helicopters have been received (and used frequently in Kampuchea). Some 50 Mil Mi-8 'Hip' and 15 Mi-6 'Hook' transports have also been sup-

plied. There are three helicopter regiments, and the same number of transport regiments. The VPAF uses at least 20 An-26 'Curl' tactical transports, with a smaller number of An-24s, and An-2s.

Flying training is mainly conducted in the USSR, but some Yak-11/18 monoplanes are in service.

The VPAF headquarters is at Bac Mai in Hanoi, which controls four air divisions situated at Noi Bai (Hanoi), Dan Nang, Tho Yuan and Tan Son Nhut (Saigon). Other bases include Binh Thuy, Can Tho, Dalat, Dien Bien Phu, Haiphong, Nha Trang, Phan Rang, Pleiku and Phu Cat.

Vietnamese Navy

Starting in 1980, 17 Kamov Ka-25 'Hormone' helicopters and six Beriev Be-12 'Mail' amphibians were supplied by the USSR, to provide an ASW force.

Order of Battle

EQUIPMENT	QUANTITY
Air defence/interceptors	
MiG-21F/PF/bis 'Fishbed'	c.150
F-5 (MiG-17)	?
F-6 (MiG-19)	?
Fighter/ground attack	
MiG-23BM 'Flogger'	c.50
Su-22 'Fitter'	c.50
MiG-21MF 'Fishbed'	c.40
Transports	
An-26 'Curl'	20 (at least)
An-24 'Coke'	?
An-2 'Colt'	?
Helicopters	
Mi-24 'Hind'	30
Mi-6 'Hook'	15
Mi-8 'Hip'	50
Training	
Yak-11 'Moose'	?
Yak-18 'Max'	?
Anti-submarine warfare	
Be-12 'Mail'	6
Ka-25 'Hormone'	17

Primary training is the responsibility of the Aerospace CT Airtrainer at Kamphong Son, although some parts of its syllabus are due to be transferred to the Fantrainer.

A few light STOL aircraft are available to Thailand, most being leftovers from the Vietnam War era. Among these are the Helio U-10 (illustrated) and Fairchild AU-23.

The RTAF's helicopter force includes examples of the Sikorsky S-58T with 201 Squadron.

...ree F27MPAs provide the main long-range patrol ...ability for the RTN. They can be armed with torpedoes ...ustrated) or Harpoon anti-ship missiles.

Normally thought of as fire-fighting aircraft, the Canadair CL-215 is also a useful amphibious transport and surveillance platform. No. 2 Squadron of the Royal Thai Navy operates two on coastal duties with Lake Buccaneers in support.

...w equipment is on order for the RTN, Dornier Do 228s ...ng procured to allow veterans such as this No. 1 ...uadron Grumman S-2 Tracker to retire gracefully.

...its operational units the Thai Army is totally dependent ...Bell products, the most numerous of which is the UH-1. ...-1 gunships are also on strength.

...e Thai Army has a large fixed-wing fleet which, apart ...n a few light transports, comprises 60 Cessna O-1 Bird ...gs, which perform spotting and liaison duties.

...e most numerous type in the Vietnamese inventory is the ...-21, which handles the air defence of the nation. ...-23s are used for attack missions.

157

INDEX

Page numbers in **bold** refer to an illustration

Picture credits

Front cover: Stefan Petersen. **4:** Tom Ross, Gabor Szekeres, G. Kromhout, Jon Lake. **5:** Jon Lake. **6:** Reuters/Popperfoto, Jon Lake, Jilly Lake. **7:** J. Sjoerdsma (two), Chris Ryan (two). **8:** Herman Pietise, William J. Mondy, Mario Carneiro (two), EMBRAER. **9:** AMX. **10:** via Robert F. Dorr, Robert F. Dorr, via Robert F. Dorr. **11:** via René J. Francillon, R.P. Clayton (two). **12:** via Robert F. Dorr, Mark A. Rankin (two). **13:** William J. Mondy (two), via Robert F. Dorr, Mark A. Rankin. **14:** Richard Gennis, William J. Mondy, Lutz Freundt, via Robert F. Dorr. **15:** via Robert F. Dorr (two). **16:** Axel Ostermann. **17:** H.J. van Broekhuizen, Harry Berger, Hans Nijhuis (two). **18:** H.J. van Broekhuizen, Hans Nijhuis, A. Vigna, H.J. van Broekhuizen. **19:** Hans Nijhuis (three), H.J. van Broekhuizen. **20:** Lockheed, Robert F. Dorr. **21:** Robert F. Dorr (both). **22-25:** Brane Lučovnik. **26-39:** Flt Lt Mike Lumb. **40-41:** Stefan Petersen, René van Woezik. **42:** Peter R. Foster. **43:** Simon Watson. **44:** Peter Steinemann, Swedish Air Force via FlygvapenNytt, M.J. Gerards. **45:** M.J. Gerards, Gabor Szekeres. **46:** J.W.R. Taylor. **47:** Stefan Petersen. **48:** Hans Nijhuis, Peter R. Foster, Peter Steinemann. **49:** Stefan Petersen, Lutz Freundt. **50:** A. Vigna. **50-51:** Gabor Szekeres (sequence). **52:** Peter Steinemann, Stefan Petersen. **53:** Alexander Dzhus 'Soviet Wings', Peter Steinemann. **54:** Stefan Petersen, Jon Lake. **55:** Hans Nijhuis, Alexander Dzhus 'Soviet Wings', Stefan Petersen. **56:** via Jon Lake, Eric Stijger, Stefan Petersen. **57:** René van Woezik. **58:** Hans Nijhuis, Simon Watson, Hans Nijhuis. **59:** Hans Nijhuis. **61-62:** Jon Lake. **67:** Lutz Freundt (two). **68:** Marcus Fulber. **70:** Jon Lake (two), Lutz Freundt. **71:** Simon Watson. **72:** Peter Steinemann, via Jon Lake. **73:** René van Woezik (two). **74:** Stefan Petersen. **75:** Jon Lake. **76:** Simon Watson, René van Woezik. **77:** Peter Steinemann, Tieme Festner (two), René van Woezik. **78:** via Jon Lake, Jon Lake (two), Marcus Fulber, Robin Timmermann, Hans Nijhuis, Jon Lake. **80:** Hans Nijhuis, Martin Baumann, Jon Lake. Martin Baumann, M.J. Gerards. **81:** Robin Timmermann, Hans Nijhuis, Peter R. Foster, Peter Steinemann (three). **82:** Peter Steinemann (seven). **83:** SIPA/Rex Press, C. Kromhout. **84:** Hans Nijhuis (two), M.J. Gerards (five). **85:** Peter Gunti. **86:** Hans Nijhuis. **86-87:** Peter Steinemann. **88-89:** Hans Nijhuis. **90:** Hans Nijhuis. **91:** Peter Steinemann, Hans Nijhuis (two). **92:** Hans Nijhuis, Peter Steinemann (two). **93:** Peter Steinemann, Hans Nijhuis, Peter Steinemann. **94-97:** Hans Nijhuis. **98:** Peter Wilson, US Air Force. **99:** Lockheed, Jeff Puzzullo. **100:** Grant Matsuoka via Bob Archer, Bob Archer/Milslides, Martin Baumann. **101:** Robert F. Dorr, René J. Francillon, US Air Force. **102:** René J. Francillon, Peter R. Foster. **103:** Paul Bennett, David Donald, Bruce Robertson, David Donald, Bob Archer. **104:** Jon Lake, Paul Bennett, Lindsay Peacock (two). **105:** Robert Shaw. **106:** Lockheed. **107:** J. Gaffney via Robert F. Dorr (two), Lockheed via Robert F. Dorr. **108:** Peter B. Mersky, Robert F. Dorr. **109:** Peter B. Mersky. **110:** Peter B. Mersky, Lindsay Peacock (two). **111:** Peter R. Foster, Peter B. Mersky, US Navy/D. Kneisler via Peter B. Mersky, Peter Wilson. **112:** Peter B. Mersky (two). **113:** David Ostrowski, Peter B. Mersky (two). **114-115:** Peter B. Mersky. **116:** US Department of Defense, Peter B. Mersky. **117:** Peter B. Mersky (two), US Department of Defense. **118:** US Department of Defense (two), Robert F. Dorr. **119:** Peter B. Mersky (two). **120:** Robert F. Dorr, Peter B. Mersky (two). **121:** General Dynamics, Peter B. Mersky. **122-3:** Gabor Szekeres. **124-5:** Karoly Gere via Gabor Szekeres. **126:** Gabor Szekeres, Karoly Gere via Gabor Szekeres. **127:** Gabor Szekeres. **128:** Aaron Bowers, Robert S. Hopkins III. **129:** Robert S. Hopkins III (four). **130:** Robert S. Hopkins III, John A. Gourley (two). **131:** Robert S. Hopkins III. **132-3:** Robert S. Hopkins III. **134:** Aaron Bowers, Robert S. Hopkins III. **135:** Aaron Bowers, Robert S. Hopkins III (two). **136-7:** Robert S. Hopkins III. **138:** Robert S. Hopkins III. **139:** Robert S. Hopkins III (two), Aaron Bowers. **140:** Peter Steinemann (four). **141:** Peter Steinemann, Chris Pocock. **142:** Peter Steinemann, Robbie Shaw (two), Northrop, Rockwell. **143:** Chris Pocock (three), Robbie Shaw (three), via René J. Francillon. **144:** Robbie Shaw, Chris Pocock (five). **145:** Robbie Shaw, Chris Pocock, via Robbie Shaw. **147:** Peter Steinemann (six), Fokker, Robbie Shaw (five), Northrop. **148:** J. Sjoerdsma, Robbie Shaw (three), Chris Pocock (two). **150:** Robbie Shaw (two). **149:** J. Sjoerdsma, Peter Steinemann (four), Chris Pocock (two), Peter Steinemann (three), Chris Pocock (two). **151:** Chris Pocock (three), Robbie Shaw, Peter Steinemann (three). **152:** Peter Steinemann (four), Robbie Shaw. **153:** Chris Pocock, Peter Steinemann (four), David Donald. **154:** General Dynamics, Peter Steinemann, Chris Pocock (three). **155:** Northrop, Peter Steinemann (five). **156:** Chris Pocock (three), Peter Steinemann (two). **157:** Fokker, Canadair, Peter Steinemann (two), Chris Pocock, MacClancy Collection.